CAMBRIDGE LATIN AMERICAN STUDIES

EDITORS

MALCOLM DEAS   CLIFFORD T. SMITH   JOHN STREET

33

MODERNIZATION IN A MEXICAN *EJIDO*:
A STUDY IN ECONOMIC ADAPTATION

For a list of books in this series please turn to page 302.

Modernization in a Mexican *Ejido*

A study in economic adaptation

BILLIE R. DeWALT

University of Kentucky

CAMBRIDGE UNIVERSITY PRESS

CAMBRIDGE

LONDON   NEW YORK   MELBOURNE

Published by the Syndics of the Cambridge University Press
The Pitt Building, Trumpington Street, Cambridge CB2 1RP
Bentley House, 200 Euston Road, London NW1 2DB
32 East 57th Street, New York, NY 10022, USA
296 Beaconsfield Parade, Middle Park, Melbourne 3206, Australia

First published 1979

Printed in the United States of America
Typeset by Telecki Publishing Services, 97 Bond Ave., Malverne, NY
Printed and bound by Hamilton Printing Company, Rensselaer, NY

Library of Congress Cataloging in Publication Data
DeWalt, Billie R.
Modernization in a Mexican *ejido*.

1.   Mexico (State) – Rural conditions.
2.   *Ejidos* – Mexico – Mexico (State) – Case studies.
3.   Diffusion of innovations – Mexico – Mexico (State)
I.   Title.
HN120.M47D48   309.1'72'5   78-3412
ISBN 0 521 22064 5

For Kathleen and Saara

Contents

Contents

Tables and figures

Tables

Figures

Preface

The major period of fieldwork on which this study is based was conducted between January and November 1973 in the Temascalcingo
region of the Mexican state of Mexico. This research and part of the initial stages of data analysis were supported by a predoctoral fellowship
(Grant No. FO1 MH54604-01) from the National Institute of Mental
Health. The Connecticut Research Foundation supported preliminary
fieldwork in Temascalcingo during the summer of 1970 and has since
provided several small grants to cover the expenses of other aspects of
this study. I am grateful to both agencies for making this research possible. Data analysis was performed using the facilities of the University of Connecticut Computer Center. A preliminary version of this
work was submitted as a doctoral dissertation at the University of
Connecticut.

Many individuals have contributed in one way or another to the
completion of this work. Robert Bee first sparked my interest in anthropology, especially in the area of sociocultural change. Kenneth Hadden
was responsible for my training in data analysis procedures and has
assisted me in putting many of my ideas into practice. Pertti Pelto
taught me a great deal about anthropology and has been and continues
to be a source of ideas, inspiration, and encouragement. Along with
many of his former students, I realize the tremendous impact that
"Bert" has had on my work and career. I also owe some intellectual
debts to individuals whose research has served as models for my own.
Studies by Frank Cancian, Everett Rogers, and Oscar Lewis have all
played an influential role in affecting my thinking about peasant studies.

Early manuscripts of this work have benefited from the critical reading of several individuals. Robert Bee, Frank Cancian, Kathleen DeWalt,
Davydd Greenwood, Kenneth Hadden, Pertti Pelto, and Heide Waldt-
hausen all made valuable suggestions for improvement.

In Mexico, Fernando Cámara B. was kind enough to provide letters
of introduction that helped to make my efforts easier. One of his letters was to Dr. Martha Fernández V., then the director of the Mazahua
Center of the Instituto Nacional Indigenista. She became a valued friend
and provided data for my research and other assistance. In Temascal-

cingo, Teresa Hernández and Pedro Romero were valuable key informants. Dr. Ignacio Ramírez helped to keep my family and me healthy; and he and his wife, Carolina, also became trusted friends. Jesús Blanco, the *primer regidor* of the *municipio*, helped us to find a house and provided letters of introduction to other local-level officials. Thanks also go to the other government officials and development agency personnel who shared their information and put up with my many questions. José María Servín de la Mora, the director of the Atlacomulco office of the Secretaría de Recursos Hidráulicos, was especially gracious in providing aid.

Eugenia Hathaway, Wendy Crosby, and Ann Ruddock typed various drafts of this work. Tom Blanchette and Jack Wright assisted me with the maps and other illustrations. Leroi Temple did a fine job of transforming my color slides into the black-and-white pictures.

A final word of thanks is to my family. My parents, Harry and Jennie DeWalt, always encouraged me in my educational pursuits and helped out whenever they could. My wife, Kathleen Musante DeWalt, and our daughter, Saara, shared this experience with me; and without their love and support it would never have been finished. The research was really a joint effort because Kathleen is also a skilled anthropologist and helped me to collect data while at the same time pursuing her own interests.

The greatest debt that I have is to the people of Puerto de las Piedras. They opened their homes and their hearts to us, and I hope that someday I may be able to repay their kindness.

November 9, 1978   *Billie R. DeWalt*

1

Modernization and nonmodernization among peasants: theoretical and methodological perspective

In 1973, a rusting metal sign provided a stark indicator of the state of planned change programs in the Temascalcingo region of the Mexican central highlands. The sign was similar to those erected near construction sites and other markers of progress in many countries of the world: It detailed the purpose of the project, the community it was designed to benefit, and the sponsoring agencies. This one read:

GOBIERNO DEL ESTADO DE MEXICO
TEMASCALCINGO
Programa para aumentar la
producción de maíz a nivel ejidal
Financiamiento: Gobierno del Estado de México
Asistencia Tecnica
Gobierno del Estado de México
Secretaría de Recursos Hidráulicos
Plan Lerma Asistencia Técnica[1]

The striking feature, however, was a skull and crossbones clearly scratched into both the bottom left and bottom right corners of the sign.

My inquiries about the development project alluded to in the sign disclosed that there had been trouble between people in some of the farming villages and the agricultural engineer in charge of the project. The engineer reported that many of the people refused to pay back the credit they had received for fertilizers, insecticides, hybrid seeds, and tractor cultivation of their fields. The farmers, on the other hand, accused the agent of overcharging them for the materials and services he had provided (see further discussion in Chapter 2). In the face of these conflicts the sponsoring agencies withdrew funding for the project after its initial year, 1970.

1. Sign about one of the development programs in the *ejido* of Puerto de las Piedras. Note the skulls and crossbones in the bottom left and right corners.

The skulls and crossbones, I was told, are scratched on such signs by change agents whenever a program fails because the local people did not cooperate (see Photograph 1). The symbol is meant to serve as a warning to other development agencies, as well as to all passersby, that the people of that village or region are uncooperative, lazy, not interested in improving their lives, and not to be trusted.

My conversations with several development agents who had worked in the valley and with some of the local people continued the theme expressed by the sign. An agricultural engineer reported that, of the many villages, *ejidos,* and groups throughout Mexico with whom he had worked, the peasants of the Temascalcingo region were the most difficult, most suspicious, and most resistant to change.[2] The director of a school established to provide month-long courses to help peasants become more self-sufficient decried the fact that people came from all over the state of Mexico to learn but the peasants nearby refused to participate in the courses. A local storekeeper repeated many times that the trouble with the farmers was that they just "don't understand." One of the peasants reported that little progress should be expected because the people are drunkards and are lazy.

Despite these and many other statements about the peasants' unwill-
ingness to change, it was obvious that modernization was taking place.
Here and there tractors could be seen plowing fields. During the season
when farmers were cultivating their corn, children could be seen spread-
ing handfuls of chemical fertilizer from plastic buckets onto the ground
around the plants. New crops were interspersed with the corn. Farmers
willingly took their animals and their children for vaccinations. Some
made regular trips to the feed stores in town to buy processed "growth"
foods for their pigs and chickens. Despite the claims about the peasants'
negative attitudes and behaviors, at least some individuals were adopting
new behaviors and technological items and were, in fact, modernizing.

This work addresses the following questions: To what extent are the
peasants of this region modernizing their behavior, and what are the
major factors that affect their economic decision making? However,
instead of focusing on peasants as a group whose behavior somehow
differs from that of other groups or people, the analysis here is on individuals who respond to the best of their ability to the various factors
impinging on their lives.

I believe that a major reason for the many failures of development
agents as well as for the failure of social scientists to achieve a significant understanding of the processes of modernization is that they have
usually treated the peasants as homogeneous groups with undifferentiated attitudes, ideals, and behaviors. The primary purpose of this study
is to develop and illustrate a methodology for the study of the processes of sociocultural change. This methodology begins with a focus on the
variability that individuals exhibit on a wide range of characteristics –
including modernization. It is my contention that a focus on intracultural diversity is essential if anthropology and the other social sciences
are to become capable of coping theoretically with change.

The inability of the social sciences to contribute to the solution of
the many vexing problems associated with development has been noted
repeatedly. The economist Gunnar Myrdal summarized the feelings of
many when he stated:

One might have expected the behavioral disciplines, particularly
social anthropology and sociology, to provide the more broadly
based system of theories and concepts needed for the scientific
study of the problem of development. Unfortunately, they have
not done so. The tradition of social anthropology has been to
work in static terms, attempting to explain the structure and in-
ternal relations of societies in what we now call a state of stag-
nation of "low-level equilibrium." Much sociological research has
remained within this tradition. It is, for instance, surprising how
little attention has been devoted in village surveys to the effects

of population increase on social stratification. And when studies
in these disciplines are focussed on change, as they increasingly
are, the emphasis is not often placed on development, much less
on framing a more comprehensive system of theories and concepts suited to the needs of the planner. (1968:27–8)

Most anthropological fieldwork has taken place in the rural regions of
the underdeveloped world, and anthropologists have been especially
criticized because their studies of change and development lack utility
(see Barth 1967:661; Poggie and Lynch 1974:4–5; Rogers 1975:355;
and Schneider 1975:271).

The results that I present in this work demonstrate the utility of a
perspective that focuses on intracultural diversity. I find that instead of
a simple choice between traditional and modern behavior, individuals
are mixing their options to produce several different economic adaptive
strategies. My investigation of how these strategies are linked to other
domains of behavior results in a much more complicated view of individual decision making, but one that I believe is more accurate than the
simplistic models generally used in attempts to explain the processes of
sociocultural change. I find that the choices of adaptive strategy are
quite understandable when the social, political, economic, cultural, and
other factors affecting individuals are specified. The multivariate model
of analysis used allows me to make much more specific recommendations that can be followed by development planners. The methodology
presented is one that can be applied generally and should lead to a significant improvement in our theories concerning economic development.[3]

In the rest of this chapter, I will briefly outline the major perspectives in research on peasants. I will show how the failure to focus on
intracultural variability has led to the creation of some unfortunate
stereotypes about peasant behavior and has hindered the study of sociocultural change. I will then discuss some positive trends arising from recent research, especially by economic anthropologists, that rejects a
focus on peasant homogeneity. The emerging methodology being developed in these studies will then be elaborated as I develop guidelines for
an approach emphasizing heterogeneity.

Studying peasant communities: the assumption of homogeneity

Robert Redfield's community study of Tepoztlán (1930) was the beginning of peasant studies by anthropologists. Although some similar
research followed soon after, the immediate postwar years saw a burgeon-
ing of "village" studies in India, the Far East, Latin America, and elsewhere. By the early 1950s enough material had been collected for Red-

field to suggest some general statements about peasant society and culture. He described the good life of peasants – their "reverent attitude toward the land; the idea that agricultural work is good and commerce not so good; and [their]. . . emphasis on productive industry as a prime virtue" (1960:64). Under criticism because some scholars felt that "their" communities did not reflect these aspects of the good life, Redfield was forced to admit that there were exceptions. (1960:65–72). Nevertheless, he did make a modified statement about peasant values still incorporating his view of the good life: "an intense attachment to native soil; a reverent disposition toward habitat and ancestral ways; a restraint on individual self-seeking in favor of family and community; a certain suspiciousness, mixed with appreciation, of town life; a sober and earthy ethic" (Redfield 1960:78).[4]

As more and more nations comprised primarily of peasant peoples made their appearance after World War II, the literature on these peoples increased sharply (see Geertz 1962; Friedl 1963; Anderson 1965; and Halpern and Brode 1967). Apart from the relatively humdrum description of communities from around the world, the objectives of most of these studies have been similar to those of Redfield's work. This research seeks (*a*) to describe the sociocultural milieu within which the peasantry exists, and (*b*) to determine the distinctive features that characterize peasant life. A dominant trend among anthropologists has been to try to identify those characteristics that would distinguish peasants from tribal and/or modernized societies. Economic, political, and cultural dimensions have been proposed, with a good deal of debate, as the most significant distinguishing features.

Most important from the viewpoint of economic development have been the attempts by George Foster and others to identify the cognitive orientations of peasant societies. It is interesting to note that although Foster never mentions Redfield by name, he has disagreed with some of Redfield's earlier generalizations. For Foster, reports of the good life were a Rousseauan view of rural life that did not fit the situation. From his research in Mexico, he concluded that "the picture that emerges does not conform to a belief cherished by many that in rural life one finds embodied the natural and primeval human virtues shared by all humanity prior to the development of urban life" (1967:87). Instead, Foster found in Tzintzuntzan (western Mexico) a picture he viewed as more characteristic of peasant communities: "Life in these communities is described as marked by suspicion and distrust, inability to cooperate in many kinds of activity, sensitivity to the fear of shame, proneness to criticize and gossip, and a general view of people and the world as potentially dangerous" (1967:89).

And so the good life among peasants came to be revised with further research. It was soon replaced by a view that might be characterized as the "crummy life." Banfield, in a study of Italian peasants, reported that they were characterized by what he called "amoral familism." People in such a society "maximize the material, short-run advantage of the nuclear family; [and] assume that all others will do likewise" (Banfield 1958:85). Foster preferred to talk about the "image of the limited good," the peasant view that their total environment is "one in which almost all desired things in life such as land, other forms of wealth, health, friendship, love, manliness, honor, respect, power, influence, security and safety exist in absolute quantities insufficient to fill even minimal needs of villagers" (1967:123). An individual in such a situation can improve himself or herself only at the expense of others.

Everett Rogers, in a review of the literature about peasants, identified ten traits that emerge as characteristic of the "subculture of peasantry." He reported that: "central elements in this subculture of peasantry are: (1) mutual distrust in interpersonal relations; (2) perceived limited good; (3) dependence on and hostility toward government authority; (4) familism; (5) lack of innovativeness; (6) fatalism; (7) limited aspiration; (8) lack of deferred gratification; (9) limited view of the world; (10) low empathy" (Rogers 1969:25). These characterizations are certainly in stark contrast to the idyllic, Rousseauan view of the good life.

Despite these discrepant characterizations of peasants, a common link between Redfield's studies and many of those reporting negative traits has been the tendency to treat all of the people of individual communities, or even peasants everywhere, as if they are all alike – homogeneous in cultural and psychological characteristics. In many ways, at least among anthropologists, this homogeneous view of peasants may be a legacy of the culture and personality studies of the 1930s and 1940s in which the ethnographers objective was to describe the "cultural configuration" (Benedict 1934), "modal personality" (DuBois 1944), "basic personality structure" (Kardiner 1945), or "national character" (Gorer and Rickman 1949) of a group of people. Foster, for example, explicitly states that he is searching for cognitive orientations – "sets of assumptions . . . which structure and guide behavior in much the same way grammatical rules, unrecognized by most people, structure and guide their linguistic forms" – that are typical of peasants (1967:200).[5]

The linguistic analogy which Foster used is interesting because it was the same sort of argument used by researchers interested in "national character" (Harris 1968:418–21). Margaret Mead, for example, explicitly used the linguistic analogy: "In dealing with culture, the anthropologist makes the same assumptions about the rest of a culture that the linguist makes about the language – that he is dealing with a system which can be delineated by analysis of a small number of very highly specified samples" (1953:665). These types of statements suggest that there is a single culture or cognitive orientation "out there" that can be discovered by the anthropologist. The variability in a population is not taken into account.

The search for cognitive orientations characteristic of peasants as a type of society may be intellectually stimulating and useful in some contexts. However, problems arise when these orientations are cited as the primary reasons for the failure of peasants to modernize. People who are characterized as distrustful, hostile, familistic, noninnovative, fatalistic, lacking deferred gratification, and having an image of the limited good can hardly be expected to be a dynamic sector in the process of economic development.

Another significant area in which homogeneity of the population has been posited is in regard to wealth. Many anthropologists who have studied communities in Mesoamerica, for example, have reported that there are no economic inequalities, especially in "closed, corporate communities" that have had little contact with the outside world. The *cargo* system, the traditional method of civil and religious government (see Chapter 8) in which considerable expenditures are required of officeholders, has often been cited as a prime mechanism for reducing inequalities. That is, the rich are pressed to serve more often and in positions that require greater expenditures of money, and thus the community supposedly becomes economically leveled (Wolf 1955; Nash 1961). According to Nash:

> The leveling mechanisms operate to drain the accumulated resources of the community for non-economic ends, and to keep the various households, over generations, fairly equal in wealth. They are mechanisms to keep economic homogeneity within the community, so that socially important heterogeneity – age, sex, previous service to the community, control of or access to the supernatural – remains the basis of role differentiation. They militate against the rise of social classes based on wealth and economic power distinctions. (1971:172)[6]

Many criticisms of peasant studies have challenged some of these basic assumptions, but they have failed to dispel the impression of homogeneity. A few students of peasant life are critical of research which purports to show that peasants hold beliefs and behaviors that are antithetical to development because they fail to emphasize why these personality traits exist. Harris (1975:461–74), for example, does not disagree with the view of peasants as conservative and suspicious. However, he believes that conservative behavior is often based upon a realistic appraisal of the situations in which the peasants live. Harris provides a number of examples to suggest that perhaps the peasants should have been more conservative and suspicious with regard to a number of development schemes. For various reasons, the development efforts failed, and the peasants were in worse shape than they were before.

Gerrit Huizer has very much the same sort of perspective. He also sees peasants as being resistant to change and views this attitude as a result of what he calls the "culture of repression" (1971:309). In fact, Huizer believes that the culture of repression leads to greater homogeneity because it produces a syndrome of traits that are "a means for conserving solidarity and group cohesiveness" and create a "need for sharing the poverty in a more or less egalitarian way" (1971:311).

Both Huizer and Harris apparently believe that peasants are suspicious and conservative, but they say that we should look for the causes which led to their adoption of this type of behavior. They believe these causes lie in the general ecological and especially in the societal circumstances in which the peasants find themselves.

There is no question that the ideas about peasant conservatism promoted in anthropological literature have led to the creation and/or maintenance of some popular stereotypes about peasants. Perhaps the most significant negative consequences of these stereotypes have arisen in the context of explanations of socioeconomic processes and planned change. Stereotyped descriptions of peasants have created expectations among change agents about what these people are "really like," and these expectations usually do not correspond with the realities of individual communities. This situation has led to a feeling that the most important changes needed are in the values, attitudes, and motivations of the peasant. Several major theories of sociocultural change have reinforced such views. The peasant only needs to learn a little empathy (Lerner 1958), to be injected with some mass media exposure (Rogers 1969), to take a dose of modern values (Kahl 1968), or to be instilled with some achievement motivation (McClelland 1961) and she/he is on the road to modernization. While there may be some credibility in such views, they conveniently shift the burden for the failure to modernize to the peasant, thus leaving the larger societal structure relatively free of criticism.

In addition, the stereotypes about peasant behavior provide a built-in excuse for economic development agents when their programs fail. Reasons cited for the failures of development schemes are not the inability of the pottery cooperative to make money, or the failure of a new type of wheat seed to grow, or the fact that the chickens died; rather, blame falls on the supposed conservatism of the peasants who refused to cooperate with the benevolent agents of socioeconomic modernization.

These statements about change agents' expectations are not merely conjectural. As I have shown earlier, the assertion was commonly made by development personnel and others that the people in the Temascalcingo region are very resistant to change and that the peasants do not understand the goals of the development agents. The "scientific validation" provided in the literature for the impressions and/or prejudices of the layman are unfortunate.

Aside from the creation and support of stereotypes, homogeneity-oriented studies of peasants have led to a notable inability to account for the dynamic sociocultural changes that are taking place in many communities. In Mexico alone, Chan Kom (Redfield 1950), Paracho (Kaplan 1965), San Bernardino Contla (Nutini 1968), Cuanajo (Acheson 1972), and even Tzintzuntzan (Foster 1967) are examples of peasant villages that have undergone significant cultural change. Emphasis on the *normative* personality, cognitive orientations, or cultural patterns of peasants does not account for the innovative and entrepreneurial behavior exhibited by certain people in these communities.

Studies of modernization: a focus on heterogeneity

One tradition of research related to economic development has emphasized the individual and looking at intracultural variation. This tendency is evident in studies by rural sociologists, communicationists, political scientists, and others that are focused on modernization. Modernization is usually defined in terms similar to those used by Everett Rogers: "the process by which individuals change from a traditional way of life to a more complex technologically advanced, and rapidly changing style of life" (1969:14).[7] Many of these researchers have done statistical studies in which a person's *degree* of modernization – measured by the number of new technological or consumer items adopted, achievement motivation, political knowledge, educational aspirations (Rogers 1969), empathy (Lerner 1958), modern values (Kahl 1968) or a combination of a number of these (Inkeles and Smith 1974) – is correlated with a number of other variables that are seen as causes of the adoption of modern behavior. The important point is that these indicators of modernization are operationalized and measured in order to look at the range of variation existing within populations. In the same way, the researchers assume enough variability will be found to make measurement of antecedent variables possible and desirable.

Once the variability in modernization is measured, the task is to determine the selective forces (antecedent variables) leading people to adopt modern behaviors. The modernization studies have shown that values, beliefs, social status, education, and other characteristics have a significant impact on the process of becoming more modern. Rogers (1969:304-7), for example, found in an impressive multivariate, multicommunity study of peasants in Colombia that cosmopoliteness, empathy, political knowledge, social status, and mass media exposure were important in determining which individuals would adopt new technological items in agriculture ("agricultural innovativeness") and new items for the home ("home innovativeness"). Kahl (1968) has found in Mexico and Brazil that social status is the best predictor of who will hold modern values. Inkeles and Smith, in a study of six countries, found that the best predictors of a hundred item modernization score were education, mass media exposure, and occupational experience (1974: 283). Nine other studies summarized in Rogers (1969:302-3) found many of these same variables to be important in predicting innovativeness. Additional important variables associated with modernization include extension worker contact (Junghare 1962); scientific attitudes, fatalism, and achievement motivation (Beal and Sibley 1966); information-seeking activity and knowledgeability (Whittenbarger and Maffei 1966); and authoritarianism (Cattopadhyay and Pareek 1967). I should emphasize again that these studies have used these concepts as *variables* – intracultural dimensions of variation – rather than as stereotypes of whole populations.

In spite of the progress these studies have made in showing the multivariate, complex nature of the modernization process, they have not brought us much closer to an understanding of how change takes place. The problem is that important descriptive, contextual information that would give meaning to the numbers is missing. These analyses are generally the product of survey research in which the investigators spend very little time in the community or region. "Real cases," in which we can see how *people* are responding, are needed to supplement the statistical analysis. Such information is especially important because these studies are synchronic in nature, having measured all of the variables at one point in time. Only by seeing how the various factors are involved in the lives of individuals can we get an idea of the historical associations of variables that are necessary to establish causal relationships. My view is that without this "feel" for how the variables are operating in actual situations (rather than how they are operating in the computer), we still have very little inkling about the processes involved in modernization.

Peasants and economic development: an emerging methodology based on heterogeneity

A number of scholars involved in the study of economic development have also reacted to the stereotyped descriptions utilized in homogeneity-oriented research. Especially prominent in this regard are the handful of individuals combining the deductive analysis of economics with the intensive, empirically based methods of sociocultural anthropology (see Belshaw 1967; Cancian 1972; Epstein 1962, 1973; Hill 1963, 1970, 1972; Ortiz 1973; and Salisbury 1970). This research is characterized by careful measurement of economic variables along with a wealth of ethnographic data on the social, cultural, political, and other factors affecting economic behavior.

One significant generalization that can be made on the basis of the research of these economic anthropologists and anthropological economists is that there is very little homogeneity in any behavior they measured. Substantial variability can be found in seemingly homogeneous communities if one admits its existence and sets out to take note of it. Polly Hill, for example, found that by concentrating on the economic inequality present in the village she studied, she was able to gain important insights into the workings of Hausa economics and society. She stated that:

> this approach is certainly a forceful demonstration of the dangers of regarding any farming community as composed of a group of 'average farmers' – together with (as one must always nowadays assume) a few 'progressive farmers.' It is not merely that a few farmers operate on a much larger scale than others, but that there are many richer farmers who have entirely different economic aims from many poorer farmers. (1972:5)

The focus on intracultural diversity, quantification of the range of economic behavior, and the interrelationships of economics with other elements of society and culture has led to a complication of our models of peasant behavior. No longer can we appeal to the shopworn idea of peasants clinging to tradition for our explanation of modernization or nonmodernization. Instead, as we learn more about the behavior of these peoples through careful observations and measurements, we are coming to realize that they make intelligent decisions on the basis of the information available to them and the parameters within which they operate. The stereotypes that had been created by earlier research are being contradicted. Salisbury (1970), for example, asserted on the basis of his study of Vunamami that traditional societies are not unreasonably conservative, nonexperimental, homogeneous, lacking in foresight, uncalculating, or nonentrepreneurial (see Schneider 1975:272-3). Belshaw (1967:204) and Ortiz (1973:271) concluded from their research that the peasants they studied behaved rationally; and Epstein expressed a similar view, although she would like to see the concept of "rational economic man" replaced by a new model of "socioeconomic man" (1975:45).

This research combining anthropology with economics holds great potential for recommendations to be made directly to development planners. Epstein's studies have had the most "applied" orientation thus far. In her study and restudy of two villages in southern India, she was able to document the increase in inequalities that had accompanied economic development (Epstein 1973:243). Not only had the rich become richer but the standard of living of the poor had actually declined, in absolute terms, in the fifteen-year interval following her original research (Epstein 1962). Epstein suggested a number of specific measures stemming directly from her study to help ensure that the benefits of development would be spread to all segments of the population and would not be concentrated only in the upper echelons of local societies (1975:40-1).

In another major research study of the Tolai of New Guinea, Epstein was able to provide some insights into why cocoa growers there seemed to be acting irrationally by selling their produce to independent traders for lower prices than they could obtain from a local nonprofit-making project (1975:41-4). Her explanation had to take into account the kinship system, pattern of inheritance, types of landholdings, and population growth in the region. Based upon her research, she suggested a minor change in policy. Where implemented, this change resulted in an immediate increase in sales to the project (1975:44).

Belshaw was also able to make some concrete policy recommendations. Based upon his analysis of agricultural productivity and potential in a Mexican village, he concluded that investment in this sector would not be worthwhile (1967:327). He suggested that development possibilities outside of agriculture should be explored and went on to make some specific suggestions.

These studies have been significant in reorienting our views toward a focus on the heterogeneity that exists in peasant societies, an emphasis on quantifying important socioeconomic variables, and making practical recommendations for improving development efforts. However, they have had little impact on our understanding of the *process* of modernization because they do not focus closely enough on why individuals decide to change their behavior or why certain behaviors from among the available alternatives become generally accepted while others fade away. Ortiz (1972) came closest to doing this when she focused on the decision-making process among the Paez, but she had little data of direct relevance to the model she proposed.

The problem is that most of this research is still slanted primarily toward the traditional, anthropological emphasis on description and inductive procedures. The measurement and quantification that forms the strong point of this research is only *better description* because it takes note of the variability of behavior. Too little formulation and testing of specific hypotheses is being done for us to gain insight into the dynamics of peasant communities in the process of change.

An outstanding exception in this regard is Frank Cancian, who has consistently concentrated on testing hypotheses with careful empirical studies. One of the guiding forces behind his research has been his feeling that:

a common view [of peasant-oriented research] seizes on the label "peasant" as a full description of the people who bear it. My impression is that researchers (and many others) presently give too much weight to "peasantness" as an explanation of human behavior, both in the sense that they treat peasant societies as relatively homogeneous and in the sense that they see peasants as substantially different from other people. (1972:158)

Cancian's first major contribution was his study of the effect of the *cargo* system as an economic leveling mechanism. Zinacantán, the community in southern Mexico in which he worked, had previously been described as one in which the hierarchy did function as a leveling device (Zabala 1961). However, by sampling people's participation in the system over a long period of time, Cancian concluded that "the evidence for Zinacantán clearly indicates that some degree of economic stratification exists despite [the operation of leveling mechanisms]" (1965:137). In fact, Cancian found evidence that "service in the cargo system legitimizes the wealth differences that do exist" (1965:140). Thus the view of Zinacantán as a homogeneous peasant community in which the *cargo* system functioned as an economic leveling mechanism was clearly contradicted.

More recently, Cancian turned his attention to research on differential wealth as a factor in agriculturalists' propensity to take risks. He found that he could demonstrate sufficient differences in socioeconomic status among ninety-three Zinacantán households to divide them into four economic ranks. He then looked at the percentages of households

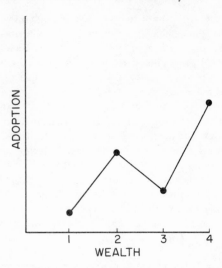

Figure 1.1   Relationship between wealth and adoption of innovations (adapted from Cancian 1972:152)

in each economic rank that were engaged in risk-taking behavior, selling corn to a government receiving center where prices above those in the local market could be obtained. The association found by Cancian between economic rank and risk taking (measured by the percentage of adopters) is diagramed in Figure 1.1.

A number of important points grow out of this research. First, significant differences in economic position and willingness to adopt new behavior patterns can be found if one looks for them. Second, much of the variability in one domain of behavior (risk taking) can be explained by variability in another (economic rank). That is, much of the variability in wealth and risk taking is patterned in the form of the model found in Figure 1.1. Finally, investigation of these patterned intracommunity variations may lead to significant cross-cultural theoretical statements. Examples that Cancian has collected from other peasant and *nonpeasant* communities have shown very much the same pattern of relationship between economic rank and risk taking (1972:154-8). Thus by taking into account the variability that exists in some aspects of peasant life, we can move toward explanation of the variability that exists in other domains of behavior. Cancian's research has also shown that the regularities discovered may be applicable to nonpeasants as well.

Cancian's research is a fine model of hypothesis testing and assembling relevant intracultural and cross-cultural empirical evidence. As important as economic rank is for explaining the propensity to take risks, however, it does not account for all of the variability in this behavior. Factors other than the economic must also be taken into account if we are to understand the process of modernization (see DeWalt 1975:165).

Homogeneity and heterogeneity in a broader perspective

Before discussing guidelines that can be used in research aimed at the heterogeneity of behavior, it would be useful to look at these perspectives in a broader context. The use of either the homogeneity or the heterogeneity perspective depends upon the question that is being asked. Anthony F. C. Wallace's discussion of these issues is instructive in this regard. Wallace (1970) distinguished between the "replication-of-uniformity" approach (comparable to a focus on homogeneity) and the "organization-of-diversity" approach (comparable to a focus on heterogeneity).

Wallace states that the replication-of-uniformity perspective focuses on "the extent to which members of a social group, by virtue of their common group identification, behave in the same way under the same circumstances" (1970:123). Such an approach is useful for "descriptive purposes serving only to delineate the preponderant characteristics of a group, particularly in comparing them with some other group" (1970:123). Every anthropologist uses this approach, no matter what his or her theoretical persuasion might be, to provide basic descriptive information about the general features of a community and its people. For example, in later chapters I report that people wear modern dress, keep animals as a kind of insurance policy, view education as desirable, and tend to frown upon divorce. Even though there is variation in these behaviors and feelings, I use the replication-of-uniformity perspective to provide some basic background material to serve as a context for what I consider to be the theoretically relevant material.

There are other cases in which it may be more appropriate to describe the community in homogeneous terms. For example, although I show that there are significant wealth differences among the people of the community that I studied, a development agent would probably not include this information in a funding proposal to a bank or government agency. The proposal only needs to show that there is relatively little investment capital present and that therefore credit funds need to be supplied. It is imperative for development agencies to be aware of the variability in wealth; but in communicating the preponderant characteristics of the community to a funding agency, a simple homogeneous description of the poverty in the region would be adequate.

All studies that focus on groups, institutions, nations, and other aggregates by necessity ignore the heterogeneity of the individuals making up these units. In many such analyses, peasant peoples have been treated as a relatively undifferentiated group·subject to exploitation by other elements at the national (Aguirre Beltrán 1967; Gonzalez Casanova 1970) and/or international level (Frank 1969). The understanding of macrocosmic relationships such as these is important because the economic, political, and social systems at the regional, national, and international levels are important determinants of the potential for economic development (Adams 1970). These social system variables impose tremendous constraints upon the actions of people in local communities. However, within the constraints of these systems, there are still options among which people are choosing. The understanding of development requires an understanding of the microcosm as well as the macrocosm, a point to which I will return later in this chapter.

Homogeneous descriptions may also be useful in terms of outlining the immediate social, structural, and ecological constraints that will bear upon the possibilities for success or failure of local development projects. Peasants have been described as part-societies with part-cultures (Kroeber 1948:248), and so they must be understood in terms of their relations with the larger society (Wolf 1966:1). Because the government establishes many of the institutional constraints under which peasants operate, how the government impinges on the peasant system will be important (Greenwood 1974:3).

The larger social structure at the local level also can be studied using a homogeneous perspective. The existence of exploitative middlemen or powerful political leaders who appropriate the peasants' surplus will affect the success of any development project. Peasants are unlikely to be willing to invest time and resources if they are not the ones to benefit from the fruits of their endeavors.

A knowledge of ecological features also can be gained from homogeneity-oriented research. It is important to know, for example, that new cash crops will not lead to marked socioeconomic improvement because there are no means available for transporting them to market. Such analyses may also show that some regions or landholding patterns are inappropriate for certain types of crops or animals.

Anthropologists have made their greatest impact on the study of planned change programs by pointing out how important ecological, social structural, and cultural conditions were erroneously ignored. Dobyns (1951), Bliss (1952), Mead (1955), Erasmus (1961), and Niehoff (1966) have been among those who have used a focus on homogeneity to good advantage in looking at the inadequacies of technical assistance programs.

The major problem with research that never goes beyond the homogeneity-oriented perspective is that theoretically important intracultural diversity is often overlooked. Wallace is very critical of those who use the replication-of-uniformity (homogeneity) approach, and he advocates the organization-of-diversity perspective. He states that "according to this viewpoint, no population, within a stated cultural boundary, can be assumed to be uniform with respect to any variable or pattern. In every instance a distribution will be found to characterize the sample" 1970:128). He feels that sound theory can be built only if the variability within populations is recognized.

In a similar vein, Pelto and Pelto recently have criticized studies which adhere to what they call "uniformism," a term they use to refer to "the various descriptions and theories that are based on an idea of common, shared, homogeneous culture, or on culture as *the* set of standards, rules or norms" (1975:1–2).

The Peltos follow a number of other recent writings (Campbell 1966; Levine 1973) in recommending an alternative based upon the Darwinian idea of natural selection. Pelto and Pelto state that: "significant breakthroughs in understanding the *processes* of biological evolution occurred only when geneticists were able to go beyond the study of species and subspecies to focus on the mechanisms of biological inheritance . . . as they are observable in physical *individuals* in *populations*" (1975:14, italics theirs). The implication for peasant studies and cultural anthropology is clear: If we wish to understand the processes of sociocultural change that are taking place, we need to have some idea of the intracultural variability within populations.

> [A]ll the ideas carried by individuals in a community, whether shared or not, are a pool of behavioral possibilities analogous to the pool of genetic possibilities carried in the genes and chromosomes of those same individuals. Each individual idea . . . *may* become of adaptive behavioral significance depending on individual life histories in particular environments. (Pelto and Pelto 1975:14, italics theirs)

Once the variability of the population is described or sampled, the task of the researcher becomes one of explaining the changes that take place over time. As with the origin, modification, and extinction of species, we need to explain the processes by which certain ideas, beliefs, values, and behaviors become dominant, others fade away, some never achieve more than a minority of adherents, and so on. The selective forces are to be found in individuals' physical qualities and social and natural environments.

The studies of Foster, Banfield, Redfield, and others cited earlier fail to explain the processes of change in communities precisely because they do not focus on the variability that exists within populations. They ignore the "pool of behavioral possibilities" from which new behaviors can be selected. Thus these scholars can only describe the persistence of tradition and cannot explain the dynamics of change.

One final point should be made about the homogeneous studies that search for cognitive orientations characteristic of peasants. This point relates to their mixing of levels of analysis. Foster (1967), for example, posits the "image of limited good" as a cognitive orientation and then cites it as a major reason for the failure of peasants to modernize. With his homogeneous approach, Foster raises the image of limited good and the failure to modernize to the cultural level as characteristics of the society. Thus he is put in the position of using aggregate information (he raises his own data to this level) to account for individual behavior (see Wallace 1970:126 for a similar view that he believes is more widely applicable). The mixing of levels of analysis ("ecological fallacy") is a common error in statistical studies, where it is relatively easy to recognize (Robinson 1950). It is more difficult to detect in descriptive studies such as Foster's but the problem is just as serious.

Fredrik Barth makes a similar argument, although he attacks the problem in a different way. He states:

> The reason for the social anthropologist's impasse when he tries to add change to his traditional description of social systems is found in the basic characteristics of the descriptive concepts we habitually use. We wish to characterize groups, societies, or cultures, and to do this we have to aggregate individual observations. We generally think of the procedure as one where we aggregate individual cases of behavior to patterns of behavior, specifying the common features of the individual cases. Such patterns we think of as customs: stereotyped forms of behavior that are required and correct. (1967:662)

Emphasizing required and correct customary behavior does not tell us much about those individuals who are adopting new, innovative behavior.

A methodology for modernization research

In the preceding review of literature on peasants, modernization, and economic development, I have emphasized both the positive and the negative aspects of previous research. I believe that, by combining the positive elements contained within these methodologies, it is possible to delineate a new methodology that will lead to a greater understanding of the processes of modernization and economic development. The utility of this strategy will be illustrated in later chapters by my case study of agricultural modernization in a Mexican *ejido.*

A focus on *heterogeneity* is the cornerstone of the attempt to understand the processes of modernization. In this study I will not be concerned with the search for shared identities, beliefs, ideologies, world views, or other factors that hold communities together and (supposedly) differentiate peasant culture from other cultures. Such research, based on the homogeneity perspective, may be valuable for certain purposes. However, there are already many studies that emphasize the "common cultural traditions" of peasants, and I prefer to leave this domain to them. As I have shown, such research cannot cope meaningfully with the dynamics of change in peasant communities, and thus it is outside the scope of my analysis. Theoretically useful statements about the processes of modernization depend upon a recognition of the intracultural variability that exists in people's behavior.

The emphasis on heterogeneity implies that the focus of inquiry is on the *adaptation* of individuals. Although adaptation is one of the key concepts in evolutionary biology and has been adopted as an explanatory principle in theories of sociocultural evolution (e.g., Steward 1955; Sahlins and Service 1960), its use in the study of modernization and economic development has not been prominent. John Bennett's definition of adaptation of *Northern Plainsmen* can be of considerable heuristic value in the development context. He defines adaptation (or what he calls "adaptive behavior") as "coping mechanisms or ways of dealing with people and resources in order to attain goals and solve problems" (1969:11). Individuals are constantly modifying their behavior to better fit both old and new conditions. The behavioral diversity existing within sociocultural systems can be seen as a result of different adaptive decisions being made by individuals in the population.

Barth, in a provocative article on social change, has some interesting ideas along these lines. He points out the necessity for explaining intracultural variability and has some suggestions about where to look:

> What we see as a social form is, concretely, a pattern of distribution of behavior by different persons and on different occasions. I would argue that it is not useful to assume that this empirical pattern is a sought-for condition, which all members of the community equally value and willfully maintain. Rather, it must be regarded as an epiphenomenon of a great variety of processes in combination, and our problem as social anthropologists is to show how it is generated. The determinants of the form must be of a variety of kinds. On the one hand, what persons wish to achieve, the multifarious ends they are pursuing, will channel their

behavior. On the other hand, technical and ecologic restrictions doom some kinds of behavior to failure and reward others, while the presence of other factors imposes strategic constraints and opportunities that modify the allocations people can make and will benefit from making. (1967:662)

The goal is to discover the determinants of individuals' behavior and the selective factors that make some behaviors successful and others failures.

Although my focus is on individuals, I should make it clear that I do not subscribe to "individual blame" theories (Rogers 1975:355). That is, the major impediments to development do not lie in the peasant mind but rather in the outside world. Economic, political, and social relationships at the regional (Aguirre Beltrán 1967), national (Gonzalez Casanova 1970), and international levels (Frank 1969) are the primary obstacles to the modernization of peasant communities. In spite of the powerful influence these external forces exert, however, peasants still continue to make adaptive decisions. In other words, as Bennett points out, there is considerable interplay between the local and the external, the *microcosm* and the *macrocosm* (1967:452). Although my focus in this study is the microcosm, the macrocosm necessarily intrudes into the analysis as a source of constraints affecting the peasants of Puerto de las Piedras. There is, however, considerable room for improvement in developing modes of analysis that can handle both the microcosm and the macrocosm as well as interplay between them.

As the preceding discussion implies, many different factors will affect the adaptive decisions that people make. Any explanation will thus have to be *multivariate* – considering as many relevant variables as the researcher can assemble. Simplistic analyses offering monistic explanations are not able to account for the great diversity in modernizing behavior.

The specific constraints and incentives involved in each case can be identified using both *deductive* and *inductive* procedures. For example, factors that are important in other contexts can be included in the research design as hypotheses to be investigated. Some variables (e.g., wealth) will be found to be important in almost every instance, while others prove to be of more limited applicability. In many of the chapters that follow, I outline hypotheses and expectations on the basis of other researchers' findings in other areas. However, the anthropological approach of spending extended periods of time in the field lends itself to the discovery, through inductive procedures, of possible explanatory features. Making preliminary observations, interviewing key informants, and collecting life histories can all lead to the postulation of relevant explanatory factors. Both inductively and deductively derived hypotheses should be systematically tested to determine their theoretical value.

One source of hypotheses for explanations of behavior are informants' statements about why they do what they do. This point brings up the distinction between *emic* and *etic* research. Harris defines emics as "descriptions or judgments concerning behavior, customs, beliefs, values, and so on, held by members of a societal group as culturally appropriate and valid" (1975:662). He defines etics as "the techniques and results of making generalizations about cultural events, behavior patterns, artifacts, thought and ideology that aim to be verifiable objectively and valid cross-culturally" (1975:662). Harris has claimed that the mixing of emic and etic research has created a morass in anthropological theory and that the two types of analysis must be clearly separated.

At the theoretical level this assessment is certainly true. I agree with Harris that "there is no error more common or devastating than to confuse what people say, wish, dream, and believe they do with what they actually do" (1975:163). However, in the process of doing fieldwork, emic and etic procedures are freely mixed. Pelto, for example, states that almost all anthropologists "accept and make use of some fundamental tenets of the emic point of view" (1970:84).

The strategy that I follow in my research is primarily an etic one: I am interested in explaining the actual behavior of human beings. However, I do use some emic data, specifically the statements that some of my informants made about how and why people acted in response to opportunities for modernization. I did not accept these explanations as true, but I treated them as hypotheses to be systematically investigated. Thus an informant's statement that, "we are not interested in development here, we are only interested in getting drunk" is an emically derived hypothesis about human behavior. By collecting data on the use of alcohol and modernization, the validity of this explanation was determined (see Chapter 9).

The constant stress on testing hypotheses means that *operationalism* is an important element of the research design. "Operationalism is a research strategy in which primary elements (terms) of descriptions and theoretical propositions are structured, *wherever possible,* in forms which prescribe, or otherwise make intersubjectively available, the *specific acts of observation* which provide the primary transformations from 'raw experience' to the language of theoretical systems" (Pelto 1970:50, emphasis his). I will be very explicit about my research methods, especially about measurement of variables, so that others will be able to evaluate the study on the basis of scientific standards and replicate the research if they desire. Only when hypotheses have been tested with careful measurements of concepts that have been adequately operationalized can we have confidence in the results.

This is clearly a study that relies heavily on quantitative data and statistical testing of hypotheses. However, as I pointed out in my discussion of other modernization research, more personal, qualitative information cannot be neglected. I have aimed, therefore, for a *quantitative –qualitative mix* in my presentation. Random sampling, careful measurement of variables, and the use of multivariate statistics are important and are utilized. In addition, however, qualitative information is provided as a context for the statistical data and to maintain the essential connection with "real people." Enough ethnographic information and case studies of individuals are included so that even a casual reader who wishes to ignore the technical statistical detail can become acquainted with the people of the *ejido* and achieve some understanding of the changes occurring. There is another reason for the collection of both quantitative and qualitative data. Statistical analyses often lead to the discovery of interesting relationships. Many times a researcher can only speculate about the reasons for these results. However, with a rich store of personal experience and qualitative description to draw upon, a perceptive scholar can often interpret such results and can sometimes even provide case studies of individuals as further evidence.

Research questions and organizational plan

Many specific hypotheses and predictions will be made in this study of modernization among individuals in the *ejido* of Puerto de las Piedras. However, three broad research questions will also be investigated. Because these will be underlying themes in all of the chapters to follow, they should be emphasized here.

First, I will be investigating the extent of homogeneity (or heterogeneity) in a wide range of behavior. All of the concepts that I use are operationalized; and in all cases, descriptive statistics are presented so that the reader can determine the extent of intracommunity variation. I believe that most readers will find the heterogeneity of behavior to be striking after having read homogeneity-oriented studies of peasants in similar communities.

Second, I will look at the patterns of modernization within the *ejido*. It is important to determine whether there is a single dimension running from "traditional" to "modern" or if there are more complex patterns of adoption of new ideas and behavior. My information indicates that the unidimensional view is incorrect and that the people of Puerto de las Piedras are choosing from among several different alternative strategies of modernization.

Third, I will determine the various factors associated with predicting which individuals will adopt each of the alternative strategies. I have found that a separate model (incorporating several different variables) is needed to explain which individuals would choose each modernizing behavior.

The following chapter presents some general information about the Temascalcingo region, while Chapter 3 is an introduction to the *ejido* of Puerto de las Piedras, whose people are the subject of this study. Chapter 4 contains a discussion of the dependent variables, the measures of modernization. Chapters 5 through 11 are organized around topics much like those that might be found in any traditional anthropological monograph. Within these chapters, however, may be found the measurements and discussion of the independent variables used in this analysis. Chapter 12 presents a series of models in which most of the independent variables discussed in earlier chapters are evaluated in terms of their combined effects on the measures of modernization. These multivariate models and their implications are further discussed in Chapter 13, which also contains a summary, predictions about the future, and recommendations to development agents.

2

The land and people of Temascalcingo: the regional perspective

The population that is the object of this study is the *ejido* of Puerto de las Piedras. No community today, however, exists in a state of total isolation from other social groupings. The purpose of this chapter is to describe the regional context in which Puerto de las Piedras exists – the *municipio* (roughly equivalent to an American county) of Temascalcingo.[8] With the general geographical, historical, social, and economic background provided in this chapter, it will be possible to view the *ejido* within a broader context.

First impressions

My first impressions of the Temascalcingo region were particularly pleasant. I can recall the few hours I spent riding from Mexico City toward a strange place that neither I nor anyone else connected with that first summer's fieldwork had ever seen. The time was late June 1970, and the summer rains had not yet returned life to the vegetation of the valleys and plateaus we passed. I watched with increasing apprehension as we drove past endless fields of newly planted corn, stunted and drying in the sun; cattle, horses, and burros, looking thin and weary, searching lifeless earth for something to sustain them just a little longer; and the mountains and hillsides, denuded of vegetation and scarred by gullies. The last few miles were perhaps the most discouraging. The road, although still paved, became more winding and pocked with holes; the houses along the road looked more austere and more isolated from one another. The erosion of the hillsides was more severe, and there were places where the gullies were buried deep between cliffs. As we drew closer to Temascalcingo, we wound down a road cut into one of the steep sides of a canyon through which a river flowed far below.

As we reached the bottom of the canyon and crossed the bridge over the Lerma River, an almost miraculous transformation seemed to occur – everything was lush and green. The mountain slopes were covered with trees, the corn was full of life, and even the weeds along the roadside were an inviting green. Soon we were rumbling over the cobblestoned streets past brightly colored houses and into the main square of Temascalcingo. We saw that the town is tucked at the base of mountains which surround it on three sides. The fourth side, to the northwest, opens into a valley which stretches toward distant mountains and the horizon.

Although I will probably never again be as impressed by the beauty of the region as I was that first time, entering the valley through the canyon never failed to provoke a reaction. At times it was of wonder and awe and then, toward the end of our ten months of fieldwork in 1973, just the feeling of home.

The valley really is a beautiful place. There is no single, striking feature; but it is a place where colors change subtly, like moods with the seasons. The winter dry season sees clear blue skies merging on the horizon with the many shades of brown which seem to cover everything. By February, people begin to irrigate their fields in preparation for planting; and the valley floor becomes a checkerboard mottled first by a few, then many, fields soaked dark brown with water. Early spring finds the mountains still brown and dry, dappled here and there with areas of red clay. Tiny young shoots of corn plants, covered with dust, stand meekly in fields now dry again despite the earlier irrigation, reflecting the apprehension of the farmers as they wait for the first rains. Then summer rains turn both mountains and valley the lush green I remember so well from that first visit, before the tassels of the maturing corn paint a floor of yellow in late summer. Soon a frost will kill the corn and everything else that is green, and the cycle will start again.

It is not hard to believe that one of the greatest Mexican landscape artists, Jose María Velasco, was born on one of the tiny streets of the community which is now known officially as Temascalcingo de Jose María Velasco. What is difficult to understand is why so few of his paintings were done in the region.

The physical setting

The *municipio* of Temascalcingo is located in the northwestern part of the state of Mexico about 155 kilometers from Mexico City (see Figure 2.1). Temascalcingo, in addition to being the name of the *municipio*, is also the name of the large town that serves as the political, economic, religious, and social center of the region. Forty-one other named communities are found within the boundaries of the *municipio*.

The central highlands of Mexico where Temscalcingo is located also encompass the past and/or present great cities of Teotihuacán, Tula, Te-

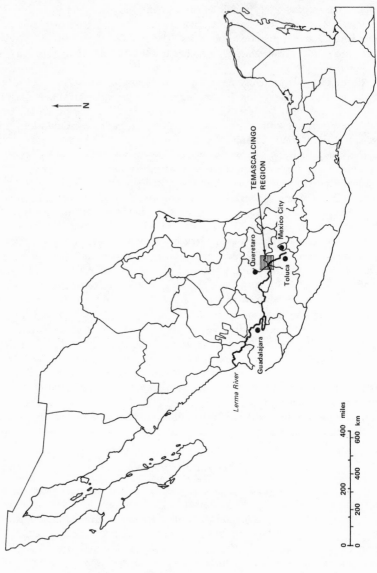

Figure 2.1 Location of the Temascalcingo region.

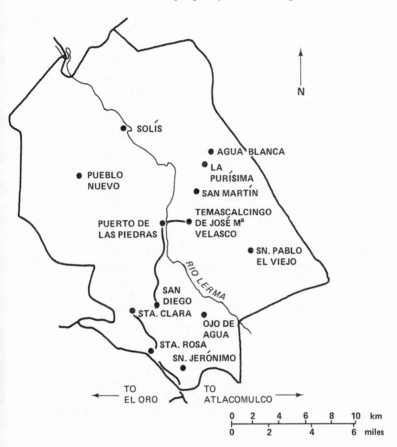

Figure 2.2 *Municipio* of Temascalcingo

nochtitlán, Puebla, Toluca, and Mexico City. As are other parts of the central highlands, Temascalcingo is characterized by a temperate climate, high mountains, and fertile valleys.

The most important geographical feature of the *municipio* is the Lerma River, which bisects a flat, fairly narrow valley known as the Valley of Temascalcingo or the Valley of Solís (Figure 2.2). Surrounding the valley, which is only 4.5 kilometers wide, are a number of mountains. Although Temascalcingo itself is 2,360 meters above sea level, some mountain peaks range up to 3,250 meters.

The climate of the region is very pleasant. The mean annual temperature is 12.9°C (about 55°F); the highest temperature recorded has been only 31.5°C (about 89°F) and the lowest −11°C (about 12°F). Normally, temperatures do not go much above 80°F even in the hottest month (June) or below 25°F in the coldest month (January). During the day, even in the coldest months, the temperature will rise to about 75°F before falling rapidly in the evening. And even in the warmest months, it is not unusual for the temperature to dip into the 40s (Fahrenheit) at night before rising in response to the warmth of the sun. Frosts are common from October through March and thus prevent the inhabitants of the region from cultivating their fields year-round. Nevertheless, the houses do not have any sort of heating system, although there are a few times during the year when it would be welcome.

The mean annual precipitation in the region is about 865 millimeters per year. Three-quarters of this rainfall (snow is very rare in the area) occurs during a distinct rainy season which runs from June through September. The six months from November through April are very dry and receive about 12 percent of the total rainfall.[9]

The mountains in the *municipio* have been exploited for centuries. Once heavily forested, they were a valuable source of timber for fuel and construction purposes over the centuries but were overused. The result, as in many other areas of Mexico, is a very serious soil erosion problem. In some parts of the *municipio,* the hillsides have been stripped of not only vegetation but the soil as well. Deep *barrancas* (gorges) have been carved in areas where the water rushes down the mountains.

These geographical and climatological features have been both a boon and a scourge to the inhabitants of the valley. On one hand, the dry season which extends into April makes irrigation desirable for the planting of the corn crop, the main means of agricultural and economic sustenance. The Lerma River and the flat valley floor have made it relatively easy to irrigate. On the other hand, the heavy summer rains produce an overabundance of water. The denuded hillsides compound the problem because there is little ground cover to hold either soil or water. Thus the Valley of Temascalcingo has been subjected to periodic flooding of the Lerma River, which has destroyed many crops in the past. In Chapter 5, I will discuss some of these features of the natural environment in greater detail because they are important in shaping the lives of villagers in the region.

The original inhabitants

The northwestern part of the state of Mexico and the surrounding area is one of diverse ethnic heritages. In the Temascalcingo region, for example, there are at present Otomí and Mazahua Indians as well as *mestizos* (people of mixed Indian and Spanish heritage). Most individuals are now classified as *mestizo,* and Mazahua outnumber Otomí. In the past, Matlatzinca also supposedly occupied the region, probably dominating the Otomí and Mazahua as they did in the Valley of Toluca (Quezada 1972). All three of these languages are very closely related (Swadesh 1960). There were also areas in which Tarascans were living interspersed with Otomí, Mazahua, and Matlatzinca (Cortes 1972:23-4), and this may have been the case in Temascalcingo. Although some information about the region can be culled from ethnohistorical studies that have been published on the Otomí (Carrasco 1950) and the Matlatzinca (Quezada 1972), any definitive study of the situation in Temascalcingo before Spanish contact will have to await ethnohistorical and archaeological investigations in the area.

The Temascalcingo region does not appear to have been a very important center in the time before the Conquest. Despite the area's probable marginality, however, it is easy to find obsidian arrow points, knives, and other cutting edges on the hillsides. Jade figurines have also been found by the current inhabitants of the region. Because neither of these types of stone occur naturally in the area, Temascalcingo must have been linked with the trade networks which seem to have been pervasive in Mesoamerica well before the Spanish conquest.

Many of the names of communities in the Temascalcingo region are of Mazahua or Otomí derivation. Temascalcingo, however, is a Nahuatl name which comes from the word *temascalli* (steam bath) and the diminutive *tzinco.* The name thus means "the small steam bath."

Colonialism and independence

It is difficult to obtain data concerning the colonial period in Temascalcingo because the documents which had been kept in the local *Presidencia* became scattered during the tumultuous Mexican Revolution. Some of these came into the hands of private citizens. According to some documents I have seen, the town of Temascalcingo was founded about 1571. The *haciendas* (great estates) in the area date from a much earlier time, however. The manager of the Hacienda Solís wrote in 1851:

> With respect to this estate, although I do not have the titles in front of me to give you the exact dates and names of the original owners, I believe that it was deeded between the years 1542 and 1555 by the Viceroys Don Antonio de Mendoza and Don Luís de Velasco to Don Francisco de Villegas. He passed possession on to Don Manuel de Villegas who gave the estate to his daughter

Doña Francisca. She married Don Gaspar de Solís, from whom we
suppose the *hacienda* got the name which it now carries. (Villas
1851, my translation)
Other *haciendas* in the region were established about the same time.

Temascalcingo was located close to two very important mining centers during and shortly after the colonial period. During the late sixteenth
and early seventeenth centuries, Tlalpujahua, only about thirty miles
from Temascalcingo, was an important silver mining community. Then
in the early part of the nineteenth century, El Oro became a very important gold mining center. This development took place soon after Mexican
independence, and the mines were controlled by British interests. Although Temascalcingo was not an important mining center, it probably
contributed to the support of the mines with its agricultural and livestock production.

By 1910, the Hacienda Solís had become an important producer of
corn, wheat, barley, and cattle and was the sixth largest estate in the
state of Mexico (Southworth 1910). A former school teacher at the
Hacienda Solís reported that:

The *hacienda* was one of the leading areas of wheat production
during the time it was in existence – and for a time it was the
most productive in all of Mexico. The average harvest was 35,000
cargas of wheat each year [or, 5,250 metric tons]. Corn was
grown only for personal consumption and not as a cash crop.
There were many *jacales* [large storehouses] which were owned
by the *hacendado*: San José, San Miguel, San Antonio, San Nico-
lás, Cerritos, Calderas, La Huerta, San Francisco, San Vicente,
Juanacatlan, Solís, and San Isidro. At one time there were about
200 bulls available in the area for plowing. Each *jacal* had a distinctive color bull – San Miguel had black bulls, San Antonio and
San José had *colorado* [reddish], Cerritos had *pinto* [mottled],
San Isidro *oscos* [color between black and red]. The *peones*
earned about 20 *centavos* per day plus 2 *cuartillos* of corn. (Bee
21 July 1971)

A man who had worked for the *hacienda* as a small boy gave me
some idea of what life was like for the common people during those
days:

The *hacendado* owned all the valley and the people of my village
lived up in the hills. We had *milpas* [fields] on the hillsides but we
got very poor yields of barley and corn. Everyone had to work
for one *peso* fifty *centavos* per week and the *hacendado* gave us
twelve *cuartillos* of corn every Wednesday. Children also worked.
The *hacendado* would round up the children to work the fields of

wheat. They would line up and weed a row while a man with a whip watched over them. When they had finished a row, the man would inspect the rows and for each weed that was left, he would give the children a lash with the whip. It was the same for older people. If a man came to work late, he would be sent home and not allowed to work. Since the *hacienda* was the only source of labor, this was a serious problem for the tardy worker.

Despite occasional floods which plagued the valley then as they did until recently, the Valley of Temascalcingo was one of the best agricultural regions in the state of Mexico just before the Revolution. Flooding was controlled by the managers of the *hacienda*, who had plenty of cheap labor to employ cleaning drainage and irrigation canals and building up the banks along the river.

Revolution and its aftermath

The Revolution never had much of a direct effect on Temascalcingo. Troops from both sides are reported to have passed through the valley; but some informants said that whenever an army passed, the populace would give them food, provision, and anything else to avoid having the town burned. Not even the Hacienda Solís was damaged during the civil war. I never talked with anyone who had a relative or friend who fought in the Revolution.

The major effect of this tumultuous period on Temascalcingo seems to have been to contribute to "buried treasure" stories. According to a number of informants, some of the wealthy families of Temascalcingo buried their fortunes in the mountains to prevent them from being stolen by the armies. These stories are occasionally fueled when someone finds a few old coins. In addition, previously poor people who have been able to succeed in some way are rumored to have found some part of the "buried treasure," which ostensibly accounts for their success. Similar treasure tales are common in Tzintzuntzan (Foster 1967: 145–50) and other areas of Mexico (Schryer 1976: 708).

The period following the Revolution was one of considerable activity. The peasants had to wage a long, hard struggle against the *hacendados* before the land was finally redistributed. Only when Lázaro Cárdenas came to power were the people successful in their struggle. Even then, the *hacendados* did not give up. There are reports that the government official sent to be in charge of the redistribution was assassinated (Iwanska 1971: 22). People in some of the communities closest to the *hacienda* were so fearful of the consequences that they refused to apply for land until after much of it had been redistributed. As a result, these communities reportedly received less land than communities situated further away from the *hacienda*. Another informant reported that the government organized a group known as Defensas Rurales among the new *ejidatarios* for protection against the Guardias Blancas, a group armed and supported by *hacendados* whose lands were expropriated.

The struggle for redistribution of the lands was successful. Between 1930 and 1940 almost all of the lands in the valley were taken from the *hacienda* and given to the peasants who had formerly worked the lands. Sixteen *ejidos* were formed to receive the lands in and around the valley. All of these *ejidos* allocated parcels to each individual. None chose to work the lands communally. Although over 17,000 hectares (1 hectare equals 2.46 acres) were redistributed to about 3,500 *ejidatarios*, only slightly more than 3,000 hectares are good, irrigated land. The rest is temporal or mountain land. Nevertheless, those individuals who received an *ejido* grant now had their own lands on which they could attempt to make a living.

Some people in and around Temascalcingo were not as fortunate. They were convinced by one of the wealthy landowners who lived in Temascalcingo not to ask for the redistribution of his lands. Although this man and his father had accumulated considerable land by lending money to small landowners and then taking the land in payment (one of my informants had a document which listed 104 separate transactions of this nature), he was reportedly a benevolent *patrón*. In addition, his brother was a very popular priest in the community and preached against the land reform (see Chapter 9). Thus this family was able to retain its lands. A group of people from the town of Temascalcingo even formed a militia to depose some members of an Indian community who had occupied the land for a while and had called for its redistribution.

This landowner had succeeded in convincing his workers that he would take care of them forever if they supported him. Other *hacendados* in the region had tried to do the same but were not as successful. Some of this man's former employees now recall bitterly that, despite his promises, he sold his lands a few years later. His "taking care of them forever" amounted to a 350-*peso* gift to each of them. Most of these people and their descendants now work for the current owners of the land – earning only 12 *pesos* (about one dollar) a day, far below the government's minimum wage for the region.

Although the region had been spared the violence of the Revolution, considerable conflict was connected with the redistribution of lands. There were conflicts between communities that were trying to obtain

2. The municipal *cabacera* of Temascalcingo, which is the political, religious, social, and cultural center of the region.

the same lands; murders were carried out by individuals who were try-ing to fill the power vacuum left by the *hacendados*; boundaries were disputed; and complaints were lodged by those who felt they had been cheated in the distribution of lands (see Chapter 3).

The population of the municipio today

The *municipio* illustrates some of the stark contrasts found in de-veloping countries today. The municipal *cabacera* (head town) of Temascalcingo (see photograph 2) is well articulated to centers of activ-ity in modern Mexico. The merchants, doctors, and teachers who live there are a part of the growing middle class of Mexico. They are well aware of events taking place within Mexico and around the world. Some of them take frequent vacations to Acapulco, Mexico City, and occasionally the United States. They live in houses with indoor plumb-ing, gas stoves, water heaters, beds, color televisions, telephones, and stereo phonographs; and they drive automobiles or trucks.

In contrast with these "modern" people, there are individuals in some of the outlying communities (and more than a few in the town of Temascalcingo itself) who live in one-room *adobe* houses, carry water from polluted water sources, ride burros for transportation, cultivate their fields with animal-pulled plows or even digging sticks, do not wear shoes, and have only candles to light their homes. Some of these individuals do not speak Spanish, and others have never traveled beyond the borders of the *municipio*.

Between these two extremes there are infinite variations in life style among the people of Temascalcingo. For this reason it is impossible to give a description of the "typical person" or to generalize easily about the culture and behavior of the people in the region. I will, however, describe the kinds of goods and services available, networks of communication with the outside world, and some general characteristics of the population. It should be kept in mind that the applicability of much of what follows for any one individual is very dependent on the variations (especially in terms of wealth) which exist within the population. Many of these variations in one *ejido* will be described in the following chapters.

The population of the *municipio* exhibits characteristics similar to most developing areas of the world. Over 50 percent of the population is under fifteen years of age. Table 2.1 is arranged by five year intervals; and as we see, the largest proportion of the population is concentrated in the younger categories. The population is increasing at an annual rate of about 3 percent.

The *municipio* is made up of forty-two different communities. The predominantly rural character of the region is obvious, for the communities range in size from 86 people in the smallest to 3,476 in the largest. Although Temascalcingo is the political, religious, and economic center (and has been since the colonial period), it is not the largest community (see Table 2.2). Temascalcingo, however, is surrounded by seven *barrios* which, if included, would bring its population closer to 5,000. Nevertheless, the makeup of these *barrios* differs significantly from *El Centro* (the center), for they are primarily inhabited by Indians and poor *mestizos*. Although some poor *mestizos* and perhaps a few Indians live in El Centro, most of its inhabitants are *comerciantes* (businessmen), skilled tradesmen, teachers, doctors, landowners, and others who are somewhat better off than the general population of the *municipio*. The significant point that I wish to emphasize is that the people in the town of Temascalcingo politically, economically and socially dominate the *municipio* despite the fact that they are only a very small minority of the total population.

In addition to the differences between the well-articulated, socially dominant center and the poorer, more backward communities, there is another important area of social cleavage. This division is a result of

Table 2.1. *Population of* municipio *by age and sex*

Age group	No. of males	No. of females	Total	Population (%)
0–4	2,971	3,144	6,115	18.3
5–9	3,032	3,028	6,060	18.2
10–14	2,422	2,336	4,758	14.2
15–19	1,650	1,445	3,095	9.3
20–24	1,179	1,222	2,401	7.2
25–29	987	1,041	2,028	6.1
30–34	825	855	1,680	5.0
35–39	877	829	1,706	5.1
40–44	619	619	1,238	3.7
45–49	591	575	1,166	3.5
50–54	372	344	716	2.1
55–59	349	330	679	2.0
60–64	299	302	601	1.8
65–69	260	259	519	1.6
70–74	183	140	323	1.0
75–79	87	75	162	.5
80 and over	76	63	139	.4
Total			33,386	100.0

Source: Dirección General de Estadística 1971.

Table 2.2. *The largest communities in the Temascalcingo region*

Predominantly mestizo	Population	Predominantly Indian	Population
Temascalcingo	1,966	San Jerónimo	3,476
Agua Blanca	1,311	San Diego	2,324
Pueblo Nuevo	1,123	La Purísima	2,169
San Antonio Solís	1,093	Santa Clara	1,682
Solís	1,012	San Pablo el Viejo	1,450
		Santa Rosa	1,256
		San Pedro Potla	1,215
		San Juanico	1,045

ethnic differences which exist in the *municipio*. As I mentioned earlier in the chapter, the population is comprised of Otomí and Mazahua Indians as well as *mestizos*. According to the latest census, almost 40 percent of the population of the *municipio* over five years of age still speak an Indian language (*Dirección General de Estadística* 1971). However, only about 4 percent of the population are classified as monolingual Indians. Nonetheless, the ethnic background of the communities is an important point. Indian communities tend, in general, to be located outside the valley and in the hills, to have fewer services (despite the fact that some of them are quite large), and to have a significantly poorer population. Such Indian communities as San Jerónimo and Santa Rosa have very large populations but are not served by electricity, water, or decent roads.

Communication and commerce

The communication network within the *municipio* is not very well developed. A paved road does connect Temascalcingo with the highway which runs between Toluca and Querétaro. Two good dirt roads link Temascalcingo with Solís and the neighboring municipal *cabacera* of Acambay. Two other recently constructed roads are important for transportation purposes. These were built to service the irrigation canals that were constructed on the perimeter of the valley. Although these roads incidentally link some surrounding communities with Temascalcingo, their main purpose was not to aid communication among the communities in the *municipio*. Many communities still depend upon footpaths and/or frequently impassable dirt roads to get to one of the main arteries of travel.

The transportation network along these main arteries is quite ample. The bus system is remarkable for such a small region. Buses run hourly, except late at night, between Temascalcingo and Mexico City. They also run less frequently to Solís and beyond, El Oro, Acambay, Jilotepec, and points between all of these communities. On Sunday, market day in Temascalcingo, there is special bus service to some communities within the *municipio*.

For those who miss the bus, have some special cargo, or wish to ride in more comfort, there are also eight taxis that serve Temascalcingo. These taxis and those from Atlacomulco and El Oro constantly circulate among these three communities. A bus to San Diego from Temascalcingo costs only two *pesos*, whereas a taxi costs ten *pesos*. Usually the taxis stay on the main roads, but occasionally a driver will make a special trip into one of the more difficult to reach communities if the fare is high enough.

The important railway link between Mexico City and Morelia passes through the *municipio*. It does not seem to carry much traffic from Temascalcingo, however, because the nearest station is not conveniently located. Most goods that enter or leave the valley do so on one of the many small and large trucks serving the region.

There are only two post offices in the region. The main one is located in Temascalcingo, and there is a substation in Solís. Postal clerks reported that about seventy letters and parcels, including newspapers, came into the post office every day. Only about four or five were mailed each day. One of the large parcels which arrived daily was a shipment of newspapers. A man employed by a local store delivered about forty-five newpapers a day to regular customers. Some of these were "sports" newspapers, whereas others were the major Mexico City dailies *El Sol* and *Excelsior.* One of the little stands in the marketplace also sold ten to twelve copies of *Novedades,* another newspaper from Mexico City, each day.

Telephone service in Temascalcingo is growing. There were twenty-eight telephones in homes and offices in 1973. All calls have to go through the switchboard which is located in the largest restaurant in town. This restaurant also has two telephone booths available for use by the general public. A messenger is often available and is sent out to try to find individuals in town who do not have telephones in their homes. Telephone service is often slow because calling anywhere outside of town necessitates going through the regional switchboard in Atlacomulco. In addition, service is only possible during the hours when the restaurant, and thus the switchboard, is in operation. Nevertheless, it provides a very important and relatively rapid system of communication. During most days a steady stream of people uses the telephones in the restaurant.

Temascalcingo and most of the communities located around the edge of the valley have electricity. The more isolated communities have yet to receive this service, but most villages that we visited seemed to have some plans or hopes for electrification projects in the future. The major problem is that each community must pay a portion of the costs for extending existing services.

The town of Temascalcingo receives its water from the distant town of Ojo de Agua through an aqueduct built in the 1930s. The water comes from underground springs and is very pure at its source. Because the aqueduct is cement and is broken in places, the purity of the water probably suffers somewhat by the time it reaches the taps of users in Temascalcingo. Nevertheless, the water is considerably cleaner than that used by communities that depend on water holes and other easily polluted sources. Intestinal diseases are rampant in towns that do not have sources of potable water.

Temascalcingo is also the main commercial center. There are a few

Table 2.3. *Stalls and Vendors in the Sunday market in Temascalcingo,*
18 March 1973

No.	Type of stall or vendor	No.	Type of stall or vendor
43	Fruits and vegetables	2	Shoes
9	clothing	2	Plastic and tin goods
8	*Tortilla*	2	*Tacos*
6	Beans	2	Bread
5	Bangles (mirrors, combs,	2	Peanuts
	ribbons, etc.)	2	Ambulatory bangle vendors
5	Limes	1	Medicinal herbs
5	*Pulque* (fermented alcoholic	1	*Tortilla* baskets
	beverage)	1	Truck with oranges
5	Pottery	1	Cloth (material)
5	Smoked fish	1	Ice cream vendor
5	Steamed mutton	1	Ambulatory vendor with baskets
3	Chilli	1	Plastic net bags (also had a video
3	Potatoes		master and a "penny" scale)
2	Lima beans	1	Avocado
2	Garlic	1	Soap Total = 127

major grocery stores, a hardware store, a few clothing and shoe stores, a
furniture store, a number of butchers, a printing shop, and a small hotel,
as well as restaurants and many *miscelaneas* (small stores that mainly
sell cigarettes, bread, soft drinks, candy, etc.). The selection of merchan-
dise may not be as varied as that found in a larger city, but a surprisingly wide range of goods is available. In the smaller towns, only *miscelaneas* serve the needs of the people.

A majority of the commercial transactions take place on Sunday,
market day in Temascalcingo. Late Saturday, many small and large
trucks roll into town, and people begin setting up their stalls in the
main plaza. Many people stay until Monday afternoon before moving
on to other communities. Table 2.3 lists the types of nonpermanent
businesses that were found on a typical Sunday in the Temascalcingo
market. Days when there is a major holiday of significance to the populace also find a large number of these nonpermanent businesses in town.
The primary holidays during 1973 were January 1 (the largest), September 29 (the festival of San Miguel, the patron saint), and *Jueves de Corpus* (Corpus Christi).

There is little in the way of industry in the *municipio* except for the
pottery made in a few villages. The pottery is very plain; but according

to local informants, it is the best cooking ware made in Mexico. A number of entrepreneurs have made it the basis of a large pottery-marketing network. They collect pottery from many parts of Mexico and store it in warehouses in one of the villages outside Temascalcingo. These entrepreneurs distribute the locally produced and other pottery throughout Mexico (see Papousek 1974).

In the early 1970s the state government established a number of small factories in the region. These factories manufacture high quality pottery that resembles stoneware. These products are made in gas-fired ovens at very high temperatures, thus eliminating the lead hazard present in traditionally made pottery. The new "stoneware" is sold in the state artisans' markets in tourist centers throughout Mexico. It can also be bought in some of the shops located in the most elegant hotels in Mexico City. The president of Mexico ordered many sets of the dishes and decreed that they be used at all state dinners hosted by Mexican embassies throughout the world. However, the effect of these factories on the region's economy has thus far been fairly small because they employ fewer than two hundred workers.

The majority of the population of the region depends upon agriculture for a living. There are over 3,500 *ejidatarios,* some private property owners, and many other individuals who work as agricultural laborers. All of these depend directly upon the potentially fertile lands for their sustenance.

Agriculture in the valley had not fared well since the redistribution of lands in the 1930s. Soon after the *ejidos* were formed, a series of disastrous floods occurred. These floods were primarily due to the deterioration of the water control system, which had been established by the *hacienda.* The *hacienda* managers had been able to control the flooding of the Lerma by constructing levees, drainage canals, and dams. The *hacienda's* cheap and plentiful labor supply made it possible to build and maintain the flood control system as well as canals for irrigation purposes. After the redistribution, the *ejidatarios* were no longer able to organize effectively to perform the necessary maintenance. Thus after 1940, the *ejidatarios* often lost their crops during the heavy summer rains because of flooding of the Lerma River.

In spite of the disastrous flooding, the agricultural potential of the region has been recognized for a long time. As a result, a number of development agencies have been involved in attempts to improve the socioeconomic situation in the valley ever since the expropriation of the *hacienda* lands. I will briefly describe some of the earlier efforts in this direction before providing a more detailed examination of development efforts in the decade preceding 1973.

Development projects

The first development efforts in the valley after the redistribution of the land were in the form of loans provided by the Banco Ejidal, a bank established by the government explicitly to give aid to the newly established *ejidos*. Informants reported that soon after the *ejidos* in the Temascalcingo region formed, the Banco Ejidal provided funds for people to buy oxen, plows, and other agricultural necessities. The experiences of the *ejidatarios* with this first form of aid have set the tone of all subsequent encounters. Some of the officials sent by the bank to collect debts were dishonest and never reported payments that were made. Some *ejidatarios* were harassed and even jailed for reneging on obligations they had actually fulfilled.

Another development effort dating from that period was an attempt to establish a sheep-raising industry in the region. Some very fine sheep were introduced without regard for their ability to adapt to the climate. The sheep quickly died, and the result was another loss for the *ejidatarios* who participated in the program.

Around 1950, there was a program designed to improve the wheat crop in the valley. A hybrid variety of wheat was distributed, along with fertilizer. Instead of increased yields, the *ejidatarios* found that their crops were smaller than in most years. Although the agricultural engineers discovered that the specific variety of wheat was wrong for the area on the basis of the poor yields, the *ejidatarios* quite logically concluded that hybrids and fertilizers had no value.

After all of these bad experiences, the people of the region became convinced that "development" meant bilking them out of money for the enrichment of those promising to help them. This attitude was still held by many *ejidatarios* in 1973.

Meanwhile, the situation of the Temascalcingo region was becoming more desperate each year. The river flooding occurred almost annually and in a few years wiped out most of the crops in the valley. In these years, the Mexican government had to send food, blankets, and other aid to save the people from starvation. Another growing problem was the increasing population. When the land was redistributed there was enough for almost everyone to receive some of it, but *ejidal* laws prevent subdividing plots. Thus many sons and daughters of the original *ejidatarios* had no possibility of acquiring land. Temporary and permanent migration to Mexico City in search of work was the only answer for many.

In the early 1960s, the Department of Hydraulic Resources (a cabinet-level agency in the Mexican government) decided to make a major investment in the Valley of Temascalcingo. They obtained loans from the

Inter-American Development Bank and other sources for the construction of flood control and irrigation facilities. The region was fortunate in that a prominent politician who owned a ranch in the valley had by then become the secretary of Hydraulic Resources. His position as head of this agency was almost certainly instrumental in beginning the program in Temascalcingo.

A massive input of capital and technology was necessary in order to construct the facilities to control the Lerma's flooding. A whole new river bed was dug in one part of the valley, and the formerly meandering Lerma was rerouted into it. Where logistical problems prevented this, the river was dredged and its banks were reinforced. Two large dams were built further upstream to enable engineers to control the amount of water flowing into the valley. Drainage ditches were dredged and cleared of overgrowth. Finally, irrigation canals were built along the perimeter of both sides of the valley to enable the *ejidatarios* to sow their crops before the onset of the summer rains and thus reduce the dangers of damage caused by early frosts.

A number of other agencies established socioeconomic development projects in the valley during this time. Quite rightly, it was thought that the technological improvements being carried out would renew the people's confidence in development efforts. One of the primary agencies that became involved was called Plan Lerma. Patterned after the massive development projects being carried out in the Papaloapan and Balsas River basins (Barkin and King 1970), Plan Lerma was supposed to accomplish much the same thing in the Lerma River valley – an integrated program of regional development crosscutting political boundaries.

Plan Lerma established three small pilot projects, one of which was located in the Temascalcingo Valley. Housed in the former Hacienda Solís, Plan Lerma personnel began by gathering economic, social, political, and agricultural data on the region. Unfortunately, the agency never received the amount of funding it needed to bring its programs to fruition. Thus the actual accomplishments of Plan Lerma were minimal – a small housing renovation program took place in one community; some fruit trees were distributed; and technical advice on fertilizers, herbicides, insecticides, animal diseases, and other agricultural matters was provided. By 1971, the agency had decided to concentrate its minimal funds and personnel in a different region and left the Valley of Temascalcingo.

The most visible development scheme being carried out during our first fieldwork in the region in 1970 was under the aegis of Plan Maíz, although several other agencies were also cooperating. Plan Maíz was a program sponsored by the state of Mexico. Its goal was to introduce "Green Revolution" (Griffin 1974) techniques to peasant farmers in the state. It was patterned after the famous Puebla Project (CIMMYT 1969) in which an enormous amount of technical and socioeconomic research had been done in connection with promoting the adoption of modern agricultural techniques.

Plan Maíz sought to improve corn yields in the region by organizing *ejidatarios* to consolidate blocks of land that could be farmed semicooperatively. Tractors were hired to plow, plant, and cultivate; hybrid seed was sown; chemical fertilizer was applied; and herbicides and insecticides were utilized. The *ejidatarios* received all of these items on credit with the understanding that they would pay off the debt with part of the extra profit they would make from the improved corn production.

The whole program was carefully watched over by an agricultural engineer who was not above threatening or forcing *ejidatarios* to carry out the tasks he deemed necessary. In Puerto de las Piedras, he became incensed when the people refused to thin the corn plants. He reacted by barring them from working on their own fields and hired laborers from another village to do the thinning and weeding. He added the cost of this labor to the *ejidatarios'* debt. Everyone agreed that he did achieve significant improvements in corn production. However, many people reported that the increased yields were not large enough to pay off all of the debts they had accumulated. Many *ejidatarios* felt that they were cheated; and some refused, or were unable, to pay the money they owed. Plan Maíz reacted to this latest example of peasant "uncooperativeness" by withdrawing funding for the program and transferring the engineer to another area.

The program did succeed in convincing the *ejidatarios* of the benefits to be gained by using chemical fertilizers. Many continued to use fertilizer on their crops even when no credit was available. By 1973, Plan Maíz was working in the valley again, although on a much-reduced scale. This time credit was provided for fertilizer; but no other aid, advice, or strings were attached.

In late 1972, another agency took over the former Hacienda Solís. This organization was a part of the Institute for the Development of Human Resources in the State of Mexico (IDREHM). The *hacienda* was refurbished and refitted and turned into a school for *ejidatarios* and their sons. A one-month course was established to "cosmopolitanize" peasants. The course included lessons on making telephone calls and writing letters, becoming acquainted with various government agencies, learning some of the country's history, learning about other countries,

and discussing problems common to *ejidatarios*. Although some attention was given to agricultural and livestock techniques, the course clearly
seemed designed to change the cognitive orientation of the *ejidatarios*.
Most of the students who came for the one-month stay at the *hacienda*
were from other regions. Only a few *ejidatarios* from the valley enrolled
in the course.

Personnel from Hydraulic Resources have become the primary devel-
opers working in the region, mainly because all of the other agencies
with which they were working have been discontinued for one reason or
another. Although Hydraulic Resources is only peripherally concerned
with socioeconomic (as opposed to technological) development, they
have poured millions of *pesos* into the flood control and irrigation
works. To date, this major capital investment has yielded a very poor
return. The *ejidatarios* pay only a nominal fee each year for the irrigation water they need, a sum far below what is required just to maintain the canals and other facilities. Because the techniques used by the
ejidatarios are rudimentary, the amount of corn produced is small; and
most of it goes for subsistence. Little corn ever reaches the national
market. Thus despite the improvements, there has been little economic
development in the region; and migration to the cities has continued
unabated.

Hydraulic Resources has been working on a plan to change all of this.
Around 1968, they established a number of experimental fields of different clovers, alfalfas, and other pasture crops in the valley. On the basis
of their experiments, they developed a combination of different grasses
which are well suited to the region and which provide an excellent supply
of food for animals. The ultimate goal of Hydraulic Resources is to form
cooperatives in the *ejidos*. These cooperatives will sow the forage crops
and will build stables for fine dairy and beef cattle. The cattle will be purchased with the aid of bank credit. By late 1974, a number of *ejidos*
had been persuaded to sow the forage crops. These have grown fairly
well, the stables have been built, and some cattle have been introduced.
Although it is still too early to tell whether the hopes for a dairy region
will be realized, a number of problems have already been encountered.
First, credit from the banks has been very difficult to secure. Second,
there is some question as to whether the animals will be able to adapt
to the climatic conditions of the region. Finally, it is not known whether
enough technical assistance will be available to help the *ejidatarios* until
they learn the proper care of the animals and the forage crops. The scar-
city of funds, as always, seems to be a major problem.

Although it is still too early to evaluate the results of this last program, a number of comments about the development efforts are in

order. In general, the succession of development programs has had little impact on the population and the economic status of the region. Development agents feel that there is apathy and distrust among the *ejidatarios*. On the basis of the evidence I have presented in this chapter, I think it would be fair to conclude that these attitudes are perfectly rational responses to the experiences the *ejidatarios* have had with change agents. These experiences have been fraught with dishonesty, unfulfilled promises, hopes that have been raised and then destroyed, and different agencies that have come and gone like shoppers in a supermarket. The people have become so accustomed to this "revolving door" approach to development that most of them take little notice when the designs and names on the jeeps and trucks change.

This is not to say that the development programs have had no effect on any of the population. There are always some individuals who will be better able to take advantage of opportunities than others; and as I pointed out in Chapter 1, the basic premise of this work is to investigate the variability of behavior with regard to a number of different attributes. One of these attributes is the adoption of innovations. After describing the particular *ejido* chosen for study, we will look at the range of variation in the adoption of innovations in Chapter 4.

3

The *ejido* of Puerto de las Piedras: the research population

The selection of a community or other group to be studied always involves a series of decisions. The choices are often made on the basis of such practical matters as accessibility, availability of housing, or having personal contact with some member or members of the group. In other cases, theoretical concerns dictate the selection.

In this chapter, I will give the several reasons why I chose Puerto de las Piedras as my population of study. I will then go on to describe some of the general characteristics of the *ejido*, including its geographical features, history, and population and occupational structure. In the final section of the chapter, I will describe my sampling procedure and briefly describe some of the methods that I used in collecting the data.

Choice of research site

The Valley of Temascalcingo was selected for study because of all the efforts designed to achieve the economic development of the region. The first summer of fieldwork in 1970 was to conduct a pilot study to determine what development efforts were under way and to ascertain whether future studies would be possible and encouraged. On the basis of our experiences then, other researchers and I returned to carry out more detailed studies. Although each one of us has studied different communities and different aspects of life, our general, overarching objective has been a regional study of modernization (preliminary results from several summers of fieldwork may be found in DeWalt, Bee, and Pelto 1973).

With the resources available to me in 1973, it would not have been possible to study a *municipio* of 33,000 people. Thus I chose one *ejido* as my population of study. The term *ejido*, as I have mentioned earlier, refers to agrarian communities that received land in accordance with the agrarian laws growing out of the Revolution of 1910. The boundaries and populations of *ejidos* do not necessarily coincide with either prerevolutionary or modern communities. That is, there are some large communities whose inhabitants belong to several different *ejidos*, while other *ejidos*, such as the one to be described in this chapter, are made

45

up of more than one community. The only requirement for the formation of an *ejido* was that groups of twenty or more individuals be formed to petition for land (Whetten 1948:182).

There are two types of *ejido* in Mexico, collective and individual. The collective *ejido* is one in which lands are held and worked cooperatively. In individual *ejidos*, individuals work their lands apart from other *ejidatarios* (members of an *ejido*). The *ejido* remains as an organization to deal with problems common to all of the individual landholders. The overwhelming majority of the *ejidos* in Mexico are individual (Whetten 1848:203), and all those in the Temascalcingo region are of this type.

I did not choose the *ejido* of Puerto de las Piedras because it is a typical population. The research that I have conducted around the region has convinced me that there is no such thing as a "typical" community. The variations in modes of subsistence (e.g., potters, agriculturalists, charcoal makers, and itinerant peddlers), ethnic status (Otomí, Mazahua, *mestizo*, and mixed communities), and other characteristics make each community fairly unique.

I selected the *ejido* for study because it has a number of characteristics that were of importance for my theoretical focus. First, I was interested in studying agricultural modernization. By making my population of study the *ejido* rather than the community, I was eliminating from consideration all of those individuals who did not have access to land.

Second, because all of the individuals in my study were agriculturalists and had access to land, they would be expected to be more homogeneous than the population as a whole (see DeWalt 1975:152). Thus my purpose was to explicitly select a group where diversity would be minimized and then to explore the range of variability within that population. As will become clear in later chapters, the heterogeneity of behavior among the members of the *ejido* of Puerto de las Piedras is quite pronounced.

A third reason for my choice was that this *ejido* has had considerable contact with many of the change agents who have worked in the region. Its possession of prime agricultural lands and its location just outside the town of Temascalcingo made it a likely target for development efforts.

Finally, the number of individuals in the *ejido* was small enough to allow a comprehensive study to be done. I was able to collect a wide variety of both qualitative and quantitative materials.

In addition to these more scientific reasons, Puerto de las Piedras was also a good choice in several practical respects. The lands and villages of the *ejido* are accessible, for they are located on the road near the town of Temascalcingo. We were only able to find a vacant house in town, and so it was desirable to study an *ejido* nearby. The mile or two distance to Puerto de las Piedras met this criterion. Finally, although the *ejido* had a Mazahua Indian heritage (see Chapter 11), by 1973 it was well along in the transition to being *mestizo*. Everyone spoke Spanish; thus it was not necessary to learn another language or to work through interpreters.

The physical setting

The physical entity known as the *ejido* of Puerto de las Piedras lies on the western side of the Lerma River just beyond the point where the river enters the Valley of Temascalcingo (see Figure 5.1). The people who farm this land come primarily from three small communities – El Puerto, Las Piedras, and El Jardín. In addition, there are a few individuals who now live in other surrounding communities but still maintain their land rights in the *ejido*.

The most important lands of the *ejido* are those which lie on the flat valley floor. The *ejido* has about 400 hectares that are relatively flat and irrigable. Less important are the 545 hectares that lie on the surrounding hillsides. Little of this land is cultivable, and in general, it is used primarily as pasture for animals.

In addition to the *ejido* lands, the communities of El Puerto and Las Piedras also have access to communal lands in the mountains above the villages. These are lands to which the communities have title and therefore are available for use by all of the inhabitants, including non-*ejidatarios*. These lands are important because they serve as pastures, provide a source of firewood (only dead wood is supposed to be gathered), and contain the quarry that is worked by some members of the community (see Photograph 3).

History: the struggle for land

People from the Temascalcingo region never became directly involved in the fighting during the Mexican Revolution. However, in the struggle for land reform following the Revolution, events in the region parallel those in most other areas of Mexico.

The first communities to receive the benefits of the agrarian reform were some of the isolated Indian settlements. The land redistributed to the people of these communities was mountainous and rocky and of little value. The prize was the rich, fertile land in the Valley of Temascal-

3. Part of the *ejido* of Puerto de las Piedras, with the community of El Puerto on the hillside in the background. Also note the quarry in the communal lands on the mountain behind the village.

cingo. Everyone agrees that two principal local figures were the leaders of the agrarian struggle in the region, Naciano and Claudio. According to informants, Naciano led raids on some of the *jacales* of the *hacienda*; Claudio was even bolder and raided the *hacienda* itself.

As far as the people of Puerto de las Piedras are concerned, the hero of the struggle was Naciano (they invariably call him by the respectful term *Don* when talking about him). He was from the village of Las Piedras and was a Mazahua Indian. He not only fought for the expropriation of hacienda lands but also had to fight to prevent people from Temascalcingo (such as Claudio) from gaining control over all of the valley lands that were redistributed to *ejidos*. Naciano, like many revolutionary leaders (e.g., Emiliano Zapata), was not a simple, poor peasant. Informants report that he already had private property of his own and a herd of fifty or more cattle before the land reform.

The redistribution of the land for the people of Puerto de las Piedras came in 1933. According to some informants, there was considerable conflict at this time between people from Temascalcingo and those from Puerto de las Piedras. The people of Puerto de las Piedras say that those from Temascalcingo were trying to grab all of the valley land for themselves. Naciano and his followers decided that they would fight, if need be, to protect their newly won lands. Federal troops were brought in to prevent violence. People from Puerto de las Piedras point to the other *barrios* of Temascalcingo that only received mountainous land for their *ejidos* and say that this would have happened to them, too, were it not for the efforts of Naciano.

Naciano and others from Las Piedras dominated *ejido* affairs in the years immediately following the redistribution. Informants report that people from the community of El Puerto were only invited to sign the list requesting *ejido* land in order to strengthen (with numbers) Naciano's bargaining power with the government. Even today, the 146 *ejidatarios* in the *ejido* of Puerto de las Piedras are a small number when compared to the more than 300 in the neighboring *ejido* of Temascalcingo. It is interesting that, as I will show in Chapter 5, people from El Puerto now hold a numerical advantage over those from Las Piedras, in complete contrast with the situation immediately after the formation of the ejido.

There is still some enmity and conflict between the *Ejido* Puerto de las Piedras and *Ejido* Temascalcingo. Part of the problem stems from the lands that were given to the two *ejidos*. The *ejido* of Puerto de Las Piedras was given the lands on the west side of the river. Temascalcingo was given lands on the east side of the river and north of Temascalcingo itself (Figure 5.1). However, Temascalcingo petitioned for more land, claiming that it had too little for its large number of *ejidatarios*. Later, more land was given to Temascalcingo; but these lands were on the *west* side of the river, just north of the lands of the *Ejido* Puerto de las Piedras. These lands are very distant from Temascalcingo, in part because the *ejidatarios* are forced to travel to El Puerto or Solís to cross the river. This distance makes these lands almost useless to the *ejidatarios* of Temascalcingo, and many rent or give these lands *a medias* (sharecrop) to people who live on the other side of the river. There is some resentment on the part of the *ejidatarios* of Temascalcingo who must pass by the fields of the *Ejido* Puerto de las Piedras before they can get to their own fields. In addition, there is still some contested land between the two *ejidos*.

Ejidatarios and non-ejidatarios: the communities

El Puerto and Las Piedras are both considered *barrios* (named locality groupings) of the town of Temascalcingo. Six other communities are also considered *barrios;* and each has its own church, patron saint, and religious organization (see also Lewis 1963:19). There has been a tendency to merge the two *barrios* of El Puerto and Las Piedras for bureaucratic and other purposes ever since the founding of the *Ejido* Puerto de las Piedras. Census materials and other official government records usually list the two communities together as one entity. In addition, only El Puerto has a church; and the religious organization of the two *barrios* is combined (see also Chapter 8). People of the two localities try to maintain the distinctness of the *barrios,* however. Individuals report that they live in El Puerto or Las Piedras but never Puerto de las Piedras. In fact, some of the factionalism in the *ejido* (see Chapter 7) may be seen in part as conflict between the two communities. In addition, El Puerto and Las Piedras have separate sets of *delegados,* representatives of the community to the *municipio* government.

Both El Puerto and Las Piedras have been described as being "very Indian" in the past. Informants say that until forty or fifty years ago, the people wore traditional Indian-style clothing – white pants and shirt for the men; long multilayered skirts and *quechquemitl* (capes) for the women. At present, both communities are in the process of becoming *mestizo.* No one in either community wears any articles of clothing that can be identified as Indian – except for some of the more urbane female teen-agers who now define as fashionable the wearing of the beautiful "Indian" *quechquemitl.* Although some older individuals still speak Mazahua, nearly everyone speaks excellent Spanish (see also Chapter 11).

El Jardín is the third community whose inhabitants belong to the *Ejido* Puerto de las Piedras. In contrast with El Puerto and Las Piedras, El Jardín is not a *barrio* of Temascalcingo and does not have an Indian heritage. In the past, the community included an old *hacienda* and associated buildings and a few houses of *mestizos* who worked at the *hacienda.* Since the formation of the *ejido,* the community has slowly grown as people have moved from El Puerto or Las Piedras to be closer to their fields (see Chapter 5). As Figure 5.1 shows, El Jardín is much closer to the *ejido* than either of the other two villages.

It is difficult to give accurate population figures for the three communities. The major problem is that the Mexican census has not been consistent in the treatment of Puerto de las Piedras. The 1960 census lists the two communities together and gives the population as 949. The 1970 census continues to list the two together but gives the population as only 583, a gross underestimate. The population of El Jardín was 114 in 1960 and 189 in 1970, figures that do seem reasonable.

I estimated the populations of the three communities in 1973 in conjunction with mapping the settlement pattern of each village. A key informant accompanied me while I roughly plotted the location of each

Table 3.1. *Approximate population of El Jardín, El Puerto, and Las Piedras (1973)*

	El Puerto	Las Piedras	El Jardín
Number of households	130	85	26
Approximate population	793	519	159

house site. As we worked, he would tell me the name and occupation of each household head. In situations where he was unsure of any information, I obtained it from other informants or the inhabitants of the house. Later, I compared my maps of the house sites to aerial photographs of the region (taken in 1969) to be sure no houses were overlooked.

Interviews, which I will describe later in this chapter, established that the average number of people per household among *ejidatarios* of Puerto de las Piedras was 6.08. The 1970 census for the *municipio* as a whole indicated that the average number of people per household was 6.1. Thus by multiplying the number of households by 6.1, I obtained approximate population figures for the three communities. These figures are given in Table 3.1.

Rapid population growth since the land redistribution in 1933 has led to a situation in which approximately half the households in Puerto de las Piedras were without land by 1973. Everyone in the three communities who wanted land in 1933 was able to obtain it, and the land was allocated to 146 individuals. Because Mexican agrarian reform laws prohibit dividing the land among heirs, the total number of *ejidatarios* should never exceed 146. Thus the number of people holding land rights has remained stable while the population of the communities has grown steadily. Only 120 of the 241 households in El Puerto, Las Piedras, and El Jardín had rights to *ejidal* land in 1973 (see Table 3.2).[10]

In the space of four decades, the economic situation of the communities has changed from a condition where having land rights was more or less ubiquitous to one where half of the households in the community now are without land. This situation would be even more serious if a substantial number of individuals had not migrated to Mexico City. Even some of those who maintain households in Puerto de las Piedras work a few months of the year in Mexico City.

Since *ejidal* land is no longer available for much of the population, many people from Puerto de las Piedras have had to rely upon other economic activities in order to earn a living. Table 3.2 provides a listing

Table 3.2. *Occupation of household heads in the three communities (only primary occupation listed)*

	El Puerto	Las Piedras	El Jardín	Total
Ejidatarios	58	48	14	120
Unskilled Workers	30	21	6	57
Day laborers (agriculture)	15	11	6	
Wage laborers (nonagricultural)	7	5	0	
Itinerant peddlers (sell fruit, flowers, wood)	4	2	0	
Tortilla sellers	2	3	0	
Clothes washers	2	0	0	
Skilled trades	31	14	5	50
Quarry workers	16	0	0	
Mason	9	7	3	
Rope maker	1	4	0	
Baker	2	1	0	
Cantor	0	0	1	
Curandero	0	1	0	
Carpenter	0	0	1	
Blanket maker	1	0	0	
Teacher	1	0	0	
Violin player	0	1	0	
Tinsmith	1	0	0	
Merchants	11	2	1	14
Stores	3	0	1	
Pulquería	4	2	0	
Corn mill (*molino*)	1	0	0	
Middlemen (buy and sell pigs, stone, pottery)	3	0	0	
Total				241

of the primary occupations held by household heads in the three communities. The most important means of making a living is obviously working *ejidal* land. However, people are engaged in a wide range of other activities.

The most common occupation, apart from being an *ejidatario,* is working as a wage laborer in agriculture. This activity is highly seasonal; and except for a few days during the preparation of the soil, the weeding season, and finally the harvest, there is little work available. Competition for those jobs that are available is even more severe because many *ejidatarios* try to supplement their incomes by working as wage laborers (*jornaleros*).

The stone quarries in the mountains around Puerto de las Piedras provide more steady employment. One quarry is located high above El Puerto and actually lies within the communal lands of the *ejido*. The preferred quarry, however, is located in the communal lands belonging to San Diego (see Figure 2.2). The stoneworkers have to pay ten *pesos* (eighty cents) each per week to work there. However, a road to the quarry is occasionally passable by truck, which simplifies the transportation of the stone. Stone from the other quarry must be hauled down on trails by horses, burros, or men. The trip is exhausting and time consuming, and very few stones can be carried at one time. The stone from both quarries is eventually used on the facades of buildings in Mexico City. For those who are skilled, earnings from work in the quarry may be as high as fifty to seventy-five *pesos* (four to six dollars) per day, depending on the vein of rock that is being worked.

Another common occupation is that of a mason. Many of the individuals practicing this trade have little skill apart from knowing how to build *adobe* houses and perhaps how to plaster a wall. Others, however, are experienced in bricklaying, in working with stone, and even in reading and working from blueprints. There is little more than sporadic demand for the services of either type of mason in the Temascalcingo region. Many, if not most, of these men spend a few months each year in Mexico City working in construction. Those who are less skilled work primarily as laborers (*peones*), whereas those who have more knowledge obtain better jobs.

The other occupations held by the household heads in the three communities are shown in Table 3.2. Although this table does show the range of occupations that people hold, it does not reflect the fact that most individuals are involved in more than one occupational pursuit. Two-thirds of the *ejidatarios*, for example, had other jobs. Their secondary positions ranged from working as wage laborers and selling *pulque* to operating stores and being a judge. In a region where there is little in the way of stable employment, having a diversity of activities or skills is perhaps the best means of coping. Although there clearly is specialization of labor in the occupations of the household heads surveyed, I also want to make it clear that there is considerable diversification in the activities of almost every individual. Beals (1975:25) stresses this same point regarding Oaxacan peasants.

Selection of a sample

As we have seen, there is considerable diversity in the economic activities of these three small communities. However, the focus of my research was not on the communities but on the *ejido*. I was interested in the changes taking place among individuals who had access to land and were being exposed to new ideas and techniques. In fact, the focus of agricultural development agents in the region has also been on the *ejidatarios*. Thus I should emphasize again that, although much of the descriptive ethnographic data that I collected refers to the *communities*, my focus for the statistical data and the delineation of the processes of change is the *ejido* of Puerto de las Piedras and the individuals who belong to it.

I selected a sample of *ejidatarios* to whom I would administer a fairly lengthy interview schedule (see DeWalt 1975c:355–66). A list of the *ejidatarios* was obtained from *ejidal* officials, and a one-half random sample was selected using a table of random numbers (see Blalock 1960: 437–40). The interview schedule was then pretested among a few *ejidatarios* with whom I had become friendly and who were not in the random sample.

It quickly became apparent that there were some problems with the sampling procedure. I discovered that some individuals were cultivating both their own lands and the lands of other individuals. Often, a father was cultivating the lands of a son who had decided to seek a living in Mexico City rather than in the *ejido*. Another common case was that of brothers who were cultivating the lands of widowed sisters. Because the individuals who were not cultivating their land did not know production techniques or even, in many cases, the productivity of their land, it did not seem profitable to interview them.

At this point, I asked two key informants (separately) to provide me with information about individuals who were working the lands of other people. Thus I was able to cut the original figure of 146 *ejidatarios* down to 110 who, according to my informants, were actually cultivating the land. I then assigned a number to each individual and again proceeded to choose a 50 percent random sample with the aid of a table of random numbers. At the same time, based on my pretesting, I modified my original interview schedule.

During the course of my interviews, I occasionally came across contradictory or erroneous information that had been provided by my key informants. These cases often involved individuals who really were cultivating their own land, usually in conjunction with another individual, and had been reported as not doing their own farming. I kept a listing of these and toward the end of my fieldwork chose a random sample from among the thirteen names erroneously reported as not cultivating their own land. Because these individuals were not in my original listing, I randomly chose seven from among this second list. This step ensured that in the total sample of 123, every individual had an equal chance of being selected. Thus the final random sample consisted of 62 individuals.

I believe that this sampling procedure had the result of giving a better picture of the realities extant in the *ejido*. Had I simply interviewed my original random sample, I would have received a lot of meaningless data and/or incomplete information from people not actually cultivating their land. By limiting myself to the individuals actually working the land, I feel that I obtained more accurate information. The sources of error that might have been introduced by this procedure were minor compared to the problems inherent in the first sampling method.

The actual interviewing was not difficult, thanks to the cooperation of the *ejidatarios*. Only one individual was hesitant to be interviewed, and he finally agreed on my second visit to his home. Three individuals in the sample could not be found during my period of fieldwork. All three were in Mexico City during the whole period. Three other individuals were randomly selected to replace them as the time for my departure from the region began to approach.

One further caveat should be noted. My interviews were conducted with the household head – usually male. At the same time, my wife was conducting interviews with the female household head concerning medical care and nutrition (see K. DeWalt 1977). In cases where the head of the household was a female, I administered a brief version of my interview schedule, for it was soon discovered that two forty-five- to sixty-minute interviews with the same person were a great imposition on the hospitality of our informants. My brief schedule was designed to get the most crucial information about land use, productivity, techniques in agriculture and livestock raising, and so on. Thus in many of the tables that follow, statistics are sometimes based upon only fifty-three cases (there were nine widowed or single women in the sample) rather than sixty-two.

4

Innovation adoption in the *ejido*: choosing alternative adaptive strategies

This chapter explores the effects that the development efforts described in Chapters 2 and 3 have had on the *ejidatarios* of Puerto de las Piedras. Although I use the term *modernization* as a general descriptive label for the process of change in the *ejido,* I find that this concept has been too broadly defined and has been too variable in its operationalization to be of much utility in my analysis. Because my concern is to determine the extent to which different individuals in the *ejido* have changed their productive techniques, I focus on the *ejidatarios'* "adoption of innovations" – the extent to which they have begun to use new ideas, crops, and techniques to improve their agricultural and livestock production.

In contrast with previous research, I do not find that individuals can be ranked from "traditional" to "modern" on a single unidimensional scale. Instead, I demonstrate that there is selective adoption of innovations; *ejidatarios* are not randomly accepting the new techniques but are picking and choosing sets of items from among those available. The concept of "adaptive strategies" is introduced to describe the *ejidatarios'* diversification of economic activities, which is occurring in response to the new opportunities.

The different adaptive strategies that I identify in this chapter are used as the *dependent variables* in subsequent chapters. My purpose in the remainder of this work is to determine the characteristics of individuals who are opting for each of the new adaptive strategies.

Measuring the adoption of innovations

The primary goal of this study is to provide understanding of the processes of socioeconomic development in the *ejido* of Puerto de las Piedras. "Development" can be defined as: "a type of social change in which new ideas are introduced into a social system in order to produce higher per capita incomes and levels of living through more modern production methods and improved social organization" (Rogers 1969: 8-9).[11] Concentrating on change at this level is macroanalytic in that the social system is the usual unit of analysis. The emphasis in this work, however, is on change at the individual level; and the concept most frequently employed in such analyses is modernization.

Rogers's definition of "modernization" as "the process by which individuals change from a traditional way of life to a more complex, technologically advanced, and rapidly changing style of life" (1969:14) has been widely employed. Many different indicators have been utilized to measure degrees of modernization or modernism among individuals.[12] Empathy (Lerner 1958); achievement motivation (McClelland 1961); modern values (Kahl 1968); educational aspirations, political knowledge, household and agricultural innovativeness (Rogers 1969); and household and farm possessions, farm inputs employed, knowledge of agricultural officials, and house and compound construction (Shapiro 1975) are among the variables that researchers have used to measure this concept. The process of modernization is admittedly complex and involves changes in values, attitudes, and social, cultural, and economic behavior, as these diverse indicators reflect. However, I would also argue that modernization has been so broadly defined and its operationalization has consequently taken on such varied forms that the results of modernization studies are only incidentally comparable, if at all. Goldberg has made the same point: "The most distressing feature of the research on modernism is the demonstrable fact that modernism has about as many meanings as there are researchers on the topic. In addition, what is defined as modern for setting A may not be modern for setting B" (1974:7).

One way of avoiding the morass surrounding the modernization literature is to use a concept that can be more specifically defined and more precisely operationalized. Because my interest was in economic development, I wanted a measure or measures that would tell me the degree to which people were adopting behaviors that had the potential for increasing their overall productivity and welfare. I was not concerned with measuring empathy, modern values, achievement motivation, or other mentalistic characteristics of individuals that might or might not indicate that socioeconomic development was taking place.[13] I therefore decided to focus on the agricultural innovativeness of the *ejidatarios* of Puerto de las Piedras.

Rogers has defined "innovativeness" as "the degree to which an individual is earlier than others in his social system to adopt new ideas" (1962:159). The search for those factors associated with innovativeness (or "adoption of innovations," the term I prefer when talking about the process of people accepting ideas or techniques communicated to them) has been a popular topic of research in anthropology, sociology, communications, and other disciplines over the years. I do not wish to review the many studies of innovation adoption that have been done (see Rogers with Shoemaker 1971), but I should point out that in many cases the researcher is only interested in tracing the spread of a single item through a society, a region, or a profession (e.g., Ryan and Gross 1943; Katz 1961). Measuring adoption of innovations in these cases is very simple: Has or has not the item been adopted?

In the majority of development contexts, however, we are interested in determining the adoption pattern of a large number of new items in a community or region, especially in areas such as Temascalcingo where new ideas and technology are becoming available at a rapid rate. The tendency in such research has been to construct scales of innovation adoption by assigning one point to each new item that a person has reported adopting. Thus Rogers, for example, utilized a scale of agricultural innovativeness that included twelve to fifteen new techniques and ideas available for adoption by Colombian farmers. These ranged from weed sprays to fertilizers and farm machinery (1969:294). He also constructed a simple, additive "home innovativeness" scale composed of from ten to twelve health, nutrition, and sanitation items. Sexton (1972) and Woods and Graves (1973) used similar procedures in measuring innovativeness in Guatemala.

One of the obvious problems with such scales is that each item is given the same weight as every other item in the scale. Thus Sexton, for example, treats "ability to speak Spanish" and "wearing shoes" as equal components of his innovativeness scale. Learning Spanish is clearly a much more difficult task (and one could argue that the type of change it produces is qualitatively different) than the act of acquiring a pair of shoes. Sexton does discuss a technique for assessing the unidimensionality of a set of such items; and while these are a step in the right direction, other methods are needed that will more adequately measure innovation adoption.

This problem was one that I tried to keep in mind during my fieldwork. I felt that by focusing only on items that were in the realm of improved agriculture and livestock production techniques, I might be able to construct a cohesive scale. In a previous analysis of some data from rural Mexico, for example, I had found that a number of items reflecting improved agricultural and livestock-raising technology formed a satisfactory Guttman scale (DeWalt, Bee, and Pelto 1973:109–10). The Guttman scaling procedure indicates the degree to which a set of items measures a single dimension (cf. Guttman 1944; Rogers 1969:103; Pelto 1970:338–43).[14]

As my interviewing of *ejidatarios* progressed and I became more familiar with the modernization taking place in Puerto de las Piedras, it became clear to me that the adoption of innovation items (see Table 4.1) was not going to form any sort of Guttman scale; that is, the items

Table 4.1. *Numbers and percentages of people adopting innovations*[a]

Innovation	Number adopting	Percentage adopting
Fertilizer use – 1972	25	40.3
Fertilizer use – 1973	47	75.8
Tractor use – 1972	18	29.0
Tractor use – 1973	18	29.0
Own a cart (*remolque*) for hauling	10	16.1
Sow forage crops (*pradera*)	9	14.5
Feed forage to animals	15	24.2
Vaccinate horses, mules, burros	41	66.1
Feed processed foods to animals	11	17.7
Wash animals	11	17.7
Vaccinate cows and/or pigs	16	25.8

[a] Of the sample of 62 *ejidatarios*.

did not appear to constitute a single, unidimensional scale. Some individuals were adopting very expensive items, which I had expected to be among the "least adopted," while ignoring other "more adopted" practices and ideas. No clear pattern seemed to be emerging. To be sure, I probably could have patched together an acceptable Guttman scale by eliminating certain items from my analysis. Shapiro, for example, began with 115 indicators of modernization in his Tanzanian study. By eliminating items that did not scale and combining variables, he ultimately used only 45 of his original indicators in constructing nine Guttman scales of modernization (Shapiro 1975).

I chose not to resort to the elimination of items to build a Guttman scale because it seemed that a unidimensional indicator was simply unrealistic in portraying the process of modernization in Puerto de las Piedras. The more I thought about the information I was collecting, the more it seemed that the individuals in my sample were following several different strategies in making decisions about the new items and ideas they were adopting.

The situation in Puerto de las Piedras became more intelligible when I began to analyze it in the terms used by John Bennett in *Northern Plainsmen*. In that work, Bennett identifies several different adaptive strategies being followed by people in the region of Canada that he studied. By "adaptive strategies," he means "the patterns formed by the many separate adjustments that people devise in order to obtain and use resources and to solve the immediate problems confronting them" (Bennett 1969:14). Adaptive behavior involves the choice among several alternative behaviors. The increasing availability of new practices and ideas in agriculture and livestock raising has opened up new possibilities for the *ejidatarios* of the region, and I concluded that my data lacked patterning because I was not thinking in terms of there potentially being several different adaptive strategies. That is, implicit in my thinking, and I believe in that of most individuals who try to induce or study modernization, there is a bias toward thinking about the peasant in terms of having to make a choice between traditional practices and modern practices, perhaps between rationality and irrationality or economizing versus noneconomizing.[15]

However, peasants confronted with a variety of new techniques and practices probably do not think of their choices in these terms. The new items are simply a part of a cultural repertoire – their major means of coping with the natural and social environment in which they live. The "modern" and "traditional" ways of life are not mutually exclusive. Instead, they are each made up of potentially useful means of adaptation. Thus peasants may select only those techniques they feel may be useful in helping them to better adapt to their particular situation. When the anthropologist can detect patterns in the ways in which these elements are combined, she/he can talk about adaptive strategies.

I have belabored the process by which I arrived at my analysis of innovation adoption items to show how my original expectations were modified and revised as I became acquainted with the community of study and as my interviewing progressed. Finally, before I began the data analysis of the materials I had collected, I formulated some specific hypotheses about the results that I expected from my statistical analyses. I was able to identify eleven possible new agricultural or livestock-raising techniques or ideas people in the region could adopt. These are listed in Table 4.1 along with the numbers and percentages of *ejidatarios* adopting each. If different adaptive strategies were being selected by the *ejidatarios*, I felt that these would show up in some patterning of the innovations being adopted. That is, the *ejidatarios* were not expected to be *randomly* choosing items or to be adopting items in some sort of set sequence (thus forming a Guttman scale).

Among the eleven potential items for innovation adoption, it seemed that there were two potential new directions in which *ejidatarios* could move toward modernizing production. As a result, I felt that I could identify at least three different adaptive strategies: (1) a new improved corn production strategy, which would include the use of both fertilizers and tractors on corn fields; (2) a new forage-raising and livestock production strategy, which would include vaccinating animals, planting forage crops, and feeding animals processed foods and forage; and (3) the traditional subsistence pattern, which would simply involve continuing to practice traditional techniques of corn production (i.e., non-adoption of the new items).

Factor analysis of the innovation adoption items

The preceding adaptive strategies constituted predictions about the patterns that I expected to emerge in the data analysis. One of the best ways of looking at patterning of data is by using factor analysis (Rummel 1970). The purpose in using factor analysis was to look at the correlations among the innovation adoption items "to see whether some underlying pattern of relationships exists such that the data may be 'rearranged' or 'reduced' to a smaller set of *factors* or *components* that may be taken as *source variables* accounting for the observed interrelations in the data" (Nie et al. 1975:469, italics theirs). That is, in terms of the data being used here, are the various innovation adoption items correlated with one another in a patterned way such that a smaller number of factors (the hypothesized adaptive strategies) can account for these interrelationships?

The four factors in Table 4.2 were identified in the factor analysis.[16] Those variables with a loading (i.e., a correlation with the factor) of more than ± .40 on any factor are in italics and may be taken as indicators of the underlying structure of the factor. These four factors accounted for 69 percent of the total variance in the data.

A perusal of the variables which load highly on each of the four factors gives us some indication of what the factors mean. Thus on Factor 1, the variable with the highest loading is "sow forage crops." The other two variables with loadings above .40 on this factor are "feed forage to animals" and "own a cart for hauling." All of these have to do with forage crop production, use, and marketing; and I have labeled the factor "forage production." On Factor 2, the highest loading is "vaccinate cows and/or pigs." Other variables which load highly are "wash animals," "feed processed food to animals," and "vaccinate horses, mules, burros." It seems clear to me that these items all have to do with improving livestock, and I have labeled this factor "animal improvement." Factor 3 includes only two variables, "tractor use - 1972" and "tractor use - 1973"; and I have labeled it "tractor use." Factor 4 also includes only two variables, "fertilizer use - 1972" and "fertilizer use - 1973," and is labeled "fertilizer use."

The two new adaptive strategies that I had predicted do not appear in the factor analysis. Comparing the four factors to the predicted adap-

Table 4.2. *Varimax rotated factor matrix of innovation adoption items*

Variable	Forage production (Factor 1)	Animal improvement (Factor 2)	Tractor use (Factor 3)	Fertilizer use (Factor 4)	Communality
Fertilizer use – 1972	.127	.111	-.016	*.733*	.566
Fertilizer use – 1973	-.025	-.094	.258	*.428*	.260
Tractor use – 1972	-.004	.185	*.782*	.139	.665
Tractor use – 1973	.159	.159	*.835*	.058	.752
Own a cart for hauling	*.633*	.154	.048	.010	.427
Feed forage to animals	*.735*	.087	.023	.188	.584
Sow forage crops	*.828*	.210	.092	-.046	.740
Wash animals	.120	*.659*	.066	-.038	.454
Vaccinate cows and/or pigs	.110	*.864*	-.006	-.026	.759
Vaccinate horses, mules, burros	.185	*.470*	.175	-.007	.286
Feed processed food to animals	.112	*.485*	.234	.216	.349

Factor loadings more than ± .400 are in italics.
A total of 68.6% of the variance is accounted for by the first four factors, which had an eigenvalue of more than 1.00.

tive strategies, we see that the two new strategies each split into two separate factors. That is, Factors 1 and 2 together would identify what I called the forage-raising and livestock production strategy. Factors 3 and 4 would identify the predicted improved corn production strategy. It appears that the clusters of items (adaptive strategies) being adopted are more numerous than I had thought. That is, those individuals who use tractors on their fields are not necessarily using more fertilizer; and those individuals who havè gone into forage crop production are generally not also adopting livestock-raising innovations. If only two new adaptive strategies were being adopted, then the patterning of these variables would not have produced four orthogonal factors.

In Table 4.3, I have presented factor scores for each of the individuals in my sample of *ejidatarios* on each of the four factors. Factor scores are computed by multiplying an individual's score on each variable by the factor weight for that variable. The sum of these weight-times-data products for all variables yields the factor score of each individual on each factor (Rummel 1970:437–41).[17] An easy way of looking at these scores is to view an individual with a positive score as adopting that adaptive strategy. Any negative score indicates that the individual is rejecting that strategy.

Table 4.3 is organized in a special way. I have lumped individuals into five different categories on the basis of the number of factors on which they have positive factor scores. Thus we see that only two *ejidatarios* had positive factor scores on all four factors; they are investing in all four new adaptive strategies. Eight individuals are investing in three of the four adaptive strategies; thirteen are investing in two of the four; and twenty-four are investing in only one of the four. Fifteen individuals have been unable or unwilling to invest in any of the new adaptive strategies. The point that I wish to emphasize with regard to Table 4.3 is that even if we know an individual's score on any one of the four adaptive strategies, we are still unable to predict anything about his or her scores on any of the other adaptive strategies. This fact emphasizes the distinctiveness (i.e., noncorrelation) of the four factors. It seems that these four areas of possible investment are currently perceived by the *ejidatarios* as separate domains, despite the fact that there are potential areas of overlap.

One more point needs to be emphasized with regard to Table 4.3. As we see, fifteen individuals have elected not to invest in any of the new adaptive strategies. It is these individuals who are continuing the subsistence agriculture strategy – continuing to cultivate corn without fertilizer, tractors, or any other improved technique. The subsistence agriculture score was computed by adding all of the scores on the other

Table 4.3. Factor scores on the four different "adaptive strategies" (organized according to number of strategies adopted)[a]

Household number	Forage production	Livestock improvement	Tractor use	Fertilizer use	No. of strategies adopted
15	2.08	1.17	1.10	0.79	4
48	1.95	1.69	1.09	0.75	"
40	0.19	-.46	1.50	1.21	3
24	0.19	-.46	1.50	1.21	"
17	1.84	-.31	1.48	0.91	"
11	2.51	-1.09	0.50	0.63	"
2	-.87	1.92	1.29	0.94	"
49	-.87	1.92	1.29	0.94	"
12	0.02	0.81	0.53	-.67	"
32	0.79	1.45	1.28	-1.14	"
27	-.67	-.45	0.21	1.03	2
34	-.59	-.26	0.26	0.98	"
3	-.01	1.93	-.95	1.25	"
20	-.57	1.10	-.93	0.74	"
54	-.08	1.33	-.88	0.97	"
55	-.70	1.62	-.94	0.69	"
35	2.49	-.68	-.77	0.67	"
39	0.37	-.15	-.42	0.11	"
41	0.38	-.45	-.66	1.20	"
31	-.73	1.09	1.38	-.56	"
18	1.64	1.52	-1.01	-1.27	"

64

	= =	1 =		0 =
23	2.13	1.44	−1.03	−1.26
60	−.59	0.10	0.44	−.55
10	0.85	−.54	−.52	−.11
13	0.29	−.65	−.55	−.06
4	−.57	1.15	−.82	−1.02
57	−.69	1.98	−.76	−.84
61	−.22	−.67	0.90	−.55
58	2.49	−.63	−.66	−1.09
53	−.66	−.46	0.37	−.28
52	−.57	1.15	−.82	−1.02
51	−.56	−.67	1.69	−.38
22	−.49	−.47	1.74	−.43
16	−.49	−.16	1.81	−.20
14	−.50	−.42	1.69	−.88
9	−.13	−.03	1.71	−.47
7	−.30	−.86	0.85	−.49
6	−.40	−.65	−.62	0.92
46	−.40	−.65	−.62	0.92
43	−.33	−.45	−.57	0.86
42	−.33	−.45	−.57	0.86
37	−.40	−.65	−.62	0.92
36	−.34	−.40	−.63	0.42
29	−.40	−.65	−.62	0.92
26	−.41	−.59	−.68	0.47
56	−.40	−.65	−.62	0.92
25	−.44	0.06	−.42	−.49
1	−.32	−.46	−.41	−.45
5	−.39	−.65	−.46	−.39

Table 4.3. (cont.)

Household number	Forage production	Livestock improvement	Tractor use	Fertilizer use	No. of strategies adopted
8	-.40	-.60	-.52	-.84	"
19	-.39	-.65	-.46	-.39	"
21	-.39	-.65	-.46	-.39	"
28	-.39	-.65	-.46	-.39	"
30	-.32	-.46	-.41	-.45	"
33	-.33	-.40	-.47	-.90	"
38	-.40	-.60	-.52	-.84	"
44	-.40	-.60	-.52	-.84	"
45	-.39	-.65	-.46	-.39	"
47	-.40	-.60	-.52	-.84	"
50	-.32	-.46	-.41	-.45	"
59	-.32	-.46	-.41	-.45	"
62	-.32	-.46	-.41	-.45	"
Total no. of individuals with positive factor scores	16	18	22	26	

[a] Factor scores are standardized to have a mean of 0 and a standard deviation of 1. Positive factor scores here are taken to indicate adoption of an adaptive strategy. Negative scores indicate rejection of the strategy.

four adaptive strategies and then reversing the sign. I reversed the sign because high positive scores on other adaptive strategies would indicate a rejection (i.e., a negative score) of the subsistence agriculture strategy.[18]

In the following pages, I will discuss in greater detail these factors and the variables comprising them. I will provide more descriptive information about the different innovation adoption items – when they were introduced, by whom, their cost, their availability, and so forth. Discussing the pattern of investment by several *ejidatarios* will give the reader a better impression of how these adaptive strategies are being put into practice in actual situations and will provide qualitative evidence for the patterns identified in the quantitative analysis. Those readers who are not interested in this type of information may skip to the chapter conclusions.

Forage production

In addition to its major construction activities in flood control and irrigation, the Department of Hydraulic Resources has also been involved in a major program for the socioeconomic modernization of the Temascalcingo region (see Chapter 2). The ultimate aim of Hydraulic Resources is to form cooperatives in the *ejidos* of the valley. These cooperatives will sow forage crops and build stables for fine dairy and beef cattle. While this program is currently in its initial stages of implementation, Hydraulic Resources has had experimental fields of clover and other grasses for a number of years. On the basis of their experiments, they have developed a combination of clovers and forage grasses that are well suited to the region and provide excellent food for animals.

Some *ejidatarios* have asked for technical assistance from Hydraulic Resources and have begun to establish fields of forage crops on their own initiative. Others have learned from the original adopters, and there are now many hectares sown with forage crops (*pradera*) in the valley region. Nineteen members of the *ejido* (nine in the sample) had begun to sow forage crops by 1973 (see DeWalt 1975:156).

Establishment of a field of *pradera* costs a considerable sum of money. First, the land must be well plowed, harrowed, and graded. This work is best accomplished with a tractor. Then seed must be purchased. If bought in large quantitites, the seed is not very expensive; but the price is fairly high for the small landholder because of the relatively small amount needed and the requirement that there be a mix of different seeds. Once established, the *pradera* does not require replanting for about seven years. By far the major expense, however, is for the fencing around the field. Fences are necessary because animals are often left to roam in the *ejidal* lands, especially after the harvest in the dry season;

and they would quickly eat up the production of a piece of land. Barbed wire fencing costs are very high.

In general, most people cut the forage and bring it to the animals rather than allowing them to graze on the fields. This practice requires some form of transportation. The back of a burro or horse serves well enough for small quantitites; but when the forage is to be sold to other buyers or when the *ejidatario* finds it burdensome to make frequent trips to bring in small amounts of *pradera*, some other form of transportation is required.

The ideal solution, perhaps, would be a truck. Only one individual in the *ejido* owns a truck, however. José lives in Temascalcingo and uses his truck for various sorts of hauling for others. He does have a field of forage crops and sells most of his production.

Trucks are out of the question for most *ejidatarios*, however. Even the twenty-year-old pickup recently purchased by José cost over 1,000 dollars.[19] Repairs, gas, oil, and tires periodically require considerable additional investments of money. The next best solution is some sort of cart. In the days of the *hacienda*, there were many carts. These vehicles had very large wooden wheels with iron rims. But when the land of the *hacienda* was redistributed, the *hacendado* took all of the carts with him. The *ejidatarios* were left with only animals and their own backs for hauling purposes.

A few of the wealthier private landowners in the valley had carts that could be hitched to tractors. These were obviously far beyond the means of the *ejidatarios*, however. Around 1957 it occurred to one of the men of the region that animals could pull similar sorts of carts, but he had difficulty obtaining materials to make such a cart. A junk yard soon provided the answer in the form of the axle, wheels, and tires of an old automobile. This individual then persuaded one of the blacksmiths in Temascalcingo to weld two struts onto this axle. He then built a platform of wood on the struts. Two long poles bolted to the platform served as a harness for a horse. The blacksmiths in town have improved upon this original cart; but the basic ideas, as well as the raw materials, are still the same. Blacksmiths will sell a completely finished cart for one thousand *pesos* (eighty dollars) or the axle, wheels, tires, and struts for five hundred *pesos* (forty dollars). With the latter, the *ejidatarios* complete the carts themselves by building the wooden platform and harness.

Until recently, there was not a great deal of demand for these carts. They were only used extensively during the corn harvest. To be sure, those who owned carts could and did rent them to others during this period; but few individuals had cash for renting carts to haul their corn, despite the potential great saving in their own labor and the wear and tear on their animals. In some years, because of the flooding, there was really very little corn to harvest.

Now that the flooding has been eliminated and harvests are more predictable, a number of *ejidatarios* have bought carts. Others are talking about trying to raise the capital to buy them. My field assistant, Pedro, sold his bicycle to help raise enough cash to purchase a cart in 1973. While useful for harvesting corn, anyone who has *pradera* finds it almost essential to own one. Otherwise, much of the *ejidatarios'* time is taken up transporting the forage from the field to buyers or to their houses. As we see in Table 4.2, "own a cart for hauling" does load highly on Factor 1, indicating the relationship between sowing forage crops and cart ownership.

The third item loading on this factor (in fact, it has the highest loading) is "feed forage to animals." As would be expected, those individuals who raise forage crops also feed them to their animals. As I have previously indicated, I thought that Factors 1 and 2 would be combined as one strategy. However, it appears that those who have forage crops and who do feed it to their animals may not have enough capital to invest as well in vaccinations and other items necessary for maintaining the health of their animals. Perhaps as time goes on and more capital becomes available, these two will merge to form one strategy. However, at present it appears that there is little tendency for those involved in animal production to become highly involved in the raising of *pradera* and vice versa. Only six individuals have adopted both the animal improvement and forage production adaptive strategies (households 15, 48, 12, 32, 18, and 23 in Table 4.3).

Sixteen of the sixty-two individuals in the sample have positive factor scores on the forage production factor. One of these individuals is Juan. Juan has been a president of the *ejido* and has managed to accumulate considerably more than the amount of land allowed each *ejidatario* (see Chapter 7). While he does not use fertilizer on his corn and only has two mules for his *yunta* (team for pulling agricultural implements), Juan has about three hectares of *pradera*. He has had the *pradera* for a number of years and has also owned a cart for a number of years. On many afternoons he can be seen in the *ejido* checking on the *peon* who is cutting the *pradera*. Other days he can be seen hauling a load of *pradera* to sell to someone in Temascalcingo or elsewhere. Although he does feed *pradera* to his mules, he is raising the forage primarily as a cash crop.

Felipe also had a very high forage production factor score. He began sowing *pradera* in 1973. He has a cart and also feeds *pradera* to his animals. He has expressed an interest in sowing more *pradera* apart from the 0.38 hectare that he has now. However, he said that he has no other field in which it would be feasible to grow this crop. Felipe is also very interested in getting into the business of raising animals. He already has four head of cattle and four pigs. He has recently moved to a house on the road near the *ejido*. This location makes it possible for him to use his cart to haul the *pradera* to his home (see Chapter 5) and is also much more convenient for taking animals to graze in the fields after the harvest. In late 1973, he was building a small corral and house for his pigs. However, he has not seen fit to vaccinate his animals, and he does not wash them. It will be interesting to see whether he can continue to build up the number of animals he has or whether some disease will wipe out his current holdings.

Those individuals with low positive scores on Factor 1 (see Table 4.3) have only a cart or have only sown forage crops or only feed *pradera* to animals. Those individuals with high factor scores have adopted two or three of the items which comprise this adaptive strategy.

Animal improvement

Perhaps the first and most distressing contact of the *ejidatarios* with modern methods of livestock production came in the late 1940s when a hoof-and-mouth epidemic was destroying vast numbers of livestock throughout Mexico. The threat that the epidemic might spread prompted the United States government to reach an accord with Mexico. Veterinarians and other personnel from the United States traveled throughout Mexico vaccinating animals that had not yet been infected and destroying those that were already diseased. In 1948, a veterinarian from the United States entered the Temascalcingo region. He was accompanied by a few Mexican soldiers who were assigned to protect him from individuals who did not understand the purpose of this program.

To be sure, there was a lot of room for misunderstanding. Cattle, horses, and other animals were dying, thus creating considerable consternation and economic hardship. Suddenly, a North American appeared and, in addition to vaccinating animals, began killing off some of the remaining animals. One day, as the veterinarian was riding along a path in one of the most isolated and poverty-stricken Mazahua communities, he was attacked by a large number of men. He managed to get free and began to ride away, but some of the women of the community were able to stop his horse. The men caught up, and he was killed. The Mexican soldiers were allowed to escape.

The people of Puerto de las Piedras seem to have been better informed about the purposes of the fight against the hoof-and-mouth disease. The *ejido* appointed one of its members to watch over the old bridge to make sure that animals from the west side of the river did not cross over to the east side and vice versa. This step was taken to prevent the spread of the disease.

In any event, this was probably the *ejidatarios'* first significant exposure to the idea of vaccinations to prevent diseases in their animals. Since 1948, periodic government campaigns have reached out to communities such as those in the Temascalcingo region. At such time, word is spread throughout the community for individuals to bring their animals to a central location where they are all vaccinated. Most of the horses, mules, and burros in the region have been vaccinated in this way.

The fact that most people have vaccinated their horses, mules, and burros (see Table 4.1) may reflect the importance of these animals in agriculture; most draft teams used by the *ejidatarios* are made up of horses or mules. The other possibility is that there has been a greater effort on the part of the government to wipe out diseases damaging to horses by making vaccines widely available. "Vaccinate horses, mules, burros" does load on the animal production factor.

Vaccination of other animals is still not widespread despite the fact that there are now two locations in Temascalcingo where vaccines (as well as other veterinary supplies) can be purchased. Nevertheless, "vaccinate cows and/or pigs" is the variable that loads most highly on Factor 2. Vaccination of these animals is very important in economic terms because they currently are in great demand in the regional market. The butchers in Temascalcingo complained in 1973 about their difficulty in getting enough meat to sell. While this was a local problem, it is perhaps even more severe on the national and international levels. Increasing demand for meat has outstripped supply. Prices for pork and beef almost doubled in both local and national markets during the period from January 1973 to November 1973. There is also regional and national demand for milk; and again, supply has not kept up with the demand. Many individuals in the region were aware of the demand for these animals and expressed their interest in buying a few head of cattle or a few small pigs. Because many cattle and pigs die annually in the region, raising these animals will probably be profitable only if they are vaccinated.

"Feed processed foods to animals" also loads highly on Factor 2. Processed foods are special mixes meant to promote rapid growth in animals, especially young chickens and pigs. These special foods usually are used only for a few months. Later, the animals are fed primarily with corn. The mixes are available in two local farm supply stores in Temascalcingo.

The final item that loads on Factor 2 is "wash animals." While certainly not a new technique, it is a practice that has been stressed by the development agents in the region. It was included as an item that had minimal cash cost and yet would indicate whether individuals were committed to caring for their animals. It is notable that it does load on Factor 2, along with animal care items requiring cash outlays.

All of these items obviously have to do with the care of animals and define what I will call a commitment to "animal improvement." Eighteen of the sixty-two individuals in the sample had positive factor scores on this factor.

The strategy of raising animals certainly is not a new alternative. Animal raising has always been practiced in the region, as well as in other agricultural communities throughout Mesoamerica. Most of the livestock raising has been for home consumption, as a supplement to the diet. However, rural peasants in Mexico also have raised animals because having a few around is a form of insurance and savings investment. They are a capital good which is always marketable; and in general, the value of the animal increases with maturation and then remains fairly stable for a long period of time. When an emergency arises and the family needs some cash very quickly, animals can be sold to provide the wherewithal to buy medicine for a sick child, to cover the costs of ceremonial expenditures, to pay off a debt, or for myriad other reasons (Nash 1964). This form of insurance policy is still very much in the minds of most of the *ejidatarios*. In fact, 98 percent of them do have animals of some variety.

Those who have begun to use vaccinations to protect their animals, to wash them, and to feed them commercial processed foods to aid in their growth and fertility are moving a step or two beyond the strategy of keeping animals as a form of insurance. By trying to keep their animals in good health, the *ejidatarios* have a greater chance of developing animals into a "cash crop." A description of some of the individuals who have begun to invest in animal improvement can give a somewhat better impression of this potentially profitable adaptive strategy.

Ramón is an *ejidatario* who had invested heavily in the production of pigs. Ramón got the capital to begin raising pigs by working as a chauffeur for the Mexican government. People take pride in pointing out that he sometimes drives for some of the most powerful people in the country. He usually is only able to get to Temascalcingo to tend to his business a few days each month. However, his brother Audón takes care of the pigs in his absence. Ramón makes sure that his young pigs are vaccinated, has them washed regularly, and feeds them a processed food, which he buys in the local Purina store, to make them grow quickly. Once they reach a certain age, he feeds them heavily with corn and forage to fatten them for market.

Audón has followed his brother's lead and now owns six pigs of his own. He plans to use these for breeding purposes and will try to build this activity into a profitable business. He has had the animals vaccinated, washes them regularly, and reports that he feeds them about twelve kilos of corn daily. Audón already has a large flock of turkeys (about seventy), which he also vaccinates and cares for quite successfully. In 1972, much of his corn was lost because of a lack of fertilizer and local flooding. Thus he had to spend considerable cash to buy corn for the pigs, turkeys, and his family. In 1973, he decided to use fertilizer on his fields and also planted a half hectare of *pradera,* which he plans to use to feed his growing number of pigs. Barring some unforeseen disaster, Audón should soon have a profitable business.

Lest we receive the impression that all of those becoming involved in animal production are very rich or are working on the same scale as Audón and his brother, let us consider the case of Francisco, a man of more modest means. Although he cultivates his own fields, he puts a minimum of effort and investment into his *ejido* land. Other *ejidatarios* say that he is more interested in working with his team of animals (*yunta*) for others in the *ejido* and in nearby communities. The horses that comprise his *yunta* are vaccinated. Francisco also has three head of cattle, all of which are vaccinated. Although he does not buy forage to feed these animals, he reports that he does buy barley to feed his horses when they are working. It is difficult to tell whether Francisco may eventually realize an increase in the size of his cattle "herd"; he does seem to be trying to protect his investment by vaccinating these valuable animals (they are worth about three thousand *pesos* each). There is little doubt that Francisco is interested in maintaining the health of his horses. The fact that they are his primary means of support at this time undoubtedly has something to do with this interest.

Mechanizing agriculture: tractor use

Several individuals in the Temascalcingo region who have fairly large pieces of private property have had tractors for a number of years. In addition to using the tractors to cultivate their own land, these individuals have also been willing to perform agricultural work on the lands of those *ejidatarios* who can pay the 140 *pesos* (in 1973) to rent a tractor for a day.

Perhaps the best model of the benefits of tractors (as well as various other agricultural advances) is a large ranch situated on the other side of the Lerma River from the *ejido* of Puerto de las Piedras. Almost all of the *ejidatarios* pass the ranch daily, and some even have a view of the neatly manicured fields from their houses. The owners of the ranch are proprietors of an agricultural equipment and supply store in Atlacomulco, a large town near Temascalcingo. In addition to tractors and other mechanized agricultural equipment, they make extensive use of fertilizers, hybrid seeds, insecticides, and herbicides. The demonstration effect provided by their fields has made the *ejidatarios* who live nearby aware of the benefits of modern agricultural techniques. At the same time, this family's affluence underlines the *ejidatarios'* awareness that increased production resulting from use of modern technology has substantial investment capital as a prerequisite.

In the minds of most of the *ejidatarios,* a tractor is perhaps the most desired piece of new technology. And, in fact, they have been within the *ejidatarios'* grasp in recent years. In the early 1960s, a few of the wealthier members of the *ejido* decided to form a cooperative. They raised enough money for a down payment on a tractor. Payments on the machine were to be made from the money earned by renting it to other members of the *ejido*. The idea was good, and the logistics of paying off the debt on the tractor were reasonable. Unfortunately, the participants made the mistake of buying a European-made tractor. Soon after the machine was acquired, it broke down. When the members of the cooperative tried to fix it, they were unable to locate anyone who sold the parts they needed. Many of the *ejidatarios* referred to the rusted hulk of the tractor as an example of what happens to cooperatives. Some said that the person who formed the cooperative and operated the machine never did pay his share and that the other members of the cooperative had to bear the burden for paying off the broken-down tractor.

In 1971, the government of the state of Mexico made a number of tractors available to the *ejidos* of the region. An *ejidatario* from Temascalcingo, one of the powerful leaders of *ejidos* in the valley, was put in charge of the tractors. He was to collect the rental fees and assign the machines to plow the fields of those who had paid or promised to pay. The government was soon investigating the whole project. The man in charge claimed that many of the *ejidatarios* asked that their fields be plowed and then refused to pay, claiming that the government should not charge them for this service. Other *ejidal* leaders disagreed and said that the *ejidatarios* had paid the fees but that the person in charge had stolen the money. The government, according to some of my informants, became irritated about the whole matter and removed the tractors. Another development scheme had failed, and the *ejidatarios* no longer had access to the tractors.

Thus for the past few years, the *ejidatarios* have only had access to those tractors they can rent from individuals in Temascalcingo. The machines are utilized almost exclusively for plowing by those who rent them. Once the plowing is accomplished, the *ejidatarios* rely on traditional tools for the other agricultural tasks. The primary reason for this is the pattern of landholding. Sections of the *ejido* are split up into many handkerchief-size plots (see Chapter 5). This arrangement creates a number of problems. First, when tractors need to cross other people's lands in order to gain access to "inside" fields, disputes often result. If the tractor crosses after another person has plowed and harrowed, it packs down the dirt, making it difficult if not impossible for the germinating seed to break through. If the tractor crosses after the seed has come up, it destroys many small plants. Second, a tractor's turning radius can be a very large proportion of a small field. Those machines that turn around in another person's fields often cause disputes. Even when the driver is careful to confine movements to the field being worked, corn can be destroyed. I once watched a tractor, trying to turn around in a field, back over a dozen hills of corn. A careful farmer can guide his animals to minimize damage to the maturing corn.

Only one person had a tractor perform tasks other than plowing on his fields in 1973. He and his son, who is also an *ejidatario,* have managed to consolidate their holdings (by trading plots) in one section of the *ejido.* Their 2.5 hectares are easily accessible from the road, and the size of their holding in this one section makes it possible and practical to use a tractor for seeding and cultivating.

"Tractor use – 1972" and "tractor use – 1973" both load highly on Factor 3. Twenty-two *ejidatarios* had positive factor scores on the "tractor use" adaptive strategy. The following descriptions give some impression of the individuals who use tractors.

Pedro has hired a tractor to plow four of his best fields for the past two years. He reports that the land in one area of the *ejido* contains a lot of clay and thus is very hard. It is difficult to plow this area with a team of animals. Perhaps the major reason why Pedro uses a tractor, however, is his job. He works daily for Hydraulic Resources. For the past two years, the agency has made a tractor available to its employees at the going rental rate in the valley. This offer is a tremendous boon for the workers because the only time they have to tend their fields is after work in the late afternoon or on weekends.

Another individual who has used tractors extensively is Margarito. He managed to secure a tractor to plow most of his fields in 1972, but he plowed only one field with a tractor in 1973. No machines were available when he needed to plow his other fields. In addition to farming, Margarito makes *tabiques,* a kind of brick that is very desirable for house construction. The best time for making these is during the dry season when the rain will not spoil the raw materials and the finished products. If he had to take time out from this work to plow his fields, Margarito would lose perhaps a whole month of the dry season when he could be making *tabiques.* Thus when he has the cash and when he can find one available, Margarito hires a tractor to plow his fields while he continues making *tabiques.*

Fertilizer use

Chemical fertilizers were first used in the *ejidos* of the Temascalcingo region around 1950. At that time, a government-sponsored program provided credit to enable the *ejidatarios* to use a new hybrid wheat seed and also to use fertilizer on this crop. The yield was worse than in most normal years because the seed was not well suited to the region; and as a result, the *ejidatarios* concluded (quite logically) that fertilizer was not worth the investment.

The next large-scale use of fertilizers by *ejidatarios* came in 1970 when an agricultural engineer visited the region to promote a program designed to improve corn yields in the valley. He supplied credit for hybrid corn seed, fertilizer, insecticides, and plowing by tractors. As has previously been mentioned, in his zeal to make the program a success, the engineer became very demanding of the *ejidatarios* and attempted to bully them into performing various tasks at the specific times he designated (see Chapter 2). In spite of the overall negative effects of this experience, corn production was improved. People attributed the increased yields primarily to the fertilizer, and many have since continued to use it. Use of fertilizer in 1973 was aided by a credit (for fertilizer alone) provided by the state government.

"Fertilizer use – 1972" and "fertilizer use – 1973" are the two variables loading on Factor 4. Twenty-six of the sixty-two individuals in the random sample had positive factor scores on this strategy. The following descriptions will provide an impression of the kinds of individuals who are adopting "fertilizer use."

Vicente is a very poor individual. Most of his income is derived from his work as a mason. He also is a part-time barber, an occupation he practices primarily on Sundays and *fiesta* days. His one hectare of land is in three small pieces. All of the lands are in poor locations and, in fact, were lands that had been unclaimed until he asked the president of the *ejido* for them in 1962. Vicente's best plot is a half hectare on which he has applied small quantities of fertilizer in each of the last two years. Although this land had a yield of thirty-eight *costales* (one *costal* equals approximately fifty kilograms) in 1970 when the agricultural engineer directed cultivation, Vicente only harvested fourteen in 1972. Because of the small amount of corn harvested, Vicente and his family had to buy corn from March until the next harvest in November. Undoubtedly, Vicente is trying to cut down on his need to purchase corn; he thus is fertilizing the piece of land on which he can expect to harvest a reasonable crop. In 1973, he also sowed another smaller portion of poorer land but did not fertilize, perhaps expecting that he would lose his investment.

Much more successful in fertilizing his land is Marcos. In 1972, when no credit was available, Marcos was only able to fertilize a half hectare of land. He is lucky to have another piece of land which yields well even without fertilizer. The total of eighty *costales* of corn which he harvested in 1972 was sufficient to feed his family and his animals for the whole year. In 1973, when credit for fertilizer was available, Marcos took advantage of the opportunity and fertilized all of his 2.38 hectares. He even applied fertilizer twice on his best piece of land. Marcos was hoping for a *cosechón* (huge harvest) in 1973.

Continuing an old adaptive strategy: subsistence agriculture

Even though many of the *ejidatarios* have adopted one or more of the new adaptive strategies, all of them still raise corn for the needs of their family on at least some of their plots. Most have one or two parcels of land on which they do not use fertilizer, tractors, or any other modern technique. These individuals are still practicing traditional techniques of subsistence agriculture. However, I am reserving the term *subsistence agriculture* to refer to the scale that is the summation of the scores on all the other four adaptive strategies. As I indicated earlier in this chapter, the individuals who receive the highest scores on this variable are those who have *not* invested in any of the innovation adoption items.

Although most *ejidatarios* may be cultivating some fields in a very traditional manner, those who received the highest scores on the subsistence agriculture adaptive strategy are those who are using this strategy exclusively. The fifteen individuals who received negative scores on all of the four new adaptive strategies are most clearly maintaining this traditional subsistence agriculture strategy.

This fact does not mean that these individuals are making no attempts at modernization, however. Cruz, for example, has a number of cattle, which he uses for milk production. He has crossed some of his animals with a part-Holstein bull in an effort to improve the paltry production he currently receives (about three liters per cow). He sells all of the milk to individuals in the village. Nonetheless, he has not vaccinated his animals, and he does not feed his cattle *pradera*. As a result, he lost two cows to disease in 1972 and receives minimal milk production from those remaining.

In essence, the individuals in this category have been unable (or unwilling) to adopt new techniques that might better serve them in their attempts to cope with their environment. Instead, they are depending for their survival on the old adaptive strategy of subsistence corn production.

Other adaptive strategies

I should make clear that these are not the only adaptive strategies possible in the region. They are, however, the adaptive strategies that are linked to the agricultural base of the community, in which almost all *ejidatarios* are heavily involved. However, two other adaptive strategies were brought about by the failure of the agricultural and livestock base to produce in the past. These are: (1) temporary and permanent migration, and (2) wage labor.

Migration from the Temascalcingo region, in general, has been very heavy. The flooding that destroyed so many crops disenchanted many people, who simply abandoned their lands and left to try to find work elsewhere. However, in relation to the individuals in this study (who have kept their lands), our main interest is in temporary migration. That is, some individuals maintain their land rights but periodically leave to work in Mexico City and then return to the community. While not as common in the *ejido* I studied, where individuals have a fair amount of land, temporary migration is very heavy from other *ejidos* in the valley, especially those in which landholdings are as little as one hectare per *ejidatario*. Nevertheless, a few people in the community of study plant their corn fields and then leave during the months of June, July, August,

September, and October. This is a period when there is little work to be done in the fields and also when work is available in construction in Mexico City (see Chapter 11).

A much more prevalent adaptive strategy, however, is that of wage labor within the region. Many *ejidatarios* have managed to find some other job in which income is much more stable and which provides the main basis of subsistence. The corn or forage raised on the *ejido* land provides a nice supplement to the money earned in other pursuits (see Chapter 6).

Temporary migration and wage labor predate the other adaptive strategies. In addition, both of these can be combined with the adoption of any of the other strategies. People who work as wage laborers can still adopt forage production, for example. Therefore, I will use migration (see Chapter 11) and wage labor (see Chapter 6) as independent variables in order to determine their potential effects on the adoption of the other adaptive strategies.

Summary

In this chapter, I have identified five different adaptive strategies that individuals in the *ejido* of Puerto de las Piedras are adopting. Rather than simply adopting some of the new, modern items in a random fashion or adopting all of them wholesale, the *ejidatarios* practice selective adoption. While a few years ago everyone in the *ejido* was involved in subsistence agriculture, there is now a diversification of activities. Some individuals are engaged on forage production, some in animal improvement, others in trying to improve their corn yields through fertilizer use, and still others in trying to improve their corn yields through tractor use. Some people have not adopted any of the new items and are still exclusively involved in traditional subsistence agriculture. Two other adaptive strategies, migration and wage labor, were present before the river improvement and development programs.

The five primary adaptive strategies that I have identified in this chapter – forage production, animal improvement, tractor use, fertilizer use, and subsistence agriculture – will be used as dependent variables in the chapters that follow. I will investigate a wide range of social, cultural, and ecological variables in order to determine which factors are related to the patterns of choosing among the alternative adaptive strategies.

5

Microecological differences
in the communities and the *ejido*

The most obvious starting point in looking at the determinants of production techniques is in a group's relationship with its physical environment. Although peasant farming, like other aspects of their lives, often appears to be homogeneous in terms of the methods utilized to extract a living from the environment, significant variation is usually present in any region. This variability in production techniques, animals raised, and crops planted can be traced to ecological differences not immediately apparent to an observer but which are clearly perceived by local people (see Johnson 1974). Because of this variability, it should also hold true that decisions about which new innovations to adopt may be based upon an individual's microecological circumstances.

On the surface, it would seem that the *ejidatarios* of Puerto de las Piedras have to adapt to almost uniform environmental conditions. The land reform laws were designed to ensure that all of them received equal amounts of land. In addition, all of the *ejidatarios'* fields are located on the irrigable flat valley floor, a landscape that again gives the appearance of uniformity. However, such a conclusion is not warranted. This chapter demonstrates that there are significant microecological differences in the communities that make up Puerto de las Piedras and in the *ejido* lands and that these differences affect the individual's choice of adaptive strategies.

The three primary communities in which the *ejidatarios* live – El Puerto, Las Piedras, and El Jardín – are all shown to have some desirable and some undesirable features. Thus certain adaptive strategies are more feasible than others for adoption by people living in the various villages. Some predictable associations are found between community and adaptive strategy, while other expected relationships do not occur.

The second microecological feature discussed is the variability of the *ejido* lands. Contrary to appearances, the land in the valley is not completely flat. Some areas can be irrigated more easily than others, and significant variability exists in soil characteristics and fertility. In addition, the amount of land held by individuals is by no means uniform. Some individuals were found to have accumulated much more than the

2.38 hectares they are supposed to have, while others have somewhat less than this amount. The land quality–quantity index that I created to measure access to land is one of the better predictors of who will be adopting several adaptive strategies.

Finally, I consider the distance from the place of residence to the *ejido* plots. Some individuals live less than two hundred meters while others live as far as seven kilometers from some of their fields. One might expect people who live closer to their land to be able to take better care of their crops and perhaps to be more willing to invest resources in increasing production on their fields.

Geographical features of the three communities

El Puerto, Las Piedras, and El Jardín are all situated on the rocky hillsides that skirt the valley floor. Despite this modicum of uniformity, however, there are some important geographical and ecological differences among the three communities.

El Puerto is the largest of the three communities; and it is situated very close to the *ejido*, the main road into Temascalcingo, and the Lerma River (see Figure 5.1 and Photograph 3). Proximity to the river does not confer any great advantage because the water is not fit for drinking (except by animals) or for washing clothes. Proximity to the road and the *ejido* do have certain advantages. Being close to the road is very convenient for individuals who wish to walk into Temascalcingo or catch a bus to Atlacomulco, Toluca, or Mexico City. The road is also useful during the harvest season. *Remolques* (carts) and trucks can use the canal roads to pick up corn near the fields and transport it rapidly to the church in El Puerto, located just on the east side of the old bridge over the river (see Figure 5.1). The corn is unloaded there and transported to the houses either on animals or on the backs of the people. Proximity to the *ejido* makes it more convenient for people to work in and watch over their fields, a fact which is especially important during the summer when afternoon rains put a sudden stop to work in the fields.

A further advantage of living in El Puerto is that approximately two-thirds of the houses lie below the aqueduct bringing water from the springs in Ojo de Agua to Temascalcingo. Most of the houses below the aqueduct have pipes that bring water directly to their homes. For those living higher on the hill, wash basins have been constructed to provide a convenient place to wash clothes and get drinking water. The water from Ojo de Agua comes from very pure springs. In contrast, the local water holes in El Puerto are very polluted.

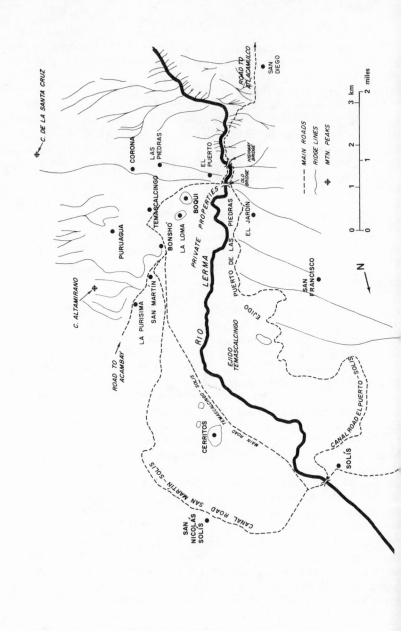

Those houses that are situated on the main road have also been able to hook into the electrical lines that run into Temascalcingo. Although other individuals in El Puerto would like to acquire electricity, there has yet to be an effectively organized effort to raise the necessary money (see also Chapter 7).

Finally, El Puerto is the only one of the three communities to have its own school. The school is situated on the canal road across the old bridge from El Puerto. Two new buildings have recently been completed, and at present the school has all six primary grades.

El Puerto is the most densely populated of the three communities. From my mapping, I found that there were 130 house sites in El Puerto (compared to only 85 in Las Piedras). Calculating the number of house sites in relation to the approximate amount of land in the community, I found a density of *approximately* 2.9 households per hectare. This figure gives some impression of the population concentration, but most of the houses are concentrated in the area around the church and on the main road into Temascalcingo. Thus one part of the community is more densely populated than the others.

This density of population is recognized by the people of El Puerto. They do not, outwardly at least, feel that their neighbors are too close. Instead, population density is conceptualized in terms of being inconvenient for raising animals. People say that there is too little room for the animals to roam without disturbing other families. The animals have to be taken high into the mountains behind El Puerto or to the other side of the river before they can be released to graze.

There is also very little cultivable land within the boundaries of the community. El Puerto is built primarily around outcroppings of rock. Only in the higher part of the village is there any private property that can be cultivated. Even there the land is poor and does not produce much.

To sum up, El Puerto is situated on the main road close to the *ejido*, receives water from the aqueduct, and has its own school. It is in a good location from the standpoint of accessibility to transportation, *ejido* land, water, and in some places, electricity. However, there is little private land that can be cultivated profitably, the community is densely settled, and there is very little grazing land for animals.

Las Piedras is situated slightly closer to Temascalcingo than is El Puerto. However, the road linking the two communities is only dirt, is very rocky, and is more difficult to walk on than is the main paved and cobblestoned road from El Puerto to Temascalcingo. Las Piedras is a considerable distance from the *ejido* (see Figure 5.1). In fact, even the houses closest to the bridge over the river are from one and one-half to

two kilometers away. The fields themselves may be a number of kilometers further beyond the bridge.

Las Piedras also is not in a good location from the point of view of
its proximity to water. The aqueduct comes only to a small corner of
the community, where there is a tap and a number of wash basins. This
location is inconvenient for all but a handful of households, and most
rely upon the springs and water holes in different areas of the community. This water is polluted and especially scarce during the dry season.
I would expect that water-borne diseases are probably more prevalent
in Las Piedras than in El Puerto.

In the past, the road leading from Temascalcingo to Las Piedras was
a viable route of transport. However, heavy erosion has wiped out large
sections of this road and has made it impassable for trucks and carts.
Attempts were being made in 1973 to repair this road (see Chapter 7),
for there was a great desire among the *ejidatarios* to use it to transport
crops during the harvest season. The long, difficult trip from the *ejido*
to house sites is very hard on both man and beast, especially during the
harvest when fifty or more round trips may be needed before the corn
is safely stored in the house. If the community were accessible to trucks
and carts, considerable labor could be saved.

Children from Las Piedras must use the school in Temascalcingo. Although the walk to school may be long and difficult, the primary problem is the fact that the children from Las Piedras attend school with
those from Temascalcingo. Time and again we were told stories about
children in Las Piedras who refused to go back to school because they
were picked on by the town children or were berated by the schoolteachers.

Despite these ecological disadvantages, Las Piedras is very favorably
situated with regard to private land. Some of the lands on the lower
slopes of the mountain produce very good crops of corn or barley.
Most families have enough land around their houses to grow some beans,
squash, and corn. There is also enough land to raise animals. There are
only eighty-five house sites in Las Piedras, with a total land base of
approximately 67.5 hectares. The density of house sites is only about
1.3 per hectare compared to 2.9 in El Puerto. There is some concentration of houses in certain areas, although this pattern is not nearly as
pronounced as around the church in El Puerto.

Thus Las Piedras has a larger and more productive land base than El
Puerto; but its ecological position is further from transport facilities,
the school, water, and especially the *ejido*. Migration from Las Piedras
to other communities or out of the region has been heavier than from
either El Puerto or El Jardín. The long distances from Las Piedras to the

ejido lands may have discouraged many *ejidatarios,* especially during the years in which river flooding caused periodic crop losses.[20] Evidence suggests that more people from Las Piedras have given up their lands than have individuals from El Puerto. Many of my informants reported that in the past the majority of the *ejidatarios* were from Las Piedras. In fact, it is said that people from El Puerto were invited to become members of the *ejido* only to add a few more names to the lists (see Chapter 3) in order to give greater weight to the petition for land. Currently, however, a larger proportion of *ejidatarios* is from El Puerto (43.5 percent) than from Las Piedras (32.3 percent), suggesting that the migration patterns have not been the same in the two communities.

El Jardín, the smallest of the three communities, appears to be the most dynamic. Census figures show that its population climbed from 114 in 1960 to 189 at the time of the 1970 census.[21] Perhaps the primary reason is the excellent geographical position of the community. It is situated on the canal road that passes along the fringe of the *ejido* lands (see Figure 5.1). Thus individuals who live there are very close to their land and have no difficulties with transportation. They can hire trucks or use carts to haul their corn. Even if they have to use animals, the short distance from the fields to their houses is much less difficult to traverse than that between the fields and El Puerto or Las Piedras. The land in the hills behind El Jardín is part of the noncultivable portion of the *ejido* and is easily accessible for grazing animals. A deep well in the community is a local center for drawing water, washing clothes, and bathing. Through the efforts of a community leader, all of the houses in El Jardín recently acquired electricity. The school, located midway between El Jardín and El Puerto, is a short walk for the children.

Perhaps the only drawback to living in El Jardín is that it is slightly farther from Temascalcingo than the other two communities. However, on market days (Sunday) a bus runs along the canal road. This service makes Temascalcingo accesssible for those who wish to go to church, to market, or to engage in other activities there. Temascalcingo is also well within walking distance, all on good roads.

A number of individuals with whom I talked in 1973 reported that they were considering moving to El Jardín. The proximity of the community to the *ejido*, grazing lands, and the school, coupled with the fact that it has recently acquired electricity, make it an attractive location. Although at present El Jardín has only a well, efforts are being made to extend a pipe from the aqueduct that serves Temascalcingo. While this arrangement would not result in piped-in water for most houses (because they are situated on the hillsides), a communal water

Table 5.1. *Means of the different adaptive strategies for the three communities*

	El Jardín (N = 9)	El Puerto (N = 27)	Las Piedras (N = 20)	All other (N = 6)
Forage production	.737	−.081	−.296	.246
Animal improvement	.315	−.135	−.324	1.214
Tractor use	.104	.143	−.309	.230
Fertilizer use	.252	−.179	.123	.018
Subsistence agriculture	−1.408	.252	.806	−1.708

tap and wash basins near the canal road would make El Jardín an ever more desirable place to live. Already people are pressing *ejidal* officials to allocate land plots on the hillsides around El Jardín to individuals for use as house sites. Until recently, the land had simply been available for grazing the *ejidatarios'* animals.

Intercommunity differences in adaptive strategies

On the basis of the preceding descriptions of the communities, certain predictions were made about which adaptive strategies might be feasible for adoption by individuals in the various communities. In the following comparisons, I have divided the sample into four groups – those who live in El Jardín, El Puerto, Las Piedras, and other communities (primarily Temascalcingo).

Because of its favorable location close to the *ejido*, its easy access for carts and trucks, and its proximity to grazing lands for animals, I predicted that those in El Jardín would have mean positive factor scores on all of the new adaptive strategies and a mean negative factor score on the subsistence agriculture adaptive strategy. As Table 5.1 shows, all of these predictions are confirmed. The mean score on all four new adaptive strategies is positive for the 9 individuals who live in El Jardín. These individuals have the highest mean score on the forage production adaptive strategy of any of the groups. El Jardín also has a very high negative mean score on subsistence agriculture. This fact indicates that these individuals are not content to grow corn in the traditional manner but are investing in the new opportunities becoming available.

El Puerto is a moderate distance from the *ejido*; carts and trucks can get to parts of the community; and it is densely populated, thus making the raising of animals difficult. I predicted that individuals in El Puerto would have factor scores that were positive or near zero on the forage production, tractor use, and fertilizer use adaptive strategies. I expected that there would be a mean negative factor score on the animal improvement strategy. Table 5.1 shows that there does not appear to be any propensity for people in El Puerto to choose certain adaptive strategies. As predicted, there is a negative mean score on animal improvement and a positive mean score on tractor use; but these, like the scores on the other adaptive strategies, are close to zero.

Because Las Piedras is quite far from the *ejido,* I predicted that the twenty individuals in this community would have negative factor scores on the three adaptive strategies requiring investment in the land – tractor use, forage production, and fertilizer use. I expected there to be a positive mean score on the animal improvement strategy because Las Piedras does have room for grazing animals. Finally, I expected that people in Las Piedras would be those most likely to be continuing the subsistence agriculture adaptive strategy (i.e., they should have a high positive score). Table 5.1 shows that Las Piedras does have negative scores on forage production and tractor use and a positive score on subsistence agriculture. These results were all expected. However, there is a small positive mean score on fertilizer use, and Las Piedras has the highest *negative* mean score on the animal improvement adaptive strategy. Although people in Las Piedras have room to raise animals, they are not investing money to keep their livestock healthy.

Most of the six individuals in the study who live outside El Jardín, El Puerto, and Las Piedras reside in Temascalcingo. Because these people tend to have other sources of income and are wealthier than most *ejidatarios,* I felt that these individuals would be most able to invest in the potentially profitable forage production and animal improvement strategies. Table 5.1 confirms these expectations and shows that the individuals in "other communities" have the highest mean score on animal improvement. I also felt that people from Temascalcingo would have the most contact with those wealthy private landowners who have tractors. This contact should also enable them to have a positive score on the tractor use strategy. This prediction is also confirmed. No prediction was made about fertilizer use, but I expected that these people would have the highest negative score on the subsistence agriculture strategy. Table 5.1 indicates that these *ejidatarios* have a mean score of close to zero on fertilizer use and do have the highest negative score on subsistence agriculture. People from "other communities" are clearly trying to modernize their production techniques.

To sum up, there are some intercommunity differences in the adaptive strategies being selected. Residents of El Jardín seem to be in a favorable geographical setting for the adoption of any or all of the new

strategies. El Puerto is in a mixed position, and this fact is reflected by
the absence of any clear pattern of adoption of new strategies. Because
Las Piedras is quite a distance from the *ejido,* it is not surprising that its
residents do not seem to be adopting any of the new adaptive strategies,
with the exception of a slight tendency to use fertilizer. People from
the other communities (primarily Temascalcingo) have positive mean
scores on all of the new adaptive strategies. They, along with people
who live in El Jardín, are most consistent in their rejection of subsistence
agriculture and are investing in the new opportunities. *Ejidatarios* from
El Puerto and Las Piedras, on the other hand, do not seem as willing to
abandon the subsistence agriculture adaptive strategy.

One part of the explanation for these adoption patterns may lie in
the differentials in wealth among the individuals in the four groups.
Residents of El Jardín (the arithmetic mean, $\overline{X}$ = 8.33) and people
from the other communities ($\overline{X}$ = 8.17) are the two groups that score
highest in terms of mean wealth ratings (see Chapter 6). El Puerto ($\overline{X}$ =
7.26) and Las Piedras ($\overline{X}$ = 6.10) both have lower mean scores. Thus
the adoption patterns for the adaptive strategies may be due as much to
wealth differences among the *ejidatarios* as to the geographical and
ecological features of the various communities. Chapter 6 will explore
differences in wealth in relation to adoption of the various adaptive
strategies.

Ejidal lands and their characteristics

The *ejidal* lands of Puerto de las Piedras are located on the valley floor
on the western side of the Lerma River (see Figures 5.1 and 5.2). The
lands are bordered on the south by the canyon through which the Lerma
flows before entering the valley; on the west by the irrigation canal,
the service road for the canal, and the mountains; on the north by a
portion of the Temascalcingo *ejido;* and on the east by the river and (on
the opposite side of the river) by the large ranch of a wealthy family.

In general terms, the ecological position of the *ejido* lands is very
good. While there were considerable problems in the past with flooding
from the river (see Chapter 2), the irrigation and flood control projects
completed in 1970 have made the land valuable again. Currently, about
four hundred hectares of the *ejido* of Puerto de las Piedras can be irrigated.

Soil tests conducted by Hydraulic Resources in a number of areas of
the *ejido* indicate that all of the soils are of comparable quality, although
the amount of organic material present (vital for plant growth) is very

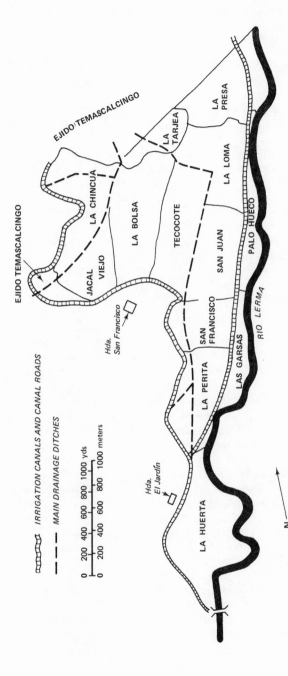

Figure 5.2 *Parajes* in the *ejido* of Puerto de las Piedras

EJIDO TEMASCALCINGO

EJIDO TEMASCALCINGO

LA CHINCUA

LA TARJEA

LA PRESA

LA BOLSA

LA LOMA

TECOCOTE

JACAL VIEJO

SAN JUAN

PALO HUECO

Hda. San Francisco

SAN FRANCISCO

LAS GARSAS

RIO LERMA

LA PERITA

Hda. El Jardín

LA HUERTA

IRRIGATION CANALS AND CANAL ROADS

MAIN DRAINAGE DITCHES

0   200 400 600 800 1000 yds
0   200 400 600 800 1000 meters

N

low. The monocultivation of corn has resulted in the deterioration of these soils.

Another general problem in the *ejido* is that, although the valley floor is relatively flat, no attempt has been made to level the land. As a result, many areas lie slightly lower than others. These areas fill up with water during irrigation and during rainstorms. There are many fields in which the collected water damages the corn, thus reducing the harvest.

The slight depressions in the *ejidal* lands make the farmers very reluctant to irrigate their fields more than once. The water that collects in the low spots during the irrigation before planting does little harm, except perhaps to delay the plowing and planting of some fields. However, irrigating after the corn is planted and has begun to grow damages the corn of individuals who have low-lying fields. *Ejidatarios* say that they will not irrigate after planting no matter how dry their crops become. To irrigate and then to have a heavy rainfall would result in so much damage and claims for indemnification that conflicts would be rife for years. So, although the irrigation facilities should eliminate worry about the onset of summer rains, it will not take place unless the land is leveled.

Another problem that arises because of the inability to irrigate after the corn is planted is the possibility of frost damage. Delayed summer rains may result in a very late maturation of the corn crop, if the corn is not completely destroyed. If an early frost should occur, some portion of the harvest could be lost. The *ejidatarios* take the possibility of frost into account and first plant areas that are out in the open valley. It is these areas that are most susceptible to early frosts. The fields that are protected by their proximity to the mountains are planted last. Informants reported that they could not remember an early frost ever harming the corn in the protected area at the base of the canyon near the bridge (i.e., the area labeled La Huerta in Figure 5.2).

Although there are problems with local flooding, nutrient-depleted soil, and occasional danger of frost damage, I should emphasize that the *ejido* is very fortunate. The average *ejidal* grant of 2.38 hectares is larger than in almost every other community in the valley; the land is irrigable; and it is located on a fairly fertile plain, which makes cultivation with animals and/or tractors possible.

Despite this generally favorable picture of the lands, there are some important microenvironmental differences in land quality. Some of these were taken into account by the early founders of the *ejido*. The allocation to each *ejidatario* was not made in one 2.38-hectare piece of land. Generally, the allocations consisted of one piece of land 1 hectare in size, two plots of 0.50 hectare, and one section of 0.38 hectare. An attempt was made to allocate these plots in such a way as to minimize the amount of difference in land quality. Thus a person with a 1-hectare piece of land that was of good quality might receive two half hectares of lesser quality. The result is that most ejidatarios have small parcels of land scattered in different areas of the *ejido*. One of my informants, for example, had one piece of land in the *paraje* (named locale) known as Jacal Viejo, another in La Huerta, another in San Juan, and a fourth in La Presa (see Figure 5.2).

The microenvironmental differences in neighboring plots of equal size can be very important, especially when one person's land lies slightly lower or higher than another's. In the course of interviewing, I often ran into statements about these very specific geographical conditions. Nonetheless, it would have been very time consuming to try to elicit statements about each one of the over six hundred separate pieces of land contained in the *ejido*. As an alternative, I decided to elicit statements about different sections of land; that is, about the different characteristics of fairly large sections of the *ejido*.

Fortunately, such a division of the *ejido* already existed in the cultural repertoire of the people. Specific areas of the *ejido* have had names since the days of the *hacienda*. These place names (*parajes*) were used to help in the redistribution of the *ejido* and, in fact, are still widely used today. The boundaries of these *parajes* do not completely reflect microenvironmental differences in the *ejido* because they are delimited by roads, canals, paths, and irrigation ditches – boundaries which do not demarcate types and qualities of soils. Nevertheless, informants were easily able to categorize these *parajes* as being generally good or poor areas in which to grow corn. In fact, these distinctions were made frequently when informants were telling me about crop yields. A typical response was, "Well, the soil in Palo Hueco [a *paraje*] is very sandy; and when the rains came late last year, I lost all of my corn there."

I will now move on to a discussion of these *parajes* as microenvironments in the *ejido,* describing the peculiar characteristics of each one and then examining production figures from 1972 to determine differences among *parajes* in terms of production potential. In all of these discussions, however, it should be recognized that the differences in land quality within *parajes* can vary greatly; and the variation may, in some cases, be greater within a *paraje* than between two similar *parajes*.

As I indicated earlier, all areas of the *ejido* can be irrigated; and the soil quality, in terms of organic material present, is fairly similar throughout the *ejido*. While *ejidatarios* sometimes talk about the differential fertility of various pieces of land, by far the most commonly made dis-

Table 5.2. *Classification of soils in parajes in the ejido*

Paraje	Soil characteristics	Numerical rank
La Huerta	Clay (*barro*) and sand (*arena*)	3
La Perita	Sand with some clay	2
Las Garzas	Sand with some clay	2
San Francisco	Clay and sand	3
San Juan	Sand	1
Palo Hueco	Sand	1
Tecocote	Clay and sand (best lands in *ejido*)	3
La Loma	Sand	1
La Presa	Sand	1
La Tarjea	Clay and sand	3
La Bolsa	Clay	1
Jacal Viejo	Clay and sand	3
La Chinqua	Clay	1

tinction is about the composition of the soils. Some soils are very sandy, while others are largely clay, and still others have a mixture of the two. Sandy soils are porous, and corn is often lost in these areas during prolonged dry spells. Soils with too much clay conserve water well, but this fact is often problematical during the heavy summer rains. Water that does not drain from these areas collects and rots the corn in a matter of a few days. The best soils have a good mixture of sand and clay.[22] These conserve some humidity during the dry season; and in the rainy season, they drain fairly rapidly.

Table 5.2 lists the thirteen most commonly named *parajes* and informants' statements about the characteristics of each one. In general, the *parajes* in the *ejido* that contain mostly sand are those bordering directly on the river (see Figure 5.2). It was these areas that bore the brunt of the river flooding in the past and where silt was deposited. An examination of aerial photographs taken in 1969 showed that, especially in the *parajes* of Palo Hueco, San Juan, La Loma, and La Presa (all of which are said to have poor soils), the effects of the river flooding are readily apparent. Walking through parts of this area was akin to trudging along a beach; my feet sank into the sand as I walked. Those *parajes* that lie farthest away from the river and closest to the mountains are found to have the most clay present in the soil (i.e., La Chinqua, La Bolsa, and Jacal Viejo).

In the final column of Table 5.2, I have assigned a numerical ranking

Table 5.3. *Average production per hectare in the parajes*

Paraje	No. of land plots sampled	Average production per hectare (in *costales*)	Ranking of *paraje* from Table 5.2
Tecocote	17	43.2	3
La Huerta	57	38.0	3
Las Garzas	27	37.2	2
San Francisco	19	35.2	3
Jacal Viejo	14	34.9	3
La Perita	31	33.3	2
La Presa	34	31.0	1
Palo Hueco	7	28.4	1
La Loma	17	28.1	1
La Bolsa	28	24.3	1
San Juan	18	23.3	1
La Tarjea	21	22.4	3
La Chinqua	10	14.1	1

to correspond to the categorizations by my informants. Lands they classified as being completely clayey or almost completely sandy were ranked lowest as a 1. Lands that were a mixture of clay and sand, although with a predominance of one or the other, were ranked as a 2. Those lands having a good or "proper" mixture of sand and clay were given the highest ranking, 3. I should emphasize that these numbers are rankings I gave to my informants' categorizations. While my informants might have been willing to perform the same ranking, I was more interested in eliciting the nominal categorizations of land when I collected the data. The rankings I have made here are a transformation imposed by me on my informants' nomothetic characterizations of land types.

Variations in production among the parajes

In order to determine whether the ratings of the different *parajes* reflected any sort of empirical reality, I determined the actual production obtained from these *parajes*. The corn production figures come from 1972, a year in which the rains came fairly late and in which the rainy season was slightly drier than average. Table 5.3 contains the data showing the average production per hectare obtained from the various *parajes*.[23]

There is a good correspondence between the rating contained in

Table 5.3 and the actual mean production per hectare.[24] There are only two *parajes* for which the ratings appear to be misleading. La Tarjea, for example, reportedly has very good soil, which is not reflected by the harvests obtained there. One reason for this anomaly is that La Tarjea is the *paraje* most isolated from the villages (see Figure 5.2). In addition, almost all of the plots in that section of the *ejido* are only 0.38 hectares. The amount of travel needed to reach this section of the *ejido* and the small size of the plots found there undoubtedly affect the amount of care given to those lands. This relative neglect is one factor accounting for the low production of these plots despite the reportedly good quality of the land. Another factor is that lands in this section are sometimes affected by flooding from a large drainage ditch that is one of the *paraje* boundaries.

The second anomaly is the case of Las Garzas. The quality of the land there is mediocre and was rated as a 2; yet the production obtained in that *paraje* was the third highest in the *ejido*. One explanation is that Las Garzas is one of the *parajes* located closest to the villages (see Figure 5.2). Also, over one-third of the land plots there were fertilized in 1972. This figure was the second highest proportion of plots fertilized among the *parajes* in the *ejido*.

Production figures for the other *parajes* closely match the rankings assigned. The Spearman correlation between the rankings and the average production per hectare was .61, indicating a substantial agreement between informants' ratings of the quality of land and the actual production obtained.

Measuring land quantity–quality

One of the most surprising findings of my research was that there was considerable variability in the amount of land controlled by *ejidatarios*. I had expected, in accordance with the figure established during the initial redistribution of lands to the *ejido* of Puerto de las Piedras, that most individuals would have 2.38 hectares of land and that only minor deviations from this amount would exist. It was true that most *ejidatarios* had only 2.38 hectares, but the deviance from this amount was shocking. Several individuals had considerably more land under their control than was legally permitted.

The most common way for individuals to gain control over *ejido* land was to have allocations placed in the names of close relatives, usually sons or daughters. During the years when flooding was common in the valley, many *ejidatarios* abandoned their land (see note 20). By law, a meeting of all the members of the *ejido* is supposed to be called to decide who will receive these abandoned lands. In practice, it was common in the past for the president of the *ejido* simply to assign these plots to landless individuals. These officials were not above showing favoritism, and many of the new *ejidatarios* were close relatives of the *ejido* president. Typically, these individuals were either too young to cultivate the land or had no interest in being farmers. The fields thus ended up under the control of the man who had "reallocated" them. As I point out in Chapter 7, this was one of the fringe benefits that accrued to *ejido* officers.

Given these circumstances, it was not possible for me to get accurate information about the amount of land controlled by five or six *ejidatarios*. Because of my rapport with several key informants and the complaints of *ejidatarios* angry about how much land some people possessed, I was aware of those cases in which individuals withheld information. Although I did collect information volunteered by informants about these "excess" lands, I did not systematically press to obtain this information. To have done so would have jeopardized my position in the community, and I would have had difficulty collecting other data. I am confident that the vast majority of people did give me accurate information about their holdings and the production they obtained from them.

My purpose in collecting information about the quantity and quality of land held by *ejidatarios* was to determine whether these factors had an affect on the adaptive strategies being chosen. To this end, I utilized the rankings contained in Table 5.2 to create an index of "land quantity-quality." This index was created by multiplying the number of hectares held in each *paraje* by the land quality rank for that area of the *ejido*. The final score for each *ejidatario* was obtained by summing the separate scores from every *paraje* in which a person had rights to land. Thus this measure combines the size of landholdings and the quality of the land.

In general, the measure of land quantity–quality is accurate for the vast majority of *ejidatarios* who have rights to only the maximum amount of land permitted (i.e., 2.38 hectares). Among those who control more land than is legally permitted, there is an attenuation of the scores due to their withholding information. However, somewhat balancing the nonreporting of "extra" plots was a tendency for those *ejidatarios* who had more than the legally allotted lands to report on the best fields under their control. In many cases, the reason why the best plots were reported was that poorer lands were not being cultivated. The *ejidatarios* were reluctant to discuss these plots because lands left uncultivated for more than two years in a row may be redistributed to other people under the terms of Mexico's agrarian reform laws. Thus the *ejidatarios* tended to report on the fields they were actually cultivating even if these were in the name of a close relative. Because they reported on their best fields all of these individuals ended up with high land quantity–quality scores, although they were not as high as they should have been.

The best example of the attenuation of scores on this variable involves Juan's lands. Juan has at least four children who have *ejido* lands registered in their names. Only one of these children now lives in the valley, and he is a schoolteacher. In addition, one of Juan's sisters also has land – land that Juan is cultivating. Finally, there is a large tract of land in one area of the *ejido* that has not been cultivated for a number of years. Some informants reported that Juan controls all of this land and has threatened *ejidatarios* who began to work it. A few *ejidatarios* reported that Juan had at least thirty hectares of *ejidal* land, and one claimed that Juan had about eighty hectares. In my interview with Juan, he reported only three hectares in La Chinqua (land quantity–quality score of 3), 1 hectare in La Huerta (a score of 3), 1 hectare in Jacal Viejo (score of 3), and 0.50 hectare in La Presa (score of 0.5). He also reported cultivating the land of one of his sons, who has 1 hectare in La Loma (score of 1), 1 hectare in La Bolsa (score of 1), and 0.38 of a hectare in La Presa (score of 0.38). Thus the total land quality–quantity score for Juan is 11.88, one of the highest scores on this variable but well below his correct score.

The scores on land quantity–quality ranged from a low of 1.00 to a high of 12.63. The mean score was 5.06, and the standard deviation was 2.40. In order to convey a better impression of the meaning of these numbers, I will discuss a number of other individual cases. Hector is the most "land poor" of the *ejidatarios*. Around 1962 he petitioned the president of the *ejido* for some small, unclaimed pieces of land (called *sobrantes*). He received one-quarter hectare in La Presa, one-half hectare in San Juan, and one-quarter hectare in La Chinqua. All of these lands are sandy and yield very little corn. The ranking assigned to each of these *parajes* in Table 5.2 was 1, and thus the total score on land quality–quantity was 1 (rank) times 1 (total hectares) equals 1. Last year Hector could only raise enough cash to sow the one-half hectare in San Juan; and despite the fact that he fertilized the land, he received a total corn production for the year of only fourteen *costales*.

Felipe's land resources are much better than Hector's. He has one hectare in La Presa (land quantity–quality score of 1), 1 hectare in La Chinqua (score of 1), 1 hectare in Jacal Viejo (score of 3), 0.38 hectare in La Tarjea (score of 1.14), 0.75 hectare in La Huerta (score of 2.25), and 0.50 hectare in San Juan (score of 0.50). Felipe's total land quantity–

quality score was 8.89. Despite the fact that he has sown *pradera* on two of his fields, Felipe was able to obtain a production of 217 *costales* of corn in 1972.

The contrast between Hector and Felipe in terms of their land quantity-quality scores is striking, as is the difference in the harvests they obtain. These two cases illustrate some of the variability in land resources present in an *ejido* where all members are supposed to have equal access to land. I will discuss the relationship of land quality-quantity with the adaptive strategies after considering another potentially important ecological variable.

Measuring distance from land

Individuals who live further away from their lands might be less able to care for their fields, and this factor could affect their decisions about whether to adopt a particular adaptive strategy. I therefore measured the "distance from land," the distance from the house site to the various plots in the *ejido*. I used aerial photographs of the region, a map of all the land plots completed in 1973 by Hydraulic Resources,[25] and my own maps of the house sites of all members of the community to determine the distance in meters from each *ejidatario's* house site to every *ejido* plot he or she owned. Distances were measured along the roads and paths that form the major arteries of travel from one location to another.

In order to better estimate the actual difficulty of the walking distance (as well as the amount of time involved), I decided to "weight" the distance an individual had to travel on hillside paths more than the distance traveled on the roads. The paths traversing the communities of El Puerto and Las Piedras are especially rocky, winding, and very steep in places. Thus the distance traveled on these paths was multiplied by one and one-half to give a better approximation of walking distance and difficulty.

Table 5.4 shows the mean distances from house sites to the different *parajes*. La Huerta, obviously, is the closest *paraje* and is a little over two kilometers from most house sites. La Tarjea is the farthest and is an average of almost six and one-half kilometers from houses. Also shown in Table 5.4 are the minimum and maximum distances from houses to each *paraje*.

My main interest, however, was in creating a variable for each individual in the *ejido* that would reflect the distance the person had to travel between the house site and the *ejido*. I decided to take an individual's mean distance from all of his or her *ejido* plots to reflect distance from land. Although the maximum distance from a land plot

Table 5.4. *Distances of house sites from different parajes in the ejido (in meters)*

Paraje	Mean distance	Minimum distance	Maximum distance
La Huerta	2,055	50	4,100
La Perita	3,694	400	5,550
Las Garzas	3,372	1,300	5,100
San Francisco	4,597	1,600	5,550
San Juan	4,541	2,150	6,400
Palo Hueco	4,150	3,050	5,850
Tecocote	5,071	3,750	6,450
La Loma	5,852	4,500	7,275
La Presa	5,924	3,850	8,025
La Tarjea	6,425	3,750	7,700
La Bolsa	4,863	2,400	6,550
Jacal Viejo	5,536	3,700	7,600
La Chinqua	6,120	3,400	8,000

might better reflect the actual distance traveled in a day (because an *ejidatario* could go to the farthest plot and then stop by every other plot on his or her way home), some of those *parajes* most distant in the *ejido* have poor soil and seem to receive less care. Thus mean distance was used rather than the maximum distance.

Scores on the distance from land variable ranged from a low of 1,712 to a high of 7,600 meters. The mean distance was 4,495.2, and the standard deviation was 1,286. To give more meaning to these scores, I will give some descriptive information on a few individuals.

Natalia is an *ejidataria* who lives high up on the hillside in Las Piedras. Her lands in La Perita, La Presa, and La Loma are an average distance of almost 7 kilometers (6.825) from her house. A large portion of this distance involves a difficult climb from the main road up the steep path to her house. Ponciano has one of the longest distances of all to travel. It is 7,550 meters from his recently constructed house in San Martín (see Figure 5.1) to his *ejido* plot in Jacal Viejo. He can travel all of this distance on level roads, but the distance is still very great. Florentino has his home in La Huerta. One of his land plots is only 400 meters from his house; and the average distance from his house to his plots is only 2,025 meters, all of which can be traveled on the canal roads.

Table 5.5. *Correlations of the adaptive strategies with the ecological variables*

	Land quantity–quality	Distance from land
Forage production	.45**	−.23*
Animal improvement	.01	.07
Tractor use	.36**	−.10
Fertilizer use	−.03	.10
Subsistence agriculture	−.39**	.08

Note: In this table and all other tables that report Pearson correlations, * will indicate $p < .05$ and ** will indicate $p < .01$. These are the levels of statistical significance.

Relationships between ecological variables and adaptive strategies

I had a number of hypotheses about the relationships of two ecological variables, land quantity–quality and distance from land, with the different adaptive strategies. I predicted that those with high land quantity–quality scores (reflecting, in part, larger amounts of land) would tend to have high scores on the tractor use strategy. With more land to plow, these individuals would be those most apt to adopt mechanization in the cultivation of their fields. Table 5.5 shows that there is a statistically significant relationship between land quantity–quality and tractor use. I also predicted that there would be a positive association between high land quantity–quality and a willingness to adopt the forage production strategy. Those individuals with more land and land of better quality should be able to allocate some portion of their land to the cultivation of forage crops and still be able to raise enough corn to satisfy their domestic consumption needs. This expectation is also confirmed. Table 5.5 shows that there is a positive relationship between land quantity–quality and forage production. I did not expect the fertilizer use or animal production strategies to be related to land quantity–quality. Those with fewer land resources would be likely to invest in fertilizers to compensate for their lack of good resources. Animal production has little to do with land resources. Table 5.5 shows that neither animal improvement nor fertilizer use is correlated with land quantity–quality. Finally, I expected that land quantity–quality would be negatively correlated with maintenance of the subsistence agriculture adaptive strategy, and this expectation is confirmed. Those *ejidatarios* who have more and better land resources are more apt (or better able) to invest in forage production and tractor use.

Distance from land was expected to be negatively associated with the tractor use, forage production and fertilizer use strategies. In general, I expected that those who lived farthest from their land would be least interested in investing any cash in their land resources, because they are least able to watch over and care for their lands and crops. Table 5.5 shows that distance from land is negatively correlated with forage production. There is very little relationship with either tractor use or fertilizer use, however. Because I expected that individuals who lived far away from their lands would not be investing cash in new crops or techniques, I thought that there would be a tendency for them to invest in the animal improvement strategy. Table 5.5 shows that there is no significant correlation between distance from land and animal improvement. Finally, there is little correlation between distance from land and the subsistence agriculture adaptive strategy. Distance from land discourages investment in forage production but has little effect on the decision to adopt the other adaptive strategies.

Correlations of ecological variables with other independent variables

Although my primary interest is in predicting who will adopt the different adaptive strategies, I am also interested in the patterning of relationships among the independent variables. Therefore, in this chapter and in the chapters that follow, I will include a section on the interrelationships among the independent variables. I will not attempt to be exhaustive or to analyze every correlation. Rather, I will be concerned with highlighting the patterns of important results. Although interesting in and of themselves, these will assume added importance when I create models of the modernization process in Chapter 12.

Land quantity—quality is positively related to all of the different indicators of wealth.[26] Only the correlation with the cash value of animals is small and not statistically significant. These correlations suggest that individuals with more land resources have been producing more and thus getting wealthier. However, it is also true that wealthier individuals have held high posts in the *ejido* in the past and therefore have been in a position to obtain the lands of other *ejidatarios*. Land quantity—quality, as Table 5.6 shows, is positively correlated with *ejido* leadership. The causal direction is difficult to establish in this case. Wealthier individuals can become leaders and then manipulate their wealth and

Table 5.6. *Correlations of the independent variables with the ecological variables*

	Land quantity–quality	Distance from land
Wealth ratings	.44**	–.19
Material style of life	.30*	–.34**
Cash value of animals	.03	–.27*
Value of agric. equipment	.33**	–.22*
Income from other pursuits	.31**	–.05
Ejido leadership	.35**	–.06
Community leadership	.21	–.06
Cargo system participation	–.24*	.16
Religiosity	–.12	.11
Alcohol use	.27*	–.09
Education	.29*	–.14
Political knowledge	.38**	.03
Mass media exposure	.31*	–.19
Change agent contact	.41**	.13
Cosmopolitanism	.11	.42**
Age	.05	.22
No. of people in the house	–.07	.10
Indian language ability	–.18	–.11
Times worked elsewhere	.03	.24*
Distance from land	–.11	—

Note: * indicates $p < .05$ and ** indicates $p < .01$.

power to acquire more and/or better lands. As I indicated earlier in this chapter, some individuals have managed to gain access to more land than is legally permitted. Having acquired these better land resources, such individuals can produce more and thus become even wealthier and more powerful (see also Chapter 7).

Table 5.6 also shows that those with high land quantity–quality scores also tend to have more education, political knowledge, mass media exposure, and change agent contact. The *ejidatarios* with more land are not only wealthier but also tend to be those who are being exposed to the modernizing influences of education, mass media, and change agents. These individuals are not likely to be interested in *cargo* system participation, a more traditional influence.

Finally, land quantity–quality is positively related to alcohol use. Those individuals with more and/or better land tend to drink more frequently. I will have more to say about this relationship in Chapter 9.

Distance from land is negatively correlated with all of the indicators of wealth. The correlations with material style of life, cash value of
animals, and value of agricultural equipment are all statistically significant. It may be that individuals who live far away from their lands are
not producing as much as other *ejidatarios* and therefore are not as
wealthy. There are two possible explanations: (*a*) these individuals are
not able to care for their fields as well as others, or (*b*) more of their
production is stolen by others. I do not have much information that
can shed light on these issues. Some people who have fields far away
from their houses did complain that others often allow animals to roam
through their fields and eat the corn. Ponciano, the *ejidatario* mentioned
earlier who lives in San Martín, reported that he had lost a lot of corn
to animals. During 1973, he went out to his fields a number of times in
the wee hours of the morning hoping to catch animals in his fields.

Distance from land is positively correlated with the number of times
worked elsewhere (that is, outside of the region). This correlation is not
surprising in light of the observation made earlier in the chapter that
people from Las Piedras (who live farthest away from the *ejido*) have
abandoned their lands more frequently than other people. It seems that
these individuals also leave the region more often to work temporarily
in the cities. If these *ejidatarios* found good jobs they might also abandon their lands. Finally, distance from land is positively related to cosmopolitanism. Part of the cosmopolitanism of these individuals probably results from their trips to work in cities. Another part may be due
to their visits to relatives and neighbors who have already left the region
to work permanently in the city.

Summary

A number of ecological variables were investigated in this chapter. First,
the different villages whose members make up the *ejido* of Puerto de las
Piedras were described. The aim was to identify potential reasons why
some adaptive strategies might be more suitable for adoption by people
in a certain community. Some intercommunity differences in the adaptive strategies chosen were found. In general, people in El Jardín and
"other communities" (primarily Temascalcingo) were found to be
adopting all of the new adaptive strategies, while people in Las Piedras
were rejecting all of them except for fertilizer use. People in El Puerto
were not found to be consistently accepting or rejecting any strategy.
These differences in strategies chosen do not seem related to a community's ecological characteristics, however; and I suggested that the variations are probably more related to the wealth of a village.

Microecological differences of lands within the *ejido* were described, and these were shown to significantly affect the potential for the production of corn. I also found that there were considerable differences in the amount of land held by *ejidatarios*. Despite the relatively equal redistribution of lands in the 1930s, some individuals have managed to gain access to more land than is legally allowed. The variability in the quality of fields and the variability in amount of land controlled were used to create a measure of land quantity–quality. Those *ejidatarios* with high scores on this variable were found to be adopting the forage production and tractor use adaptive strategies and to be rejecting subsistence agriculture.

Distance from land was also measured, for some individuals live very close to their fields while others live as far as seven or eight kilometers away. This variable does not make a significant difference in willingness to adopt any of the adaptive strategies, except that those who live far away from their fields are less willing to invest in forage production.

The correlations of distance from land with other independent variables did identify one interesting pattern. I found that people who live farther from their fields tend to be poorer. I suggested that this pattern may result because people who live farther from their land are not getting as much production, partially because of their inability to keep a close watch on their crops. Perhaps as a consequence, those who live farther away from their fields are more likely to seek work in other places and are more cosmopolitan than individuals who live closer to their land.

6

Economic inequalities

The anthropologist who does fieldwork in the rural backwaters of an underdeveloped country cannot help but be impressed with the material poverty of the population encountered. The contrast with the affluent, wasteful society from which he or she has just come is striking, if not appalling. No wonder then that anthropologists have often been unable or unwilling to see beyond what appears to be a homogenous impoverished mass to those economic inequalities that might exist.

This tendency is perhaps nowhere more pronounced than among ethnographers of Mesoamerica. The "shared poverty" of villagers has been noted repeatedly (Wolf 1957:2; Huizer 1971:311); and there have been studies of "leveling mechanisms" (Wolf 1955; Nash 1961), which supposedly act to eliminate economic inequalities among the people. According to Nash, these leveling mechanisms "operate to drain the accumulated resources of the community for noneconomic ends, and to keep the various households, over generations, fairly equal in wealth. They are mechanisms to keep economic homogeneity within the community" (Nash 1971:172). Restudies of communities (Lewis 1951) and even reanalysis of data (Goldkind 1965) have shown wide disparities among researchers regarding the existence of relative socioeconomic homogeneity among various populations. Even the *cargo* system (see Chapter 8), which had been considered to be the prime leveling mechanism among Mesoamerican populations, has been shown by Cancian (1965) to be actually mirroring stratification rather than acting to eliminate existing inequalities. Thus different ethnographers have reached very different conclusions concerning the degree and characteristics of economic inequality in Mesoamerican communities.

While part of the explanation for the ethnographers' diverse conclusions might be that they reflect differences among the communities studied, research in the Valley of Temascalcingo has produced the same sort of disagreements about a single community and region. Alicja Iwanska studied one of the communities in the region and stated that the Mazahua from El Nopal "are now not only living within a completely nonstratified society, but also have been quite outspoken about what may be called their rudimentary ideology of equality" (1971:58).

104

Furthermore, "Everybody in El Nopal today has roughly the same prestige and, within the limits of tradition, the same access to the local power structure" (1971:59). While admitting that some inequalities in wealth and material possessions existed, she steadfastly maintained that El Nopal was a nonstratified community.

Preliminary research done in the same region by other researchers and myself has contradicted these findings. Based on detailed household inventories and participant observation, considerable economic inequality and a rather stratified social system were found to exist (DeWalt, Bee, and Pelto 1973:44–9).

The importance of determining whether socioeconomic inequalities exist, and their extent, cannot be overemphasized. Socioeconomic inequalities have been found to be associated with differential rates of reproduction, adequacy of health care, and adequacy of diet, as well as many other behavioral characteristics. Understanding systems of economic inequalities may be particularly significant in relation to modernization and economic development. Determining whether individuals have the resources to invest in new opportunities, for example, is crucial in predicting whether new programs are likely to be adopted. By the same token, programs that allow only certain wealthier individuals to take advantage of them might increase the inequalities already present in a community and lead to an increasingly rigid stratification system.

The purpose of this chapter, then, will be to explore the nature of economic inequalities in Puerto de las Piedras. I will then examine the relationship of economic inequalities and adoption patterns of the new adaptive strategies. Finally, I will discuss the relationships between these inequalities and other social and cultural features.

Wealth – homogeneity or heterogeneity?

One of the primary reasons for my choice of an *ejido* as the unit of study is that these individuals should be more homogeneous in wealth and other characteristics than the general population of the communities studied. Some of the other members of these communities are much poorer than the *ejidatarios*, for they have no land rights and must depend on wage labor for their living. On the other hand, a few people are wealthier than the *ejidatarios* because they engage in fairly profitable, nonagricultural economic activities (e.g., commercial ventures, marketing stone from the quarries, or working for the government).

In addition, a number of factors should have operated to maintain relative socioeconomic equivalence among the *ejidatarios*. First, Mexican land reform laws require that members of the *ejidos* should have approximately equal amounts of land.[27] Founders of the *ejido* also tried to ensure that the quality of the land held by each *ejidatario* should be more or less equal. (One of the more damaging side effects of this ideology was the fractionalization of lands. That is, the 2.38 hectares owned by each *ejidatario* are composed of at least four widely separated small plots.) Another leveling mechanism has been the frequent flooding, which in previous years wiped out major portions of the crops. Recent development programs have also tended to equalize people's economic positions because they have been largely unsuccessful. Finally, the region has periodically been subjected to a number of illnesses afflicting the livestock. Those who had managed to accumulate some wealth in animals often lost part or all of their herds in these epidemics.

In actuality, all of these would-be leveling mechanisms have not created a situation of "shared poverty" among the *ejidatarios*. Economic differences among the *ejidatarios* are easily found. They are reflected in household possessions and construction, the number of animals owned, other business investments and endeavors, the types and amounts of food regularly eaten, capital invested in agricultural equipment, and so on. In the remainder of this chapter, I will discuss some of the inequalities that I found to exist among the *ejidatarios* and will then look at the relationships of these inequalities to the other dependent and independent variables used in the study.

Informant ratings of wealth

One of the primary reasons why descriptively oriented ethnographers frequently fail to report the existence of inequalities is their reliance on informants' statements. Thus if informants articulate a "rudimentary ideology of equality" (Iwanska 1971:58), the ethnographer may record these emic statements (the informant's view) and report that there is no inequality present. However, emic statements or the reports of key informants may have only an imperfect relationship with the situation that actually exists.

In Puerto de las Piedras, I received the usual reports of "everyone here is equal" or "we are all poor." However, Silverman (1966) and Simon (1972) studied similar peasant villages and found that, when asked, their informants were easily able to assign other individuals in the community to positions in a stratification hierarchy.

After establishing rapport with a number of key informants early in my field work, I asked three *ejidatarios* (separately) to rate other people in the *ejido* in terms of wealth. All three of the key informants

Table 6.1. *Gamma correlations among the three different informant ratings of wealth*

	Pedro's ratings	Vicente's ratings
Vicente's ratings	.95	
Felipe's ratings	.79	.85

knew most, if not all, of the other *ejidatarios*. One of the informants was a wealthy individual who had recently been president of the ruling body of the *ejido*. The second was younger, of more moderate means, and a recent first *delegado* (representative of the community in the municipal government). The third informant had held many offices in the *ejido*, occasionally sold *pulque* (a fermented alcoholic beverage) from his house, and seemed fairly well respected by almost all members of the *ejido*.

The technique of informant ratings used was similar to that employed by Silverman (1966). The key informants were given a set of cards, each containing the name of one of the *ejidatarios*, and were asked to sort these into groups on the basis of socioeconomic position. Instructions were purposely vague so as to allow the men to develop their own criteria for ratings. They were also free to use as many or as few categories as they wished. Two of the men easily sorted people into five categories, while the other used only four groups. The gamma correlation coefficients among the ratings are found in Table 6.1. The correlations are fairly high and indicate substantial agreement among the men.

Although I tried to elicit some underlying basis or concept upon which the men formed their ratings, I did not encounter such terms as *rispetto* (found by Silverman among Italians) or *categoría* (found by Simon in research among Mexicans).

All three key informants' ratings were summed to yield the final "wealth ratings" score for each *ejidatario*. The distribution of scores on this variable for the sixty-two individuals in the random sample are found in Table 6.2. As we see, the individuals perceived as poorest received the lowest score of 3, while the wealthiest individual received the maximum possible score of 14. The mean score was 7.12; the median 7.25; and the standard deviation was 2.88.

Thus economic inequalities were perceived by the *ejidatarios* themselves. In addition to these informant ratings, a number of other, more objective measures of economic inequality were collected.

Table 6.2. *Distribution of scores on the wealth rating variable*

Rating	Number	Percentage
3	7	11.3
4	10	16.1
5	3	4.8
6	8	12.9
7	4	6.5
8	6	9.7
9	12	19.4
10	6	9.7
11	2	3.2
12	1	1.6
13	2	3.2
14	1	1.6
Total	62	100.0

Material style of life

One way of measuring wealth or the relative well-being of individuals or households is to compile lists of material goods possessed. Wealth is measured not in terms of disposable income (i.e., how much cash a person has on hand) but in terms of income which has already been disposed of (i.e., has been converted into goods). The amount of material goods a household has accumulated is, in general, a good index of its present style of life. The villagers themselves appear to consider ownership of these material items as desirable and significant for assessing differential living standards.

A tool for looking at differences in household possessions is a Guttman scale, constructed using the material items that are present in the community. Guttman scaling (Guttman 1944) is a technique that produces an ordinal scale. It is most useful when items are cumulative. Thus it works well with material goods where items are accumulated (i.e., where a particular item is added to existing items in the household and does not displace them). Kay (1964), Pelto (1973), and others have used Guttman scaling of material goods in examining economic differentials.

Table 6.3 contains the "material style of life" Guttman scale constructed for the *ejido* of Puerto de las Piedras. We see that an iron (electric and nonelectric) is the item most frequently possessed in the com-

Table 6.3. *Guttman scale of material style of life*

Household	Scale type	I	II	III	IV	V	VI	VII	VIII
025	1								
047	1								
003	2	X							
005	2	X							
014	2	X							
021	2	X							
024	2	X							
038	2	X							
010	2	X			X				
037	3	0	X						
001	3	X	X						
007	3	X	X						
016	3	X	X						
020	3	X	X						
026	3	X	X						
028	3	X	X						
029	3	X	X						
040	3	X	X						
041	3	X	X						
043	3	X	X						
002	4	X	0	X					
008	4	X	0	X					
045	4	0	X	X					
027	4	X	X	X					
030	4	X	X	X					
033	4	X	X	X					
039	4	X	X	X					
042	4	X	X	X					
044	4	X	X	X					
046	4	X	X	X					
051	4	X	X	X					
052	4	X	X	X					
056	4	X	X	X			X		
018	5	X	0	X	X				
019	5	X	X	0	X				
048	5	X	X	X	X				
032	5	X	X	X	X				
050	5	X	X	X	X				
049	5	X	X	X	X			X	
013	6	X	X	X	X	X			

Table 6.3. (*cont.*)

Household	Scale type	I	II	III	IV	V	VI	VII	VIII
012	6	X	X	X	X	X			X
006	6	X	0	X	0	X			
011	6	X	X	X	0	X			
015	7	X	X	X	X	X	X		
035	7	X	X	X	X	X	X		
004	7	X	X	X	0	X	X		
031	7	X	X	X	0	X	X		
036	7	X	X	X	X	0	X		
034	8	X	X	X	X	X	X	X	
009	8	X	X	X	X	0	X	X	
061	8	X	X	X	X	0	X	X	
055	9	X	X	X	X	X	X	0	X
017	9	X	0	X	X	X	0	X	X
058	9	X	X	X	X	0	X	X	X
023	9	X	X	X	X	X	X	X	X
057	9	X	X	X	X	X	X	X	X
054	9	X	X	X	X	X	X	X	X

ITEMS:
I. Iron (electric and nonelectric)
II. Radio
III. Bed
IV. Cooking facilities off the floor
V. Sewing Machine
VI. Wardrobe
VII. Stove
VIII. Television

Coefficient of reproducibility: $1 - \dfrac{22}{456} = .95$.

munity. A radio is the next most frequent item, followed by a bed, facilities for cooking off the floor, a sewing machine, a wardrobe, a stove, and the scarcest item, a television set.

The percentage of errors (coefficient of reproducibility) is one measure of a scale's reliability. In Table 6.3, there are two types of errors. The first is marked by the symbol *O*, which indicates that the household does not possess a particular item, even though we would predict that they should, given the other items owned by that household. The other type of error is denoted by the symbol *X* in an unexpected position (i.e., the household owns an item without also owning all of the other items before it). There are only twenty-two errors in the Guttman scale of material style of life, and the coefficient of reproducibility of .95 indicates that the scale is significantly reliable.[28]

The numbers that are contained in the column headed "scale type"

Table 6.4. *Cash value assigned to different animals (in pesos)*

Animal	Average value	Animal	Average value
Cattle	3,000	Sheep	300
Mules	2,500	Goats	200
Pigs	1,800	Turkeys	100
Horses	1,000	Chickens	20
Burros	400		

were assigned to each household as the summary measure of material style of life. The mean score was 4.7, and the standard deviation was 2.3.

Cash value of animals

In rural Mexico, one of the primary means of saving for emergencies, ceremonial occasions, or other times when cash is needed is through the accumulation of animals. Animals are a kind of savings institution on the hoof (Nash 1964). Individuals with a little extra cash can buy an animal, sometimes increase its value by fattening it, and maintain it until an emergency or other need arises. Chickens and turkeys in particular are maintained by most families for use on such occasions as weddings, baptisms, confirmations, or other times when a ceremonial meal is appropriate. Some individuals are engaged in raising animals for profit, clearly intending to sell them when they reach a certain size. These individuals are engaged in a commercial exploitation of animals in contrast with those individuals who are primarily using animals as a savings account. In any event, the value of animals is a very good index of financial solvency.

Assigning a cash value to animals is, of course, dependent on many factors, including the condition, age, breed, and weight of the particular animal. A young Holstein that produces a large quantity of milk each day is obviously much more valuable than an old *criollo* (common mixed breed) that produces little or no milk. Cash value also depends upon the knowledgeability, financial position, and bargaining ability of the buyers and sellers. Nonetheless, for purposes of assigning a value to all animals held by an individual, it is useful to give an approximate market value to all animals of a given species. Thus I have used more or less common estimates of the value of an average cow, pig, goat, and other animals common to the region. Table 6.4 shows the average cash values assigned to the different animals held by the *ejidatarios*.

Table 6.5. *Average costs of agricultural implements in 1973 (in pesos)*

Item	Cost	Item	Cost
Team of oxen	6,000	Harrow (*rastra de clavos*)	800
Team of mules	5,000	Plow for cultivating	350
Team of horses	2,000	Iron plow	275
Cart (*remolque*)	1,000	Plow for seeding	250

The final "cash value of animals" score was obtained by multiplying the number of each type by that animal's monetary value. Scores on this variable ranged from a low of 0 for three individuals who had no animals to a high of 142,800 *pesos* for one individual whose holdings included forty-one head of cattle. The mean score was 9,788.9; the median was 4,690; and the standard deviation was 19,123.7. That is, the approximate median cash value of animals held by the *ejidatarios* of Puerto de las Piedras is about $375.

Value of agricultural equipment

Because all of the people included in this study are *ejidatarios*, another important index of general wealth is the amount of capital invested in agricultural equipment. Those individuals who lack a *yunta* (team of animals) and the implements necessary for working the land are forced to hire other individuals to work their lands for them. Up to seventeen *yunta* days are required to perform the minimal plowing, harrowing, cultivating, and other operations for one hectare of corn. At 40 *pesos* per day, the rental cost to an individual would be at least 680 *pesos* per hectare.

Table 6.5 shows the current costs of the various important agricultural implements used in cultivation. The cost of these items also obviously depends upon the quality of construction, bargaining ability of the buyer and seller, and other factors. For example, I once talked with two men who had come by bus from a town twenty or so miles away from Temascalcingo to buy a seed plow. They reported that they had paid 275 *pesos* for the implement at the largest blacksmith shop. Only a few days earlier, an *ejidatario* from El Puerto had reported buying one of these plows for 215 *pesos* at the same shop. Table 6.5 shows the prices that this same blacksmith reported he was charging for the implements in late 1973. The prices for the teams of animals are based upon informants' estimates.

Table 6.6. *Outside income categories and number of respondents in each*

Category	Amount of income (in *pesos*)	No. of respondents
1	< 200	22
2	201–300	9
3	301–400	12
4	401–500	9
5	501–600	2
6	601–1,000	1
7	1,001–2,000	5
8	Over 2,001	2

Note: Mean = 2.9; median = 2.5; and standard deviation = 2.1.

Twenty-three of sixty-two respondents did not have a *yunta* or any of the other items needed to cultivate the land. The highest score, "value of agricultural equipment," was 7,675 *pesos*.[29] The mean score was 1,990.6, and the standard deviation was 2,207.9. The "average" *ejidatario* has agricultural equipment worth about $160.

Income from other pursuits

As a final measure of economic inequality, the income derived from nonagricultural activities was estimated for each respondent. In the course of the interviews with each respondent, I asked what other work they did in order to earn money, the approximate number of days in which they worked at that pursuit, and what their daily wage was. From this information, the approximate monthly income of the respondents could be calculated. These estimates were grouped into eight categories. The monetary income that corresponds to each category and the number of respondents in each category are found in Table 6.6. As we see, about half of the respondents have little or no income outside of their agricultural pursuits. The other half of the *ejidatarios* do have "income from other pursuits" of more than three hundred *pesos* (twenty-four dollars) per month.

Income from other pursuits is earned in many different jobs. A few *ejidatarios* work cutting the stone in the quarry on the communal lands of the *ejido*. Another *ejidatario* earns twenty *pesos* a day by gathering wood that he sells to the pottery makers in San Diego. A few *ejidatarios* have regular jobs working for fifteen to twenty *pesos* per day for other

Table 6.7. *Interrelationships of the various wealth measurements*

	Wealth ratings	Material style of life	Value of agricultural equipment	Cash value of animals	Income from other pursuits
Wealth ratings	—	.53**	.71**	.48**	.48**
Material style of life		—	.42**	.35**	.55**
Value of agricultural equipment			—	.52**	.32**
Cash value of animals					.28*
Income from other pursuits					—

Note: * indicates $p < .05$ and ** indicates $p < .01$.

agriculturalists or for people who own stores in Temascalcingo. Other
have jobs working for the Department of Hydraulic Resources. On
man is a judge in the Temascalcingo court. Finally, a large number o
individuals depend upon sporadic work as laborers in the fields of th
ejidatarios who are somewhat better off. The mean score on this vari
able was 2.9; the median was 2.5; and the standard deviation was 2.1

Interrelationships of the wealth variables

Table 6.7 shows the interrelationships among the five different mea
sures of economic well-being. The five are all highly and significantly
correlated with one another. The two lowest correlations both involve
income from other pursuits. Value of agricultural equipment and cash
value of animals both have fairly low positive correlations with this vari
able. It seems that people who earn a significant portion of their
income from other jobs are not interested in investing in either agricul
tural equipment or animals. Their income from other pursuits has prob
ably made their ties with agriculture and livestock more tenuous.

It is also interesting to note that the informants' wealth ratings were
primarily based upon agricultural equipment, for these two variables are
most highly correlated. This finding conforms with what my informant
reported in the interviews following their ratings. They all cited the
ability to work the land without having to hire teams, equipment, and

drivers as being a major factor in differentiating some individuals from others.

Although these variables measure different aspects of wealth in general, they are all indicators of the degree of economic inequality that exists within the *ejido*. The pattern of intercorrelations shows that, in general, individuals who score highly on one measure of wealth will also tend to score highly on the other measures.

Variability in wealth: descriptions of three individuals

The information presented in the preceding section indicates the wide range of variability among the *ejidatarios* with regard to several types of wealth. In the following paragraphs, I will describe several aspects of three individuals' life styles and finances. I did not systematically try to obtain family budgets from any of the households in my sample. As Oscar Lewis points out, an accurate accounting of this type could only be obtained by an investigator living with the family for a long period of time and keeping a daily record of income and expenses (1951:213). However, I was able to collect enough information from households to provide a general impression of the economic status of *ejidatarios* and their families.

Antonio and his family are very poor, and their household is among those that consistently fell at the bottom of the various measures of wealth. A closer examination of their finances will show the difficulties faced by individuals who simply do not have any resources that can be invested in alternative ways.

Although his land is of good quality, Antonio does not have as much land as most other *ejidatarios*. He lost some of his land when one of the large drainage canals was created and later lost a little more when the canal road was built. As a consequence, his land resources have been pared down to only 1.9 hectares. Antonio does not have a team of animals or any agricultural implements, and so he has to rent them to work his fields. He reported that he performed the minimal operations necessary for growing corn and that he was able to hold his costs for *yuntas* down to about 880 *pesos* in 1973 (see Table 6.8). He fertilized one field in 1972 but did not continue this practice the following year.

Although Antonio has less than the average amount of *ejido* land and is only able to give his fields poor care, he did manage to produce approximately 2,000 kilograms of corn in 1972. This amount was sufficient to feed him, his wife, two sons, and a daughter. He sold 600 kilograms to obtain cash for hiring animals and implements to plant his fields again, but he estimated that he would have to buy about 225

Table 6.8. *Major income and expenditure estimates for two families*
(in pesos)

Antonio		Juan	
Income		*Income*	
156 days of wage labor		150 days of work in stone	
@ 12 *pesos*	1,872	quarry @ 60 *pesos*	9,000
Sale of corn (400 *cuar-*		Sale of corn (1,333 *cuartil-*	
tillos @ 1.3 *pesos*)	520	*los* @ 1.2 *pesos*)	1,600
Money sent by daughter			
working in Mexico City	??		
Major expenditures		*Major expenditures*	
Rental of *yuntas* to work		Rental of *yuntas* to work	
lands (22 days @ 40		lands (35 days @ 40	
pesos per day)	880	*pesos* per day)	1,400
Corn purchases (150		Corn purchases (80 *cuartil-*	
cuartillos @ 2.0 *pesos*)	300	*los* @ 1.6 *pesos*)	128
Food (22 *pesos* per week	1,144	Food (65 *pesos* per week)	3,380
Alcohol (8 liters per week		Alcohol (14 liters per	
@ 1.2 *pesos*)	500	week @ 1.2 *pesos*)	875
		Fiesta expenses (*carguero*)	200
		Chemical fertilizer (15	
		bags @ 35 *pesos*)	525
		Tractor rental (2 days @	
		140 *pesos*)	280
		Wage laborers (40 days @ 15	
		pesos per day)	600

Note: In 1973, 1 *peso* was worth eight cents; 12.5 *pesos* were equal to one dollar.

kilograms before the next harvest. For peasant farmers living a precari-
ous economic existence, this pattern is typical. They have to sell part of
their production at low prices just after the harvest so that they can
put in the next year's crop; then they have to repurchase their staple
food at the high prices prevailing just before the harvest.

The family is able to spend very little for food, and they do not eat
very well. Apart from corn, Antonio's wife only spends about twenty-
two *pesos* ($1.75) each week for their meals (see K. DeWalt, Kelly, and
Pelto, in press, for a description of the method used in collecting this in-

formation). They eat twice a day and rarely have meat or beans, which supply important parts of protein complementing those present in corn. It is a great sacrifice for the family to buy a half liter of milk each day for their youngest son. They said that the doctor has told them they must give milk to the boy, who is slightly retarded, if he is to remain healthy.

Antonio and his family live in a poorly constructed one-room *adobe* house that has a dirt floor, a tile roof, and no windows. Their only material possessions are an iron, a radio, a kerosene lamp, a few household utensils, and some articles of clothing. They sleep on straw mats on the floor and do not have a table or any chairs. They had ten chickens, but all died in an epidemic in 1972. They no longer own any animals.

Another major expenditure by Antonio and his family – in addition to what they spend for corn, food, and working the land – is on alcohol. It is difficult to determine exactly how much a family like Antonio's spends for *pulque*. Many families buy a liter or two of this fermented beverage to drink with meals, and many men carry a liter along with them when they go to work in the fields. In addition, Antonio was classified as a fairly heavy drinker by my informants, who rated people in terms of their use of alcohol (see Chapter 9). In Table 6.8, I have conservatively estimated that this household consumes eight liters of *pulque* per week. Even this low estimate shows that this is a substantial outlay of cash, forty dollars a year.

The major portion of the household's income comes from Antonio's various odd jobs. He estimated that he can secure work an average of three days a week. Sometimes he works in the fields for other *ejidatarios;* on other occasions he works as a mason; and at times he collects the sap from *maguey* plants for people who make *pulque*. He seems to be more successful in obtaining jobs than many other people, and the reason for this success is probably because he will work for twelve *pesos* a day (less than one dollar). Most day laborers in the region were receiving fifteen *pesos* per day in 1973.

Even though he works steadily and derives some cash profit from his corn, Antonio's expenses still are larger than his income. I should also emphasize that Table 6.8 lists only *major* expenses: It does not take into account expenditures on clothing, medical care, a daughter's school expenses; basic household necessities, and so forth. As Lewis notes, income usually is less than expenditures among poor families in both Mexico and the rural United States (1951:213). The source of income that is impossible to estimate and that probably most helps to close this gap is money sent by a daughter who lives and works in Mexico City.

Although only sixteen, this girl had been working as a domestic in a house in the city for about a year and regularly sent some money home to the family. Her seventeen-year-old brother and thirteen-year-old sister had just joined her and were also seeking employment.

Although they are poor, this family is in better shape than many others. Antonio is still young (about forty) and healthy. Three of the children have just reached the age where they can be expected to contribute some support to the household before they marry and have families of their own. Their departure for Mexico City left only three children to feed and clothe. Other *ejidatarios* who are older, who are no longer able to work, who have no working children still contributing to the household's support, and who obtain smaller yields from their crops are even poorer than Antonio and his family. Those people in the rating categories 3, 4, and 5 (see Table 6.2) are as poor or poorer than Antonio. They comprise almost one-third of the *ejidatarios*.

Juan and his family fall into the middle range of wealth. Juan has a marketable skill in addition to his *ejido* land, and thus the income and the living standard of this family is much higher than that of Antonio's household.

One of Juan's sons inherited some *ejidal* land from his maternal grandmother in 1968. Because the son now lives and works in Mexico City, Juan is working this land as well as his own. He does not sow all of the land every year; but in 1973, he was cultivating 4.18 hectares. The previous year he had cultivated 3.68 hectares, from which he harvested 106 *costales* of corn. He also harvested 4 more *costales* from a small piece of private land and thus obtained a total of approximately 5,500 kilograms of corn. Of this amount, he sold about 2,000 kilograms for 1,600 *pesos*. As the harvest in 1973 drew near, Juan realized that he would have to buy some corn and purchased some from one of his *compadres*. This purchase only cost him 128 *pesos*, and so he still made a profit of over 1,450 *pesos* (about $118) from the corn.[30]

Juan did not use any fertilizer on his fields in 1972, but he did purchase fifteen bags in 1973 at a cost of 525 *pesos*. He also used insecticide on one field. The insecticide was necessary because Juan had interplanted broad beans (*habas*) with the corn in several places. In one field, the beans were being destroyed by an insect pest. He therefore applied an insecticide. Although he reported that many of his beans were stolen, he did manage to harvest about 125 kilograms for the year. These were all for home consumption.

Although he has a team and most of the implements needed to work the land, Juan finds it more profitable to hire other people to cultivate his land for him. Table 6.8 shows that Juan spent 1,400 *pesos* to hire *yuntas*, 280 *pesos* for tractors, and another 600 *pesos* for men to perform other agricultural tasks. These investments were necessary because he wanted to continue his primary occupation, working in the stone quarry, rather than spending all his time cultivating his fields.

Juan has been working in the quarry for over thirty years. He now employs two other men, and they work about 150 days a year. Juan reported that they cut enough stone to make an average of 175 *pesos* each day. He told me that his share is 60 *pesos* (see Table 6.8). Their only expense, apart from the tools of their trade, is a weekly payment of 10 *pesos* to the *ejido* of San Diego, in whose community lands the quarry is situated. In 1973, Juan was selling the stone to a wholesaler from El Puerto who owned a large truck and to the state of Mexico. The former transported the stone to Mexico City, and the latter took it to a state building project in Ixtlahuaca (a small city about sixty-five kilometers from Temascalcingo). In both cases, the rock was destined to adorn the facade of new buildings.

Juan's comparatively good cash income (although it is only about $850 a year) makes it possible for this family to live better than many others. Although four people live in the two-room house, the main living and sleeping room has stone from the quarry covering the floor. In addition, the family was planning to move from their house high on the hill in El Puerto to a site on the canal road. Their main reason for wanting to move was so that they could have electricity and running water in the house. In the way of material possessions, the family has one bed, a table and two chairs, a radio, a petroleum stove, a bicycle, and a wardrobe. They also have a horse, a donkey, nine turkeys, and three chickens.

The size of Juan's income coupled with the fact that they produce such staple foods as corn and *habas* allows the family to eat comparatively well. They spend about sixty-five *pesos* (close to five dollars) a week for food other than corn. They drink seven liters of milk each week, eat beans frequently, have meat at least once or twice a week, and occasionally eat bread instead of *tortillas*.

Two other significant expenditures of the family are for fiesta expenses and alcohol. Juan and his wife hold positions in the *cargo* system (see Chapter 8); and their expenses, including food they are required to provide, are about two hundred *pesos* per year. Juan is one of the people who my informants reported as being a heavy drinker. Because his work in the quarry provides him with a fairly substantial income, Juan is probably able to spend a good deal each week on *pulque*. Several people commented that he and his family would be able to live quite a lot better if he did not spend so much on alcohol. I have conservatively estimated his *pulque* consumption at fourteen liters per week, resulting in an annual expenditure of 875 *pesos*.

The final family that I will discuss is the wealthiest of the *ejidatarios*. Felipe is widely known as one of the richer men in the region. Although his family was poor, people report that he has had good luck in life. As a young man, he managed to scrape together some cash, which he used to buy wheat from other *ejidatarios*. He held the wheat until the price rose and then resold it at a profit. Then a clothing dealer from Mexico City contacted him and asked if he would like to sell clothes in the region's market. He loaned Felipe the money and clothing to begin the business, and Felipe is still involved in this activity.

As he acquired capital, Felipe invested in animals. He bred these animals with considerable success; and in 1973, he had forty head of cattle, twenty-seven goats, a few pigs, sheep, and burros, as well as a team of mules that he uses to work his *ejido* land. He uses the dung produced by all these animals to fertilize his fields.

Felipe has only 2.38 hectares of *ejido* land, but he also cultivates a small piece of private property. He has all of the agricultural implements needed to work the land, including a cart that he uses to haul fertilizer and *pradera*. He has not sown forage crops on any of his fields as yet; but in 1972 he produced 113 *costales* of corn, 25 *costales* of broad beans, and 3 *costales* of beans (*frijoles*).

I have not attempted to estimate the income and expenditures for this family. Felipe is involved in many different commercial activities. In addition to selling clothing in several markets, his animals, and the corn he produces, Felipe also has a corn mill and store in his house. In 1965 he spent 8,000 *pesos* ($640) for this corn mill. In 1971 he made another capital investment when he bought a record player and speaker system. He now charges a small fee from people who wish to dedicate a record to someone else. The speakers then blare out the song, which can be heard by everyone in El Jardín and most people in El Puerto. Felipe was able to install the broadcasting system because he headed the committee to bring electricity to El Jardín.

He and his family live in a four-room house with cement floors and *adobe* walls that have been covered with cement and painted inside and outside. They have a television set, radio, sewing machine, bicycle, cupboards, wardrobe, table and nine chairs, petroleum stove, and four beds (for five people). The family is also atypical in that a doctor attended the births of nine of the ten children.

Felipe's family also eats well. They spend over one hundred *pesos* (eight dollars) a week on food. This sum is considerable in view of the fact that they get milk from their cows, eggs from their chickens, and

Table 6.9. *Correlations of the adaptive strategies with various measures of wealth*

Strategies	Wealth ratings	Material style of life	Cash value of animals	Value of agric. equip.	Income from other pursuits
Forage production	.50**	.36**	.17	.41**	.16
Animal improvement	.36**	.33**	.27*	.33**	.31**
Tractor use	.06	.04	-.13	-.14	.17
Fertilizer use	-.09	-.04	.12	-.07	.08
Subsistence agriculture	-.41**	-.34**	-.21	-.17	-.35**

Note: * indicates $p < .05$ and ** indicates $p < .01$.

occasionally meat from their own animals. They eat meat at least once each day, eat more fruits and vegetables than most people, and eat three meals a day (the majority of families eat only two).

Of these three families, Antonio's household, the poorest, is living below or barely at the subsistence level. Juan's family has the economic advantage of the husband's stone-working skill, which allows him to earn approximately three times the daily minimum wage (about twenty *pesos*) established by the government for the area.[31] Felipe's family has potential capital of well over 100,000 *pesos;* and in general, they live at a level comparable to that of some merchants in Temascalcingo.

Relationships between wealth variables and the dependent variables

Because all of the different measures of economic well-being are simply various aspects of a domain that can be generally labeled as "wealth," predictions of relationships between one of these variables and the different adaptive strategies should hold for all of them.

I expected that wealth would be significantly and positively related to the adoption of forage production and animal improvement. In fact, as we see in Table 6.9, all of the relationships between the various measures of wealth and both of these adaptive strategies are positive. The highest correlations for both the forage production and the animal improvement strategies are with the wealth ratings and the material style of life scale. Forage production is also highly related to value of agricultural equipment, whereas animal improvement has a very low correlation with this variable. However, forage production has very low correlations with cash value of animals and income from other pursuits;

whereas animal improvement is significantly correlated with both. The pattern of intercorrelations suggests that individuals who have close ties to the land, as indicated by their investment in agricultural equip ment, are much more likely to adopt the forage production strategy. In dividuals who have animals and work a large portion of the time in nonagricultural pursuit, on the other hand, are more likely to adopt the animal improvement strategy.

Wealth was not expected to be correlated with tractor use or ferti izer use. Credit has been available to aid individuals who wish to us fertilizers, and the use of tractors for plowing is comparable in price t renting a team of animals. Thus both of these strategies should be rela tively independent of wealth. As we see in Table 6.9, this appears to be the case. None of the wealth variables are significantly correlated with either of these two adaptive strategies. Income from other pursuit does have a small positive correlation with tractor use, indicating tha those who work in other occupations are slightly more likely to hire tractor to do part of their agricultural work. Also, individuals who al ready have a large amount of cash invested in agricultural tools, as indi cated by the value of agricultural equipment, are slightly less likely t hire tractors. This negative correlation might have been expected to b much higher, but it appears that those who want to hire tractors t plow their land are not affected very much by the fact that they may already have the traditional equipment needed to perform the task (i.e. a team of animals and a plow).

Finally, I expected the wealth variables to be negatively correlated with a maintenance of the subsistence agriculture strategy. Those indi viduals who score highly on the wealth variables should be able to in vest in some of the new adaptive strategies that are available. Table 6. shows that the wealth variables are all negatively correlated with subsis tence agriculture, although the relationships with value of agricultura equipment and cash value of animals are not statistically significant

Thus the indicators of wealth are correlated in predictable ways with the different adaptive strategies. There are positive relationships be tween all of the wealth variables and the forage production and anima improvement strategies. It is interesting to note some differences in the magnitude of the correlations, however. Cash value of animals and in come from other pursuits both have relatively small positive correla tions with forage production. Both of these wealth variables might be taken to indicate a lack of interest in agriculture (i.e., an interest in live stock and nonagricultural jobs). Although these individuals seem to be less likely to become involved in the production of forage crops, they do have an interest in animal improvement; and this interest is indicate by the higher correlations with this adaptive strategy.

Table 6.10. *Correlations of independent variables with the wealth variables*

	Wealth ratings	Material style of life	Cash value of animals	Value of agric. equip.	Income from other pursuits
Land quantity-quality	.44**	.30*	.03	.33**	.31**
Distance from land	-.19	-.34**	-.27*	-.22*	-.05
Ejido leadership	.47**	.36**	.35**	.61**	-.02
Community leadership	.50**	.39**	.54**	.57**	.32**
Cargo participation	-.28*	-.31*	-.17	-.09	-.29*
Religiosity	-.02	-.37**	-.16	.02	-.30**
Alcohol use	-.02	.01	.06	-.05	.05
Education	.40**	.21	.19	.34**	.23*
Political knowledge	.37**	.17	.15	.38**	.20
Mass media exposure	.41**	.55**	.22	.33**	.41**
Change agent contact	.46**	.40**	.16	.64**	.34**
Cosmopolitanism	.27*	.30*	.10	.06	.52**
Age	.11	.05	.06	.11	.01
No. of people in the house	.05	.13	-.04	-.20	.09
Indian language ability	-.34*	-.40**	-.22	-.05	-.40**
Times worked elsewhere	.04	-.15	-.11	-.02	.11

Note: * indicates $p < .05$ and ** indicates $p < .01$.

None of the wealth variables were significantly related to tractor use or fertilizer use. As I indicated earlier, neither of these adaptive strategies seems to be dependent upon a large investment of capital. All of the wealth variables are negatively correlated with subsistence agriculture. This fact indicates that those who are wealthier than others are not simply content to continue cultivating corn in the traditional manner but are investing in at least one new adaptive strategy.

Correlations of wealth variables with other independent variables

All of the wealth variables, with the exception of cash value of animals, are positively correlated with the index of land quantity–quality (see Table 6.10). Those individuals who have more control over land resources also have built up wealth in other areas. As I indicated in Chapter 5, the direction of causation is difficult to ascertain. Individuals with more and better land are in a good position to increase their wealth. However, wealthier individuals also have been able to gain leadership positions in the *ejido*. In these positions, they are able to gain access to more lands (see Chapters 5 and 7). Thus the concentration of land and wealth in the hands of a few individuals has been and probably will continue to be a trend in the *ejido*.

It is also interesting that all of the wealth variables are negatively related to distance from land. These correlations suggest that wealthier individuals may have obtained rights to land plots closer to their homes by various manipulations.

Wealth and political power are interrelated, as the correlations in Table 6.10 show. The wealth variables are highly related to both *ejido* leadership and community leadership. The correlations are all positive and statistically significant, with the single exception of the relationship between income from other pursuits and *ejido* leadership. Those who derive a major portion of their income from non-*ejidal* activities are no more likely to be elected to leadership posts in the *ejido* than are those who receive little income from other pursuits. Those with a higher non-*ejidal* income, however, are more likely to be chosen for community leadership posts. Yet those individuals who score highly on value of agricultural equipment and tend to be heavily involved in agriculture are those most likely to be chosen as the *ejido* leadership. It should be obvious from the consistent pattern of correlations that, even in this fairly poor peasant village, economic wealth and political power are very interrelated.

The wealth variables are also positively correlated with those variables indicating access to information (see Chapter 10). Wealthier individuals tend to have more education, greater political knowledge, more mass media exposure, more change agent contact, and more cosmopolitanism. Although a few of the correlations are not statistically significant, some of the differences in magnitude of the relationships are understandable. For example, those who are likely to have the highest "cosmopolitanism" scores (i.e., the most trips to cities) are those who have the highest income from other pursuits. This relationship exists because the other occupations in which the *ejidatarios* are involved take them to the city. The highest correlation of change agent contact is with value of agricultural equipment, which indicates that change agents in the region seem to be concentrating their efforts on those who are really interested and are able to cultivate their land. Mass media exposure has the highest correlation with material style of life. This relationship again is predictable, especially because two of the components of the material style of life scale are mass media items – radios and television sets.

Wealth variables are generally negatively correlated with *cargo* participation, religiosity, and Indian language ability. Individuals who take on positions in the *cargo* system have some expenditures connected with their duties (see Chapter 8). As a result, they would be expected to have lower wealth scores than individuals who do not participate in the system. Because religiosity is also positively related to *cargo* participation, the generally negative correlations observed between the wealth variables and religiosity may arise because people who are religious are also participating in the *cargo* system. The negative correlations between the wealth variables and Indian language ability mean that those who are "more Indian" tend to be poorer than individuals who are "more *mestizo*." Indian language ability has statistically significant negative correlations with the wealth ratings, material style of life, and income from other pursuits; the correlations with cash value of animals and value of agricultural equipment are lower and not statistically significant. I should point out that Indian language ability is also positively correlated with *cargo* participation and religiosity. Thus the exact causal relationships among all of these variables are difficult to determine. People with high Indian language ability scores may be poorer because they are not able to function effectively in a region dominated by *mestizos*, or they may be poorer because they participate in the *cargo* system and have to spend some cash while in office. However, the negative relationships of the wealth variables with *cargo* participation may arise because those who participate in *cargos* tend to be Indians (who tend to be poorer). The fact that some expenditures are required in *cargo* positions may have little to do with the relationship. I will have more to say about this problem in Chapter 8.

Summary

A number of different measures of wealth were employed in this chapter. These were all found to be positively correlated with one another. These measures clearly show that the *ejido* of Puerto de las Piedras is not an egalitarian community but rather is marked by considerable inequality in a number of different areas.

These economic inequalities were found to correlate in predictable ways with the different adaptive strategies. In general, all of the wealth variables were positively related to the adoption of the forage production and animal improvement strategies. All were found to be negatively correlated with subsistence agriculture, and no relationship was found with either tractor use or fertilizer use.

The wealth variables were also strongly related to a number of other independent variables. I found that wealthier individuals have accumulated more and better land; and in addition, many have been able to acquire lands that are closer to their homes. I suggested that one of the primary ways in which this land was accumulated was through parlaying wealth into political power. In fact, the wealth variables were positively associated with both *ejido* leadership and community leadership. Once in positions of political power (especially in the *ejido*), these individuals have probably been able to engage in manipulations to acquire land, thus increasing their wealth. The wealth variables were also positively associated with the information access variables but were negatively associated with *cargo* participation, Indian language ability and religiosity.

7

Ejido and community leadership

Although every community has its leaders, the quality of that leadership is often an important determinant of the well-being of the people. Dynamic leadership can bring about dramatic social changes. Sometimes these are revolutionary, such as the changes advocated by Primo Tapia in a Michoacán village (Friedrich 1970); at other times they are more modest in scope, such as those carried out by Don Eus in Chan Kom (Redfield 1950). Poor leadership can range from simple ineptitude to the excesses perpetrated by those who advance themselves at the expense of others.

Two types of leadership have been emphasized in the literature about Mesoamerican communities. The first involves what has been called the civil-religious hierarchy or the *cargo* system (Cancian 1965; DeWalt 1975). Leaders in these communities are commonly village elders who have passed through a system of hierarchically ranked civil and religious offices (*cargos*). These individuals are leaders in both the secular and the religious spheres (see also Chapter 8). The elders settle disputes, set social policy in the community, determine who will fill other less important offices, and are responsible for the spiritual well-being of the community (see Wagley 1949).

Considerable change has taken place in peasant communities in Mesoamerica, as these once isolated hamlets become more articulated with the state and national scene (Adams 1957; DeWalt 1975). In some communities, rapid change came almost overnight when a demand was created for someone who spoke Spanish. The key role in handling community affairs, especially with extracommunity groups and individuals, sometimes shifted from the village elders to schoolchildren. The children spoke Spanish and could deal with government agents and other Spanish speakers. Sometimes the post of secretary was created and filled by a *Ladino* appointed by the state or federal government (Gillin 1951) simply to facilitate communication between municipality and state. Another blow to traditional authority was dealt as a result of the land redistributions following the Revolution. The *ejidos* that were formed required leaders who were able to deal with the state and national agencies concerned with the implementation of land reform. In

127

many cases, the *ejido* leaders became more important than the traditional village leaders.

The second type of leadership sometimes results from the changes
just discussed, although historically it has been concomitant with the
civil–religious hierarchy rather than succeeding it. This type of leadership is often called *caciquismo*. In the years immediately following the
Spanish conquest, native chieftains (*caciques*) were often allowed to retain many of their former powers as long as they acted as intermediaries between the Spanish and the indigenous peoples. Powerful men in
rural Mexico who maintain control of communities through the use of
force or fear are still called *caciques*. One of the primary reasons why
these men continue to be an important force in modern Mexico (in contrast with the village elders of the civil–religious hierarchy, whose power
is diminishing) is that they function as "power brokers" (Wolf 1956).
That is, these individuals mediate between the local level and the larger
society. Helms (1975:276) states that a *cacique* "is an influential person who can 'get things done' both inside and outside the community
in a manner that is often personalistic, arbitrary, and technically illegal
– but effective."

Both the *cargo* system and *caciquismo* have played at least some historical role in leadership in the Temascalcingo region. The *cargo* system,
however, now has very little to do with civil government and will be
discussed in Chapter 8. In this chapter, I will be concerned with describing the patterns of nonreligious leadership in Puerto de las Piedras – the
roles of the leaders, the kinds of influence and power they have, and
their effectiveness in achieving goals. I will also discuss some of the factional conflicts that have divided the people; and ultimately, I will be
interested in determining the role of leadership in the region's modernization. Reference to Table 7.1 will help the reader to keep in perspective the various officials discussed in this chapter.

Community leadership

As I have previously noted, the *ejido* of Puerto de las Piedras is composed primarily of individuals from three villages – El Puerto, Las Piedras, and El Jardín. Although these separate communities have a common involvement in the *ejido*, they are autonomous with regard to rep-
resentation in the government of the municipality. Each of the three
has three *delegados* who act as spokesmen for the interests of their village in the *municipio* government. The three *delegados* serve three-year
terms and are ranked hierarchically. The *primer delegado* is almost al-

Table 7.1. *Outline of formal leadership statuses and roles in the municipio of Temascalcingo*[a]

Officials	Method of selection	Duties, responsibilities, powers
Village level:		
Delegados	Election; appointment by outgoing official, municipal president, or *ejido* president	Mediate between village and *municipio*, state, and federal officials; administer community work projects
Committee officers (water, school, electricity, etc.)	Election; volunteering	Collect fees for projects; organize work details; mediate between village and various officials
Cargueros	Appointment; "village consensus"; volunteering	Care of the church and the saints
Ejido:		
President (*comisariado ejidal*)	Election (3-year term)	Representing *ejido* to outside officials and agencies, resolve small disputes; redistribute *ejidal* land
President (*comité de vigilancia*)	Losing candidate in election for *C. E.*	Watchdog over activities of the *comisariado ejidal*
Other *ejido* officers (secretary, treasurer, *suplentes*, etc.)	Election	Miscellaneous functions indicated by title
Municipio:		
Presidente municipal	Municipal elections	Administer *municipio*; represent *municipio* to outside officials and agencies; solve disputes
Primer regidor	Municipal elections	Watchdog over activities of president; solve disputes
Other officials (*síndico, regidores*, etc.)	Election or appointment	Miscellaneous functions indicated by title

[a]Based on DeWalt, Bee, and Pelto (1973:97–8).

ways the main "broker" in the community's relations with the *munici-pio* officials.

These representatives are supposedly elected at a village meeting (DeWalt, Bee, and Pelto 1973:97). However, I also received two other versions of the selection process. The man who had served as the *primer delegado* in El Puerto prior to 1972 reported that the new *primer delegado* was chosen by him in consultation with the municipal president. The other two *delegados* were then chosen by the new *primer delegado*. Another informant provided a second version. He reported that the president of the *ejido*, who is a man from Las Piedras, chose the *delegados* in both Las Piedras and El Puerto. When a number of people from El Puerto complained, the municipal president replaced them. These two stories are not incompatible with one another; and it may be that the *delegados* from Las Piedras were chosen by the *ejido* president, while those from El Puerto were eventually chosen by the older *primer delegado* in consultation with the municipal president. It should be clear, however, that no election took place in a village meeting.

The primary function of the *delegados* is to represent the community in meetings with the municipal officials. They try to articulate the needs of the community at this time. If some special need arises, they take their request to the officials in Temascalcingo. Because of the very limited resources in the municipal budget, any requests that have to do with acquiring material aid are usually denied or are referred to the district representative in the state government or the representative in the national legislature. It is at this level that village projects can sometimes find support. Almost all resources in Mexico are held and distributed by the national government. The district representatives are often able to tap some of these resources for the local communities.

As an illustration of this process, in 1973, the villagers in Las Piedras decided to try to fix up an old road that passes through the community. The road was in a terrible state of neglect, and erosion had created large gullies that had to be bridged. The people in Las Piedras decided to begin the repairs through the use of the *faena,* which required each male member of the community to work for at least a few hours every Sunday (see Photograph 4). However, the villagers still needed concrete and other materials in order to build the bridges. The *delegados* first went to the *presidente municipal,* where they were told that there was no money for such projects. In company with the president of the *ejido,* they next went directly to the governor's office in Toluca, where they hoped to meet with the governor or his representative. There they received some encouragement and were told that the state government

4. Some *ejidatarios* from Las Piedras performing work on the road into their village as part of their communal labor obligations. The church in the background is in the town of Temascalcingo.

either would try to get the concrete for them or would attempt to secure it through the district representative to the national legislature.

This oversimplified account of the journeys of the *delegados* does not give the flavor of their actual trials and tribulations. It does not reflect the number of times they were not able to see the *presidente municipal* or the times they were told that the matter was under advisement and that they would be contacted. I should also mention that neither the *primer delegado* nor the president of the *ejido* can read or write. The picture of poor, illiterate peasants attempting to carry out such a project, given the handicaps and frustrations they had to overcome, should quickly dispel the notion that these particular peasants are conservative and passive. Whether they will ever obtain the concrete for the bridges they hoped to build probably depends upon whether they are fortunate enough to strike the right chord with the right official. One thing was certain; their hopes for completing the bridges and the road in time to facilitate transporting the harvest to their houses were not going to be realized in 1973.

The post of *delegado* does not confer any advantage to the holder as far as I was able to determine. Although there may be prestige which

accrues to the *delegados,* there is also considerable potential for alien-
ating oneself from other members of the community. *Delegados,* for
example, are in charge of administering the *faenas,* the periods of labor
required of each individual for community improvements. In the road
work just mentioned, the *delegados* frequently found only ten or
twelve men working on any given Sunday, considerably fewer than the
number of household heads in the village. The *delegados* kept a list of
those who performed their labor and turned over to the *presidencia* the
names of individuals who were frequent absentees. These men would be
brought before the municipal president, reprimanded, and fined. The
delegados often got into arguments with individuals whom they tried to
persuade to perform the *faena.* Although community opinion was on
the side of the *delegados,* there is little doubt that the *delegados'* efforts
usually went unrewarded monetarily and in prestige.

Whereas the *delegados* seem to be responsible for the everyday affairs of the community and for communicating the people's desires to
the appropriate authorities, special committees and leaders often are
chosen to head specific projects. The construction of a one-room school
in El Puerto a number of years ago and the recent addition of two more
classroom buildings (which raised the number of grades taught to six)
have made the school committee a permanent and important group in
the community. Because most children from Las Piedras find it more
convenient to attend the grammar school in Temascalcingo, the school
children and parents most concerned with the school in El Puerto are
those from El Puerto and El Jardín.

For many years the leader of the school committee was Don Juan.
Each year he was elected president of this group by the villagers. It is
difficult to assess this man's impact. It is true that during his tenure the
school in El Puerto grew from a one-room schoolhouse to three buildings and *organización completa* (having all six primary grades). However, I heard complaints from a number of individuals that his tenure
was marked by fraud. There were reports that he and his sons always
harvested the wheat or corn from the *ejido* plot allocated to the school
at the same time that they harvested their own fields. Don Juan supposedly bought a few buckets of paint to paint the school building and
then told everyone that the proceeds from the school's *ejido* plot had
all been spent. One of this man's sons has now become a teacher and
head of the school, and there are many complaints about the two men.
Primarily as a result of this criticism, Don Juan was not reelected as
president of the school committee in 1973; but he has remained a
powerful force in school affairs.

Construction and improvement of schools is a federal government priority. The two new school buildings in El Puerto are a recent outgrowth of this government commitment. In 1973, materials were made available to the community of El Puerto for constructing a chain link fence around the school yard. Sunday *faena* was used to put up this fence under the watchful eye of one of the local masons, who was paid for his work on the project.

Other committees formed in the recent past include one to bring electricity to El Jardín. Don Felipe (described in Chapter 6) collected the required sum from each family and was successful in electrifying the homes in the community. A similar project in El Puerto around 1963 quickly lost its impetus when Don Jerónimo, who headed up the committee, died unexpectedly. Since then no one has been successful in mobilizing support for the project. Part of the problem is that there is some opposition from certain individuals who do not feel the need for electricity and do not feel they are able to spare the substantial amount of money required for its installation. Another problem is that all of the houses along the road into Temascalcingo, where many of the most influential members of the community live, already have electricity. Thus those individuals who might have the power and prestige needed to carry out such a project have no vested interest in doing so because their needs have already been met. There has not been any attempt to acquire electricity in Las Piedras.

Leadership in the ejido

The structure of offices in *ejidos* has been determined by the *Código Agrario de los Estados Unidos Mexicanos,* the Agrarian Code. There are six *ejidal* officers – a president, a secretary, a treasurer, and an alternate for each of these officials. The alternate replaces an official if he is removed from office, dies, or is incapable of continuing to perform his duties. In addition, a vigilance council is also composed of six members – a president, a secretary, a spokesman (*vocal*), and alternates for each. Officers are changed every three years during an assembly of all the *ejidatarios.* Two slates of candidates are proposed and voted upon. The winning slate becomes the ruling body (*comisariato*) of the *ejido;* losers form the vigilance council.

In general, the commissariat performs all of the duties necessary for running the *ejido.* It (especially its president) is the official voice of the *ejido* in dealings with government officials and other outsiders. The vigilance council remains largely in the background, although it is charged with a watchdog function over the activities of the commissariat. In theory, the opposition of the two groups is supposed to insure honesty in the administration of the *ejido*.

The president (or *comisariado ejidal,* as he is often called) is probably the most powerful formal leader at the village level. He is in charge of the most important natural resources of the community. These include not only the agricultural lands but also the communal lands, which provide firewood, grazing, and other resources (e.g., the quarry) for *ejidatarios* and other citizens of the community.

The *comisariado ejidal (C.E.)* is a powerful person by virtue of his office. He can begin the procedures for dispossessing an *ejidatario* of lands if she/he is renting the land or has given up cultivating it. He also can redistribute these lands to persons whom he considers worthy. Although the whole body of *ejidatarios* is supposed to vote on whether to accept the new person, in recent years in the Temascalcingo region the *comisariados* have been able to redistribute lands without such approval (see Romanucci-Ross 1973:175, who reports the same trend in another area of Mexico). This fact reflects what seems to be a very high concentration of power in the hands of the *ejido* president. Even development agents reported that they would not begin a planned program among some interested *ejidatarios* because the *comisariado ejidal* of that particular *ejido* was opposed to the scheme. Negotiations with development agents, banks, and other parties outside the *ejido* always are carried out by the *C.E.* in the name of all the *ejidatarios.*

Within the *ejido,* the *comisariado* is in charge of settling disputes that arise among *ejidatarios.* Some of these go beyond the *C.E.* and are resolved in the courts of Temascalcingo. The *C.E.* is also charged with the responsibility of saying when the harvest should begin. Because people need to pass through the fields of other *ejidatarios* in order to harvest their own crops, chaos could result if everyone began the harvest at different times. In practice, some individuals have ignored these dictates. The president of the *ejido* also is in charge of organizing the communal labor projects. The most important of these is the annual removal of the silt that accumulates in the irrigation canals.

Thus the *comisariado ejidal* has a great many responsibilities. A number of men who had previously held the office agreed that there were constant demands on their time – disputes to solve, projects to organize, officials to meet. Along with the responsibilities, however, are some potential benefits. During the course of my fieldwork, I received a number of reports about past presidents of the *ejido* who had redistributed lands to close relatives or to themselves. In fact, although there is now a serious shortage of land in relation to the population of the community as a whole, most sons and daughters of past presidents of the *ejido* do have land rights as *ejidatarios*. The practice is not so galling to other *ejidatarios* when these sons and daughters actually cultivate the land. However, various informants complained that many of these sons and daughters are not even living in the Temascalcingo region. The fathers of these individuals cultivate the land. As I reported in Chapter 5, there is a significant relationship between being a former or present leader and the amount and quality of land controlled.

Duties in the other offices of the *ejidal* hierarchy are not nearly as demanding. The function of the secretary, for example, appeared to have little to do with taking minutes at the *ejidal* meetings. This never occurred. Instead, the duties of the secretary primarily seem to involve consulting with the president and helping to disseminate information to the other *ejidatarios*.

The treasurer does collect money, primarily to pay the taxes on the *ejidal* lands. These taxes were about twenty-eight *pesos* per *ejidatario* during 1973. The treasurer collects the money and then turns it over to the appropriate authorities in Temascalcingo. Otherwise, the treasurer performs the same tasks as the secretary – disseminating information, supporting the *comisariado ejidal*, and proffering advice.

The other officials in the *ejido* are relatively powerless. The alternates (*suplentes*) only become important if they are called upon to replace the president, secretary, or treasurer. Most important, of course, is the alternate to the president, for there have been past occasions when the *suplente* has been called upon to replace the *comisariado ejidal*.

Factionalism in the ejido

From informants' reports it seems that during the past few years there has been considerable conflict within the *ejido*. Some of the conflict apparently stems from the tendency of the officers to usurp more and more power, especially in redistributing lands that have been taken away from *ejidatarios*. Some *ejidatarios* also feel bitter about a development project that took place in 1970 (see Chapter 2). The president of the *ejido* joined with the agricultural engineer in charge of the project to keep *ejidatarios* off of their own lands. Workers were brought in from another community, and the costs were passed on to the *ejidatarios*. Many people believed that the *C.E.* and the development agent were in collusion and stole some of the money paid by the *ejidatarios*. They perceived this as a continuation of the illicit practices in the *ejidal* administration over the past decade or more.

The Agrarian Code forbids reelection to office. Nonetheless, according to a number of my informants, the men who have occupied the post as president during the past four or five terms have all been closely allied with two brothers, Juan and Vicente. These two brothers have also been president of the *ejido* during this period. Some *ejidatarios* even applied the label of *caciques* to the two brothers.

In the election of officers held in late 1972, a maverick group of *ejidatarios* managed to break this power group. The leader of this faction, Eduardo, had been trying to win the post of president for at least twelve years. During the last three terms, he had lost the election and was therefore the president of the vigilance council.

People who are allied with the two brothers ridicule the leader of the new group now in power. They say that he is very stupid, and as evidence they cite his inability to read or write. Some informants say that he is against progress and over the years has combated the potentially beneficial programs of the two brothers. He has been accused of stealing *ejidal* funds and has been jailed for fighting with another *ejidatario*.

According to Eduardo, the fight was provoked as a means for trying to dislodge him from power. He says that those allied with the brothers are afraid of him because he is working for all the *ejidatarios*. One of his primary goals is to get the state or national Department of Agrarian Affairs to undertake an investigation of the *ejido* and to establish the correct amounts of land and the rightful owners of land. His aim is to purify the *ejido* by having land taken away from those who are not really cultivating land or who actually have more land than they are entitled to hold (true of both Juan and Vicente). According to Eduardo, every time he sends a request for this investigation to the state Department of Agrarian Affairs, it is subverted by a son of one of the brothers. The son works in the Department of Agrarian Affairs and also holds a political office in the state government. He is thus in a position to exercise his influence for his father's benefit.

The weight of the evidence in the dispute is certainly against the faction led by the brothers. They are the ones who have redistributed large amounts of land to their close relatives and friends. Even *ejidatarios* allied with this faction admit that this has happened. Nonetheless, it also seems to be true that the brothers have been actively engaged in seeking out and encouraging programs that could lead to the development of the *ejido*. Although Juan and Vicente have an essentially negative view of the majority of *ejidatarios* (i.e., they say they are lazy, drunkards, and not very intelligent), they realize that they need the lands and the participation of these men and women in order to be successful in any venture leading toward economic development. Eduardo has thus far remained stubbornly resistant to these development programs. In the main, his objections seem to be that these programs are always controlled by, and benefit, the brothers. There is certainly considerable substance to support this view, too. During 1972 and 1973, however, the political influence held by the previously mentioned son has brought some positive benefits to the community and the region in the form of a housing improvement program.

In summary, then, there is considerable support for the view held by Eduardo and his faction that the brothers are simply modern *caciques* who want to use others to advance their own interests. At the same time, *caciques* can help to advance the development of the larger community in the pursuit of their own interests. Because of their contacts and influence outside the community, these individuals can have an impact on decisions that will affect and potentially benefit the village in which they live.

In part, the conflict between the brothers and Eduardo can be subsumed under the pattern noted by Wolf:

> Confronted by these contrasts between the mobile and the traditional, the nation-oriented and the community-oriented, village life is riven by contradictions and conflicts, conflicts not only between class groups but also between individuals, families, or entire neighborhoods. Such a community will inevitably differentiate into a number of unstable groups with different orientations and interests. (1974:76)

In contrast with traditional Mesoamerican communities in which power and prestige were vested in the *principales* (village elders), Puerto de las Piedras is an *ejido* that is divided into factions. The individuals associated with the two factions are constantly shifting. The shifts take place as individuals perceive potential benefits from supporting one group or the other. Although I have just described two factions, a large number of individuals are definitely not allied strongly with either faction. In the main, these individuals are very dissatisfied with the leadership patterns in the community and perceive both factions as equally evil.

When I asked which individuals in the community were honorable and respected and were leaders, only a minuscule proportion of my informants volunteered any names. When I asked about powerful individuals, a few respondents replied along these lines: "Oh, you mean *caciques*. Here we still have a few like _____ ." Other individuals, when asked about leaders, replied by naming an office, most frequently the *comisariado ejidal*.

In order to determine the amount of support for each faction in the *ejido*, I asked a leader of each to tell me which *ejidatarios* from my ran-

Table 7.2. *Number of supporters for each faction in the ejido*

	Support the brothers	Support Eduardo	Support not clear
Claimed by brothers' leader	36	25	1
Claimed by Eduardo's leader	22	39	1
No. agreed on by both	21	23	18

dom sample were allied with each faction. Listed in Table 7.2 are the claims made by leaders of the two factions. Leaders from both sides claimed that the majority of *ejidatarios* were on their side. The leader from the brothers' side claimed that thirty-six individuals were allied with them, while the leader from Eduardo's group claimed thirty-nine supporters. The bottom line of Table 7.2 is my tabulation of the number of individuals agreed upon by both men. Thus both men agreed that twenty-one *ejidatarios* were clearly allied with the brothers and twenty-three were allied with Eduardo. We see that these totals are very close to the number that the two leaders viewed as definitely falling in the other faction. The brothers' leader saw twenty-five supporters of Eduardo; the leader from Eduardo's side counted twenty-two people as being in the brothers' faction. The final column on the bottom line of Table 7.2 indicates that there are eighteen individuals about whom the two leaders disagreed (or both indicated were "nonaligned"). In counting their supporters, both men clearly tried to claim these eighteen individuals.

Thus two-thirds of the *ejidatarios* seem pretty clearly aligned with one group or the other, but the sympathies of the other third appear to be in doubt. The balance of power in the *ejido* depends upon which way the sentiments of these individuals sway. Many of these uncommitted individuals expressed a dislike for the leaders of both factions and saw them as equally bad. Thus far, however, there does not appear to be a third group forming in the *ejido*. These individuals who are not aligned with the two factions are politically isolated from one another and have no common ground among them.

Factional affiliation and choosing adaptive strategies

It is relevant at this point to explore whether affiliation with the factions is associated with higher participation in any of the adaptive strategies. The new opportunities in the region have become the focal point

Table 7.3. *Mean adaptive strategy scores for different factions*

	Eduardo's supporters	Brothers' supporters	Neutral
Forage production	.064	−.187	.137
Animal improvement	.077	.016	−.117
Tractor use	−.334[a]	.252[a]	.133
Fertilizer use	.178	−.183	−.014
Subsistence agriculture	.015	.102	−.139

[a]The difference between these two means is statistically significant ($t = 2.44$; $p < .01$).

of debate and political activity, as I have shown (see Bailey 1973 for some similar cases). Is it true, as members of the brothers' faction report, that Eduardo and his followers are traditionally oriented and are against progress?

Table 7.3 shows that there is little support for this view. There are no significant differences in the adaptive strategies being adopted by members of the two factions, except that the brothers' allies are more likely to use tractors in the sowing of their fields. I do not have any explanation for this finding; none of the people in either faction ever claimed that they used tractors more or less often than people in the other group. Table 7.3 does show that Eduardo's supporters are more likely to use fertilizer than the brothers' supporters, although this difference is not statistically significant. Those people who are not allied with either faction do not have significantly higher or lower scores on any of the adaptive strategies.

Thus factionalism within the *ejido* is a serious matter, but it does not appear that the battle lines are drawn between traditionalists and modernizing individuals. The decision about whether to adopt an adaptive strategy does not depend upon a person's factional affiliation. Although the brothers have tried to paint a picture of Eduardo and his followers as conservative, backward peasants, the evidence does not support this view. Eduardo himself used a tractor to plow one of his fields in 1973; was using fertilizer; had planted alfalfa; owned a cart; had vaccinated his horses, mules, and pigs; and talked about the possibility of experimenting by planting lettuce or onions on one of his fields. He and his supporters are just as interested in economic development as Juan and Vicente; they are just unwilling to commit themselves to projects that will again be controlled by the brothers.

Measuring leadership

Juan, Vicente, and Eduardo, although they are the principals in the factional dispute, have in common the characteristic of modernizing their own productive activities. All three have chosen to adopt several of the adaptive strategies. In this section, I will investigate whether there is a relationship between being a leader and being more willing and/or able to invest in the new opportunities.

In his study of modernization among Colombian peasants, Everett Rogers included leadership among the variables he measured. He was interested in measuring "opinion leadership," "the ability to influence others' opinions consistently in a desired way" (1969:23). Thus he attempted to get at villagers' perceptions of others as leaders.

In pretests of the interview schedule used in my study, a number of questions were included to obtain a sociometric measure similar to that used by Rogers. Respondents were asked to which person in the community they would go for advice on a variety of topics. Almost everyone indicated that they did not need advice on agricultural and livestock matters; and in reply to a question about the person they would consult if a child were ill, most indicated that the child would be taken to a doctor in Temascalcingo. Thus I quickly became convinced that the sociometric measure was not tapping the domain of opinion leadership.

I decided that a measure of individuals' filling of offices in formalized leadership positions would be a reasonable substitute in the attempt to operationalize leadership. By "formalized leadership positions" I mean those offices in which an individual serves as a duly elected or selected representative or authority of the community.

Although this procedure might not identify certain individual leaders whose influence is limited to more informal settings and roles, I feel that this problem is not significant. First, the number of leadership positions in these Mexican villages is large in proportion to the total population. Second, as I became better acquainted with the community, it became increasingly clear that individuals were leaders because the offices they held gave them the authority to be leaders. That is, the people who filled the offices of *delegado* or *comisariado ejidal* had certain duties and functions as leaders that they were expected to perform. Much as with the officers in the civil–religious hierarchy in other communities, in Puerto de las Piedras authority is conferred largely by title and position rather than by the individual's personal qualities. Granted, a few powerful men exercise power irrespective of whether or not they hold office. I have already discussed such individuals. But these individuals also score very high on the "formal leadership" scales because they have held and, in some cases, now hold offices in the community, the *municipio,* and the *ejido.*

There are two different spheres in which leadership is exercised in Puerto de las Piedras, the *ejido* and the *municipio.* Leadership scales were created for both of these. In the course of interviews, respondents were asked what offices they had ever held in the *ejido* and the *municipio.*

In order to take the importance of the leadership roles into account, offices were ranked; and more value was given to those of high rank. In the scale of "*ejido* leadership," for example, service as *comisariado ejidal* was worth four points; as *vigilante* or *suplente* to the *C.E.,* three points; as treasurer or secretary, two points; and as an alternate on the vigilance council or other minor offices, one point. Any individual who served more than one three-year term in any position received points for every period served. Scores on this measure of *ejido* leadership ranged from zero to eleven. Thirty-six individuals of the fifty-three interviewed had never served in a leadership position in the *ejido.* None of the women had ever served in an office.

Leadership in community government was scored similarly. Serving as first *delegado* was scored four points, second as three points, and third as two points. Service in other minor positions was scored as one point. Because two men have served as judge (*juez menor*) and police chief for the *municipio* as a whole, a score of five points was assigned for service as a municipal official. These offices are much more important than *delegado* and indicate power which extends beyond the village. Again, multiple three-year terms were given points for each period of tenure. "Community leadership" scores ranged from zero to twenty. Twenty-seven men had never served as *delegado* or in any other community leadership position.

More individuals have had an opportunity to participate as municipal officers than as *ejidal* officers. This pattern results from the marked tendency I have mentioned toward the rotation of offices among a small group of individuals in the *ejido.* A number of people have served almost continuously in various offices over the years. However, over half of the males have served in at least one office in either the *ejido* or the community.

The correlation between *ejido* leadership and community leadership is .56 ($p < .001$). Although the correlation is far from perfect, it indicates that there is a considerable concentration of political power in the community. Those people who have served in leadership positions in the *municipio* also tend to have served as leaders in the *ejido.*

142 *Modernization in a Mexican ejido*

Table 7.4. *Correlations of the adaptive strategies with ejido and community leadership*

Strategies	*Ejido* leadership	Community leadership
Forage production	.35**	.34**
Animal production	.28*	.18
Tractor use	-.03	-.29**
Fertilizer use	-.08	-.08
Subsistence agriculture	-.26*	-.08

Note: * indicates $p < .05$ and ** indicates $p < .01$.

Leadership and the dependent variables

I predicted that the *ejido* and community leadership variables would be positively associated with the adoption of forage production and animal improvement, the two most profitable new adaptive strategies. No prediction was made concerning the other two new adaptive strategies, fertilizer use and tractor use. Finally, I felt that both types of leadership would be negatively correlated with subsistence agriculture.

We see in Table 7.4 that there is a positive correlation between the two types of leadership and both the forage production and the animal improvement strategies. Forage production is most highly associated with *ejido* leadership and community leadership; the correlations between leadership and the animal improvement strategy are somewhat lower. These findings indicate that the leaders in the political sphere are also taking the lead in adopting new adaptive strategies that are potentially very profitable.

There are negative correlations between *ejido* and community leadership and the other two new adaptive strategies. All but one of the correlations are very small, however. The negative correlation between community leadership and tractor use was not expected and is difficult to explain.

The expected negative correlation between the two types of leadership and subsistence agriculture is confirmed. However, I expected that the magnitude of these correlations would be greater. *Ejido* leadership and subsistence agriculture are significantly correlated, but the correlation between community leadership and subsistence agriculture is very small and not significant. The fact that the expected high negative correlations do not appear is something that I will seek to explain in Chapter 12.

Table 7.5. *Correlations of other independent variables with ejido and community leadership*

	Ejido leadership	Community leadership
Land quality–quantity	.35**	.21
Distance	-.06	-.06
Wealth ratings	.47**	.50**
Material style of life	.36**	.38**
Value of agricultural equipment	.61**	.57**
Cash value of animals	.35**	.54**
Income from other pursuits	-.02	.32**
Religiosity	.05	-.09
Cargo participation	.00	-.12
Education	.16	.17
Political knowledge	.33**	.23*
Mass media exposure	.18	.13
Change agent contact	.70**	.44**
Cosmopolitanism	.09	.10
Use of alcohol	.02	.01
Age	.28*	.44**
No. of people in house	-.02	-.02
Times worked elsewhere	-.23*	-.12
Indian language ability	-.05	-.24*

Note: * indicates $p < .05$ and ** indicates $p < .01$.

Leadership and the other independent variables

As I reported in Chapter 6, both *ejido* leadership and community leadership have consistently positive correlations with the various measures of wealth (see Table 7.5). In Puerto de las Piedras, wealth and political power tend to go hand in hand. This pattern is true even though more than half of the *ejidatarios* have served in some office in the *ejido* and/or the community. Those who are wealthier are filling the most important political positions, while those who are poorer are only able to gain access to minor offices.

Two correlations involving the leadership and wealth variables deserve reemphasis. Income from agricultural pursuits is positively and significantly correlated with community leadership, but it is not related to *ejido* leadership. This fact indicates that wealthier individuals who derive their income from nonagricultural activities are either not interested in *ejido* leadership positions or are not chosen as leaders as frequently as individuals who have more of a commitment to the land (see also Chapter 6).

The Guttman scale of political knowledge is also positively correlated with *ejido* leadership and community leadership. This relationship indicates that people who serve in leadership positions either have or acquire more political knowledge than others who do not hold office.

The highest correlation in Table 7.5 is between *ejido* leadership and change agent contact. This relationship indicates the extent to which development agents in the region have tried to work through the existing leaders, especially those from the *ejido*. The relationship between community leadership and change agent contact is not as high and probably is as high as it is mainly because individuals who fill leadership roles in the *ejido* tend to fill community leadership positions as well.

Land quantity–quality is also positively related to the two types of leadership. The highest correlation again is with *ejido* leadership. In part, this relationship reflects one of the potential benefits of occupying *ejidal* leadership positions. As I mentioned previously, officials, especially the *comisariado ejidal*, often have abandoned lands to redistribute. Frequently, these lands have been placed in the name of a close relative of the *comisariado* or have been added to his holdings. Thus one of the benefits of *ejido* leadership has been a chance to acquire more and/or better lands.

It is interesting to note in Table 7.5 that age is apparently a more important prerequisite for leadership than is education. While age is correlated highly with both *ejido* leadership and community leadership, the correlations of education with these variables are smaller and not statistically 'significant. Schooling has only recently become more widely available to the *ejidatarios* of Puerto de las Piedras. The young men with more education have yet to take over leadership positions in the *ejido* or the community. This point is illustrated by the case of the *comisariado ejidal* and the first *delegado* of Las Piedras in 1973. Neither of these men had more than a year or so of schooling. Nonetheless they were able to acquire these responsible leadership posts.

Finally, it should be noted that there is very little correlation between Indian language ability and *ejido* leadership. We might conclude that those identified as "more Indian" have had equal access to leadership positions. Indians dominated *ejido* leadership during the early years; but recently, there has been increasing exclusion of Indians from *ejidal* offices. None of the top *ejido* officials in 1973 had a very high score on the Indian language ability variable, for example. There is fairly high negative correlation between this variable and community leadership. It seems that a shift toward non-Indians in community lead

rship positions began taking place before a similar shift in *ejido* leadership posts. This change probably resulted because *delegados* had to deal
with the *mestizo* officials of Temascalcingo. *Ejido* leaders at present
also have considerable contact with *mestizos*, but these dealings may
have been more infrequent in the past.

To conclude the discussion of leadership, I should note the insignifi-
cant correlations between *ejido* and community leadership and *cargo*
participation. As I indicated in the introduction to this chapter, leadership in civil government has traditionally been linked with religious
leadership in most rural Mexican communities. Table 7.5 shows that
there is no correlation between *ejido* leadership and *cargo* participation.
There is a small negative relationship between community leadership
and *cargo* participation. Clearly, the linked civil and religious govern-
mental system is not now and has not recently operated in Puerto de las
Piedras. The separation between the two systems is quite pronounced in
terms of the individuals who have filled the leadership posts.

Summary

Temascalcingo and the *ejido* of Puerto de las Piedras both have political
systems that are fairly congruent with those dictated by the national
structure. The *cargo* system, which once was the dominant form of
government throughout rural Mexico, no longer has a role in the civil
government in the area. *Caciquismo* is still in evidence, but even it has
changed. As recently as 1940, the Temascalcingo region was marked by
the violence of *caciques* imposing their will on others and fighting one
another for preeminence. Murders were common; and in one case, even
the municipal president was assassinated. Those who are called *caciques* no longer have to resort to violence.

Juan and Vicente, the two individuals I have talked about in this
chapter, illustrate this phenomenon very well. Both have achieved
power by using wealth and politics. A few years ago, Vicente was the
municipal police chief. In 1973, Juan became the judge in the *municipio*. Both men have built up connections in the state government as
well. Perhaps the most important of these connections is Juan's son, a
representative in the state legislature. By manipulating their offices and
their influence in high places, these men can achieve results without re-
sorting to violence.

I have pointed out in both Chapter 6 and here that economic wealth
and political power go together in the *ejido* of Puerto de las Piedras.
Very often, the leadership positions can be manipulated to the advantage of the holder. I have shown how *ejido* leadership has been used by

some in order to gain access to more and better lands, for example. *Eji do* leaders have also had the greatest contact with change agents and thus have been in a good position to acquire knowledge about poten tially beneficial innovations that can be used in agriculture.

The leadership variables were found to be associated with some o the adaptive strategies. *Ejido* leadership and community leadership are both positively associated with the adoption of the forage production adaptive strategy. *Ejido* leadership is also positively associated with ani mal improvement and is negatively associated with the subsistence agri culture strategy. Thus those who have been leaders in the *ejido* have been adopting new adaptive strategies.

8

Cargos and Catholicism: religion in the community

A dominant feature of community life among peasants in Mesoamerica since the Conquest has been religion. Along with whatever role Catholicism has with regard to the spiritual needs of the people, religion has also played a significant integrating role for the community through a form of organization known variously as the *cargo* system, civil–religious hierarchy, *fiesta* system, or ladder system. The distinctive feature of this system, as described in many of the anthropological monographs written about Mesoamerican communities, is the linkage between religious and civil authority within a single organization. All men are encouraged through social and sometimes physical sanctions to participate in the religious and political governance of the community. Service is performed without remuneration and may actually require substantial expenditures of capital, especially by those who fill the offices (*cargos*) responsible for organizing the *fiestas* in honor of the saints (Cancian 1965:284).

Cargo systems in Mesoamerica and elsewhere have often been assumed to act as barriers to economic development. Two characteristics of this institution lend themselves to such a conclusion. First, the *cargo* systems are a major factor in the integration and maintenance of communities, especially in insulating them from the outside world (Adams 1957). This insulation may restrict the availability of new economic opportunities. Second, individuals who take on *cargos* are often required to expend large amounts of time and/or money in the performance of their duties. Because the wealthy are strongly encouraged to take on the most onerous positions, the institution has sometimes been called a "leveling mechanism" (Nash 1971) that reduces inequalities in the community and creates a state of "shared poverty" (Wolf 1957:2). The net effect is conspicuous consumption of surplus capital, thus reducing the potential for investment in new economic opportunities.

The *cargo* system has changed greatly in many communities in the past few years in response to state and federal government regulations about local-level community government, increasing contact of some people with cities and towns; and also some opposition from the Catholic church to what are sometimes considered to be rituals beyond the

pale of Catholic religion (DeWalt 1975a). This chapter demonstrate
just how much the system has changed in Puerto de las Piedras. In spit
of these changes, however, many members of the community do con
tinue to spend time and money in sponsoring *fiestas* in honor of th
saints.

This chapter will describe the religious activities and organization:
now present in Puerto de las Piedras. The relationship of religion to
other aspects of society and culture will be investigated. Special empha
sis, of course, is placed upon assessing the potential negative effect that
religious participation might have on the prospects for economic devel
opment in the region. The first several sections of this chapter are pri
marily of ethnographic interest and contain historical materials and a
discussion of family chapels, the church, and the *cargo* system. Those
readers who are only interested in the relationship between religion and
economic development may skip to the section on "Catholicism in the
communities."

Religion: historical perspective

The role of religious institutions and personalities in the Temascalcingo
region after 1900 closely matches the experience of other regions of
Mexico. The priests who staffed the main church in Temascalcingo were
a very conservative element during the Revolution. Even after the Revolution, informants report that the priests continued their conservative
role and warned the people that it was sinful to accept the redistributed
hacienda lands. The peasants were hungry for land, however; and despite these warnings, the land reform was eventually accomplished.

One of the priests who preached most vociferously against land reform was Father Felipe. He was successful in saving the lands owned by
his brother near the town of Temascalcingo but could not prevent redistribution of the *hacienda* lands. Father Felipe is still respected in the region and is sometimes called a "saint" by the people, indicating that his
stand against land reform was not held against him. He is credited with
performing many "miracles" in curing people of illnesses.

The Catholic church is a powerful force in village life to this day.
Protestant missionary ventures in the 1940s and 1950s attracted few
converts. According to the 1970 census, about 99 percent of the people
report that they are Catholics. The few individuals who did convert to
Protestantism were harassed and threatened at first, but federal troops
were reportedly sent to the region to stop these actions. One *presidente
municipal* is said to have been told that he would be hanged if he did
not protect the Protestants. Since the 1950s, there has not been any sig-

nificant conflict between Catholics and Protestants. The small number of converts has probably held conflict to a minimum. The serious divisions along religious lines that plague other Mesoamerican communities (see Nash 1958; Redfield 1950) are not present in Temascalcingo.

Oratorios

Historically, a religious institution important in the Mazahua area revolved around what are called *oratorios*. *Oratorios* are tiny chapellike structures. Most of those that still exist in the Temascalcingo region are constructed of *adobe* that has been smoothed and whitewashed. The roofs are generally of tile. Even the largest of these structures can be entered only by stooping through a tiny doorway. There is room for only one person in almost all *oratorios,* and most are nothing more than a simple, covered altar. In general, the altar holds a wooden cross or perhaps a picture of a saint surrounded by containers of flowers, old bottles with candles, and some pottery incense burners.

Soustelle first described *oratorios* during a trip through the Mazahua region in the 1930s (1935; 1937:543-8). The *oratorios* pertained to specific families and were destroyed and reconstructed at certain intervals. Construction was accompanied by large feasts during which heads of other families would give gifts of food that would be reciprocated when they rebuilt their own family chapels. These rites were apparently to assure fertility of the soil and successful harvests (Soustelle 1937: 543-4). Recently there has been a much more detailed study of the cult of the *oratorios* in a very isolated Mazahua community (Cortés Ruiz 1972). Cortés Ruiz reports that in San Simón de la Laguna, a village of about one thousand and two hundred people, about thirty to thirty-five *oratorios* still exist. These structures are cared for by patrilineal, patrilateral extended families. Considerable magic and ritual are associated with *oratorios*, and care of the structures and the crosses they contain is essential if the family wishes to ward off evil. The crosses in particular can be very malevolent.

According to my informants, there formerly were many *oratorios* in the villages of El Puerto and Las Piedras. Like those described by Soustelle and Cortés Ruiz, my informants reported that these structures each pertained to an extended family.

One of my informants reported that when he was a small boy (he was about sixty in 1973), many of the *oratorios* were destroyed. He recalled that Father Felipe told the people that these buildings and the images they contained were not sacred and that, in fact, they were not permitted by God or the church. Almost all of the *oratorios* in the *barrios* and communities closest to Temascalcingo were destroyed.

Three *oratorios* still exist in El Puerto, and three more have survived in Las Piedras. With the exception of one in Las Piedras that is cared for by a fairly young nuclear family, all of these are now maintained by very old individuals. Doña Camila, for example, regularly places flowers in the *oratorio* near her house. She is reputed to be the oldest living person in the community, and some informants say that she is about ninety years old. Despite her age, until late 1973 she walked daily from her home in El Puerto to Temascalcingo to work as a housekeeper and also had retained her fondness for *pulque*. Doña Natalia, another widow, lives high on the slope of the mountain in Las Piedras. She is not as old as Doña Camila, but she also still maintains the *oratorio* situated at the side of her house.

The largest of the existing *oratorios* (and perhaps the largest ever in the area) has now become incorporated into the *fiesta* cycle and seems to be accepted as a legitimate place of worship by a large proportion of the community. This *oratorio* contains an image of San Miguel, the patron saint of the *municipio* of Temascalcingo. Yearly, during the *fiesta* of San Miguel, the image is removed from the *oratorio* and is carried in a procession to the main church in Temascalcingo. However, unlike the main church in El Puerto, the *oratorio* is not under the care of the *cargueros* (*cargo* holders). Instead, like the other *oratorios*, this building is maintained by an individual, Guadalupe de la Cruz.

The other *oratorios* do not seem to have any special meaning for the community members, although they are given some recognition. For example, the women who replace the flowers in the main church are usually delegated to put a few flowers in the *oratorios* they pass on their way home.

One other interesting and as yet unexplainable feature of the religious life of the Mazahua in the past came to light when one of my informants discovered dozens of small clay statues when digging in the area where his family's *oratorio* had stood. Subsequently, when I began asking individuals in the region about these statues, I was told of similar finds in other communities. Although Cortés Ruiz (1972:95) found no evidence of such statues, he quotes Soustelle's statement that these had apparently existed in the region around Ixtlahuaca until about thirty years before Soustelle passed through in the early 1930s: "The uncle and grandfather of my informant, now dead, made small statues of baked clay which they decorated with lime; they were representations of men and women generally unclothed . . . Every year or every two years a *fandanguito* was celebrated in honor of these idols" (Soustelle 1935:113, my translation). Not even my oldest informants were able to

ell me anything about the little statues. The statues that were uncovered
n El Puerto were similar to those found around Ixtlahuaca. However,
he statues that I saw were glazed, were not decorated with lime, and
vere not limited to statues of men and women. Also included were ani-
nals and even men with *sombreros* mounted on horses.

To sum up, the role of the *oratorios* in the religious and social organization of the community has diminished considerably in this century.
While we cannot be certain that *oratorios* in the Temascalcingo region
played the same role as in other Mazahua communities, informants report that these structures were cared for by extended family groups. In
ny mapping of the community, I was unable to find much evidence of
he survival of what may have been territorial, kinship-based units.
However, some of my informants in El Puerto were able to recall some
parajes (named places) that pertained to various locations in the community. These were no longer in use in 1973. It is possible that these
parajes pertained to extended families living in proximity to *oratorios*.
Further evidence is needed to corroborate such speculations, but it is
possible that these *parajes* may be found to be similar to the patrilineal,
patrilocal domestic units organized around a "house cross" erected on
the patio of compounds in the highlands of Chiapas (see Vogt 1969:
129–30).

Although the activities of Father Felipe in encouraging the abandon-
ment of *oratorios* certainly was of major importance in their diminishing role in religious life, the increasing contact of people in the region
with the national scene has also certainly had its effects. Most of the
customs and organizational features of the *oratorios* that I have discussed
are not remembered by most people in the region. Other religious institutions have not changed as much, and I will now turn to a discussion
of these.

The church: the focus of religious life

The religious life of the communities of El Puerto, Las Piedras, and El
Jardín revolves around the stately church situated near the old bridge
over the river in El Puerto (see Figure 5.1). The church used to be situated higher on the hill further away from the river; but according to informants, the Virgin of Guadalupe appeared one night in the 1860s and
told the people of the community that she wanted her church in its
present location. The present church was completed in 1871, and the
appearance of the Virgin is commemorated on the most important religious *fiesta* days. A gaily decorated basket filled with such items as liquor, cigarettes, chocolates, and pastry is thrown into the river. I re-

152   *Modernization in a Mexican ejido*

ceived varying answers about the significance or meaning of this event
but informants were agreed that it was "for the Virgin."

When the Hacienda El Jardín was still operating, there was a church
there. Currently, however, only El Puerto among the three communities has a church. The people of the three communities are very proud
of the church. They extol its beauty, remark about the quality of its
bells, and are fond of comparing its size to the churches in the other
barrios. In the past ten years, the communities have put considerable
time and money into renovating the church. In 1972, each family contributed one hundred *pesos* and about a month's work to help fix the
roof. A few years ago, they contributed twenty-seven *pesos* each to put
electricity into the church; and a few years before that, they contributed twenty *pesos* each to fix the floor.

Masses in the church in El Puerto are conducted every other Sunday
by one of the priests from Temascalcingo. On *fiesta* days, arrangements
are made for special masses. A special mass costs seventy *pesos* or more
depending upon how many priests are desired and the amount of time
spent in the community.

Although masses, when they are held in El Puerto, are fairly heavily
attended, the church is more important as the setting for a community
religious organization, the *cargo* system. It is to this very important feature of community life to which I will now turn.

The cargo system

Cargo systems have been the primary institution involved in carrying
out the religious and civil governance of many rural Mesoamerican communities. Traditional *cargo* systems have generally consisted of a series
of religious and civil offices (*cargos*) that are voluntarily filled on a ro-
tating basis (usually annually) by community members.

In many communities the civil and religious offices form a single hierarchy, and individuals alternate between serving in the two types of
offices throughout their lifetimes. The classic case described in the literature is that of Santiago Chimaltenango (Wagley 1949). In this community, individuals can start their service to the community in a low-level
civil or religious post. They alternate service in the two hierarchies in
succeeding years much like the career illustrated in Table 8.1. Some
individuals only serve in the lower levels of the hierarchy in posts with
little responsibility. Others, who pass through the whole system, are
accorded considerable prestige in return for their service to the community and achieve the status of elder statemen. These elders consitute

Table 8.1. *The civil-religious hierarchy in Santiago Chimaltenango (adapted from Wagley 1949:95)*

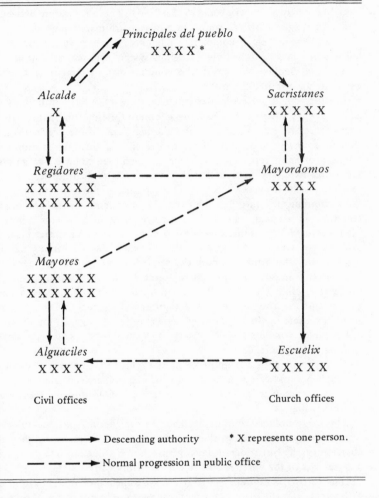

Principales del pueblo
X X X X *

Alcalde
X

Sacristanes
X X X X X

Regidores
X X X X X X
X X X X X X

Mayordomos
X X X X

Mayores
X X X X X X
X X X X X X

Alguaciles
X X X X

Escuelix
X X X X X

Civil offices   Church offices

────────────▶ Descending authority   * X represents one person.

── ── ── ──▶ Normal progression in public office

the ultimate decision-making body in the community (Wagley 1949; J. Nash 1970).

Cargo systems probably deviated from this ideal pattern in the past; and in response to government intervention, increasing contact with the outside world, the presence of Catholic priests, and other factors, they have become increasingly different in their appearance (DeWalt 1975a: 101). I have classified the hierarchy that exists in Puerto de las Piedras as a "faded system" (DeWalt 1975a:93–4). The alternation between civil and religious offices found in Santiago Chimaltenango does not exist, and the system is completely religious in nature. It is difficult to tell whether such a linked civil–religious system ever was present in Puerto de las Piedras. No one in the community can remember a time when such a system existed.

In other communities in Mesoamerica, the *cargo* system functions as an integrative institution. Outlying communities send individuals to a town center to serve in offices, and the big *fiesta* of the year turns the usually sparsely populated town center into a bustling metropolis. Some informants reported that Temascalcingo used to have a *cargo* system of its own. It is possible that this system was of the traditional civil–religious form. However, since at least the turn of the century, the outlying communities have had their own *cargo* systems. Some form of integration on a small scale does take place. A number of communities (San Martín, La Purísima, El Puerto, and La Loma) do practice mutual exchange of saints and *cargueros.* That is, when one community has its major *fiesta,* the other communities send their images and *cargueros* to help the community honor its patron saint. In addition, during many of the larger *fiestas* (e.g., Holy Week, San Miguel, Día de Año Nuevo, and Corpus Christi), the *barrios* still send groups of dancers to Temascalcingo to take part in the celebration. Other outlying towns in the *municipio* seem to conduct their own festivities and do not send representatives to Temascalcingo.

Cargo participation is limited almost exclusively to married couples, although I found a few instances in which an unmarried male became a *carguero.* Women are given the same title (e.g., *mayordoma* or *carguera*) as their husbands.

The *cargo* holders who are attached to the church in El Puerto have three primary duties. First, they are responsible for organizing the celebration of the most sacred days in the church calendar. The four primary events of the year are: the day of the Holy Cross (3 May in 1973); Corpus Christi, 8 September (to mark the appearance of the Virgin in El Puerto); and the most important, the *fiesta* in honor of the Virgin of Guadalupe, which takes place in early December. On these occasions there are processions, ceremonial meals, ritual celebrations in the church and other sacred spots, and sometimes dances. The *cargo* holders are in charge of performing in and/or organizing all of these events.

The second duty, especially for those who hold the more important *cargos,* is the maintenance of communication with the priests. They arrange for the masses the priests perform on special occasions (such as the *fiestas*); assist the priest in the biweekly masses held in El Puerto; and in general serve to link their community with the church hierarchy.

Finally, the *cargo* holders are responsible for the maintenance of the church and its grounds. Low-ranking *cargo* holders must spend a week each year living in the tiny house attached to the church. They guard and clean the church. The females must replace the flowers and perform other tasks each Wednesday.

Informants recall that new *cargo* holders were chosen every year in the past, as is the case in most Mesoamerican communities with *cargo* systems. However, since around 1950, the selection of new officials has apparently taken place much less frequently. The *cargo* holders in 1973, for example, had been in office for four years; and changes did not appear to be imminent.

The manner in which new *cargueros* are chosen to replace the old ones seems to be rather informal. Informants reported that the process begins when a person who is not presently a *carguero* decides that he and his family would like to hold a *cargo.* This individual then visits other families and tries to interest them in pressing for a change of *cargo* holders. If there is some support, then still other families are asked. The process continues until all of the positions in the *cuadrillas* (group) are filled. These individuals are known as *cargueros.* All of these individuals then hold a meeting in which they select those families that they would like to fill the posts of *mayordomo* and *fiscal.* A procession then moves to the house of the family selected to be the third *mayordomo.* The family is asked if they would like to fill the position. If they accept (and in front of so many people it is difficult to refuse), the procession then continues on to the house of the second and first *mayordomos,* where the same procedure is followed. If *fiscales* are to be chosen at this time, the procession continues. There is some question as to whether *fiscales* are always replaced at the same time as *cargueros.* Some informants reported that a good *fiscal* would be allowed to stay in office as long as the family could bear the burden or until they were discovered to be stealing money from the church.

My impression is that the impetus for changing the *cargo* holders in reality comes from individuals who feel that they have served long enough. When complaints reach a crescendo, the necessity for change becomes apparent to everyone. Change can also be initiated when *cargo* holders simply stop performing their duties. In 1973, there were many complaints in the community that some *cargueros* were not doing their duty in spending a week guarding the church. Others also complained that some *cargueros* simply did not make the required contributions for the *fiestas* or did not help in changing the flowers in the church.

A serious example of this neglect of duty took place in the summer of 1973. Normally, two *representantes* are the most important religious officials in the community. These men serve for life. However, since the death of one of them over ten years before, no successor had been chosen. There was great dissatisfaction with the remaining *representante*. Many people complained that he was too weak and could not maintain discipline over the other *cargo* holders. Others decried his inability to supervise effectively the reconstruction of the church roof about a year earlier. Finally, meetings were held to select a new *representante*. The individual chosen would become first *representante*, while the present *representante* would become the second. Four or five meetings were held over a period of about two months before a person agreed to take the position and also received the positive consensus of the villagers. In any case, the lack of a formalized procedure for choosing new religious officials and the lack of an agreed-upon duration for *cargo* holders' terms differ considerably from other Mesoamerican communities in which the *cargo* system appears to retain more of its traditional form and still has considerable importance in the integration of the community (DeWalt 1975a).

I will now discuss the offices that make up the *cargo* system in El Puerto. I will also discuss a few of the individuals who filled these offices in 1973 in order to give the reader some impression of the qualifications needed to fill the different posts.

Representantes: As I mentioned before, *representantes* are the top officials in the *cargo* system in El Puerto. They do not take part in the ritual celebrations in honor of the saints. Instead, their duties are primarily confined to overseeing the other *cargo* holders. They are supposed to make sure that the *cargo* holders are performing their duties as required and that the *mayordomos* and *fiscales* are not stealing any money from the church treasury.

In addition to overseeing the functioning of the church and its officials, the *representantes* also have at least one civil function, for they hold the title to the communal lands (the mountains above the community). When a dispute arose with the community of San Martín el Alto because individuals from this community were cutting timber in lands belonging to Puerto de las Piedras, the *representante* was in charge of seeking justice and negotiating the dispute. Normally, disputes that need to be taken to the *presidente municipal* in Temascalcingo are the province of the *delegados*. This civil role of the *representantes* recalls the civil and religious omnipotence held by the top officials in other more traditional *cargo* systems in Mesoamerica. In the main, however, the duties of the *representantes* do not overlap into the civil sphere.

Although there is some evidence that *representantes* hold both civil and religious responsibilities, they are not old and thus do not fit the mold of *principales,* the village elders who are the ultimate decision-making body in some Mesoamerican communities. Rafael, the only *representante* for ten years, is about forty-five years old. The newly elected first *representante* in 1973, José, is only about fifty years old. José does fit the mold in that he has passed through a number of religious *cargos* in the past. He was a *carguero* many years ago and also completed one term as *fiscal*. He has never served as *mayordomo*, however.

Although the position as *representante* is very important in the community, no one ever mentioned that a great deal of prestige was needed before an individual could be selected for the office. Nor does it appear that prestige automatically accrues to the individual who serves as *representante*. The considerable criticism by individuals who were dissatisfied with Rafael's performance makes this point evident. Prestige is often cited as the primary reason why individuals are willing to take on *cargos* in other Mesoamerican communities (Cancian 1965).

Fiscales: Below the *representantes* in the *cargo* system of El Puerto are the *fiscales* (see Table 8.2). They are ranked as first and second *fiscal*. The *fiscales* have extensive religious duties involving leading services in the church. Although they are clearly above the *mayordomos* in terms of the church hierarchy, there is no need to serve in lower posts before becoming *fiscal*. Only one of the seven present and former *fiscales* I interviewed had served as both *carguero* and *mayordomo* before becoming *fiscal*. In fact, two individuals became *fiscales* without having served in any other *cargo*. And a number of individuals who served as *fiscal* later participated in the system as *cargueros*.

Being a *fiscal* is the most onerous *cargo* in terms of economic commitment. During the primary *fiesta* of the year, 12 December (Virgin of Guadalupe), the *fiscales* have to give a dinner for the priest from Temascalcingo; and they must feed all of the other *cargueros* as well. The meal for the priest requires considerable expenditures of money; so much food is bought for the priest that he regularly carries off most of what is given to him during the meal. One of the present *fiscales* reported having to kill four turkeys and four chickens in December 1972. He also had to buy various quantities of beer, *pulque*, fruit, bread, and

Table 8.2. *The cargo system in Puerto de las Piedras*

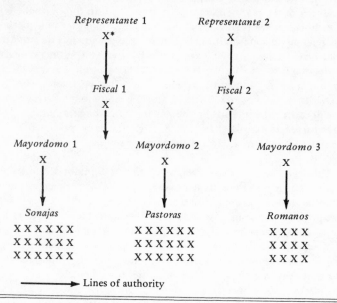

```
         Representante 1          Representante 2
              X*                        X
              |                         |
              v                         v
          Fiscal 1                  Fiscal 2
              X                         X
              |                         |
              v                         |
  Mayordomo 1        Mayordomo 2        |        Mayordomo 3
      X                  X              |            X
      |                  |              |            |
      v                  v              v            v
   Sonajas            Pastoras                    Romanos
  X X X X X X        X X X X X X                  X X X X
  X X X X X X        X X X X X X                  X X X X
  X X X X X X        X X X X X X                  X X X X

          ―――――――――――> Lines of authority
```

* X represents one person.

other items. A number of past and present *fiscales* estimated that they must spend five hundred to one thousand *pesos* (forty to eighty dollars) every year during the *fiesta* of the Virgin of Guadalupe.

The outlay of money is considerable, and I asked one of my best informants how anyone could afford to spend that amount of money. He reported that one of the two current *fiscales* has a nephew working in Mexico City who sends money to help him out. The other *fiscal* has a job killing animals in the slaughterhouse in Temascalcingo, for which he receives very good pay. Thus it seems that one of the requirements for holding this office is some extraordinary source of income that makes possible the outlay of a considerable sum of cash each year.

The office of *fiscal* holds some possibility for economic gain, however. The *fiscales* are responsible for the money donated to the church. One of the previous *fiscales* was removed from office for stealing some of these funds. The people of the community did not seem shocked by this sort of behavior, and the ousted *cargo* holder still lives in the community. I had the impression that this kind of act is not unusual and may even be expected, although it is certainly not encouraged.

Mayordomos: There are three *mayordomos* in the El Puerto *cargo* system; and they are ranked as first, second, and third. The *mayordomos* take an active part in the ritual duties of the church. They often lead the chants, say prayers, and in general are the spiritual leaders along with the *fiscales*. The *mayordomos,* unlike their counterparts in many Mesoamerican communities, do not incur heavy financial obligations in the performance of their duties. In fact, their monetary obligations are equal to those of the *cargueros*. Unlike the *cargueros,* however, the *mayordomos* are the recipients of many ceremonial meals. Thus the *mayordomos* may actually receive as many economic benefits from the office as liabilities. This assessment does not take into account the time they spend performing their duties, however.

The *mayordomos'* duties include regular (supposedly bimonthly) house-to-house collections. Each household head is asked to contribute a *tostón* (four cents U.S.) to help defray the expenses of the church (i.e., to pay for lights, water, and so on). Apparently little pressure is put on families to contribute if they say they cannot afford the contribution.

The *mayordomos* are each responsible for one of the three groups of *cargueros*. These groups are called *cuadrillas* and perform as dancers during the most important *fiestas*. The *cuadrillas* are known by the name of the dance groups that they represent. Thus the first *mayordomo* is in charge of the *Sonajas*. This group is a women's dance group, and its members wear white dresses and carry rattles when they dance during the festivities in honor of the Virgin of Guadalupe. The *Sonajas* also dance during the *fiesta* on 8 September, but at this time young girls eight to twelve years of age are the performers rather than the women. The second *mayordomo* is in charge of the group known as the *Pastoras*. These are also women who dress in white and perform only on 12 December. The third *mayordomo* is in charge of the *Romanos*, a man's dance group. The men dress in skirts, pantyhose, and colorful capes. They wear feathers and carry large horseshoe-shaped arcs of plastic flowers. They also dance on 12 December and in addition perform in the Temascalcingo *fiesta* on 1 January.

The *mayordomos* try to make sure that the members of their *cuadrillas* pay their contributions (*limosnas*), attend practice sessions for the dances, and carry out the other duties that are required of them.

Cargueros: The lowest members of the *cargo* system in El Puerto are the *cargueros,* also called *semaneros* because of the week that each must serve guarding the church. Twenty-four families are *cargueros* in the first two *cuadrillas* and sixteen in the third *cuadrilla*.

The burden of filling the position of *carguero* is truly a family responsibility. Although the wives of the *fiscales* and *mayordomos* are also *cargo* holders and play a role in village ceremonial life, the males are clearly more important in carrying out the duties of these offices. Such is not the case for the *cargueros*. Wives who also serve as *Pastoras* and *Sonajas* are obviously playing a more important role than their husbands. In addition, the wives are also important because they prepare and contribute the food required at various times throughout the year. For example, the *cargueros* are responsible for providing a ceremonial meal for the *fiscales* and *mayordomos* (and their wives) on 3 May and on other occasions. They are also responsible for providing a meal for the dance groups each night that they practice for the upcoming *fiesta*. Providing this food is in the woman's domain. When the family serves as *semanero*, it is usually the woman who is left behind during the day to guard the church while the men go off to work in the fields or attend to other activities. The women also undertake the major responsibility for changing the flowers and cleaning the church each Wednesday. Often, a larger part of their day is spent in this activity.

In addition to these responsibilities, the *cargueros* must also contribute a sum of money to help offset the costs of each *fiesta*. The sum assessed in 1973 was 20 *pesos* for *Jueves de Corpus*, 30 *pesos* for 3 May, 25 *pesos* for 8 September, and 60 *pesos* for 12 December, or a total of 135 *pesos* ($10.80). This money is used to buy flowers, candles, food, and, perhaps most important, the fireworks. It was estimated that the fireworks alone for the major *fiesta* on 12 December would cost 3,000 *pesos* ($240) in 1973. The *cargueros* also have to provide food at different times of the year. Some informants reported having to kill three or four chickens during years when they were serving *cargos*.

Although the consumption of alcohol is an institutionalized part of *fiestas* in many communities of Mesoamerica (see Vogt 1969; Pozas 1971), such is not the case in El Puerto. A good deal of drinking does occur during the *fiestas*, but alcoholic beverages are not allowed in the church or at the ceremonial meals. *Pulque* is served during ceremonial meals in nearby *barrios*, but alcohol is simply not permitted at these events in El Puerto.

In general, then, moderate cash outlays are required of the *cargueros*. They do not put in as much time as the *mayordomos* and *fiscales*, although they must spend one week each year as *semaneros*. The wives expend most of the time and effort required in this *cargo*.

Catholicism in the communities

Although the *cargo* system fulfills a number of very important ritual functions, it cannot meet all of the religious needs of the people. As I mentioned before, for example, masses are held only every other week in El Puerto. Churchgoing people who want to attend mass every Sunday thus must go to Temascalcingo at least every other Sunday. As a matter of course, most individuals in Las Piedras attend mass in Temascalcingo. It is a much easier walk to Temascalcingo than to El Puerto. In addition, the weekly market on Sunday is a further incentive for those in Las Piedras to attend religious services in Temascalcingo.

The ceremonies in the Catholic church that mark the life cycle – baptisms, confirmations, marriages, and funerals – are only available in the main church in Temascalcingo. Although a priest may agree to perform one of these ceremonies in an outlying community, the fee charged for such a service is prohibitive. The main church in Temascalcingo also serves as the focal point for *municipio*-wide *fiestas*. Often a saint's day is marked with a small celebration in the local community and then a procession (with images of saints and virgins in tow) to the main church in Temascalcingo. After this celebration, there is another procession back to the local community. Thus an individual in the *barrios* has a dual orientation toward: (*a*) the local church, which is the focal point of many community activities, and (*b*) the Temascalcingo church, which provides desired services not available in the local community.

Measuring religious participation: Catholicism and the cargo system

The measurements of religious participation were designed to reflect the dual orientation of Catholicism and the *cargo* system. On the one hand, I wanted a measure of participation in activities within the established structure of the Catholic church. On the other hand, a measure of participation in the community-based *cargo* system was needed.

With regard to participation in the Catholic church, respondents were asked the frequency of church attendance and the frequency with which they received communion. Responses on the former question ranged from one individual who attended church every morning before he went to work to a number of individuals who reported that it had been a number of years since they had attended a church service. These responses were converted to percentages. In order to eliminate the one extreme score, the maximum score was set equal to 100. (That is, only one individual went to church 365 days out of the year. The next most frequent attendance was once a week.) Thus individuals who attended church once a week received a score of 52 percent, those who attended every other week received a score of 26, and so on. The same procedure was followed with regard to communion participation. In this case, no extreme scores had to be dealt with; and so the percentages refer to number of times per year communion was received, divided by the maximum score (which was 12 times a year), times 100. My purpose in converting these scores to percentages was to give equal weight to attending church and taking communion. The two percentages were then summed to yield the final score, which reflects "religiosity" in terms of participation in the Catholic church. Scores ranged from a low of 1 to a high of 167, with a mean of 71.3 and a standard deviation of 47.3.

"*Cargo* system participation" was measured from respondents' reports about the *cargos* in which they had served as well as by the number of years served. Because offices higher in the hierarchy require more input of time and/or money, I arbitrarily decided to weight these offices more in computing the score. Thus serving as a *carguero* was worth only one point, *mayordomo* two points, *fiscal* three points, and *representante* four points. A person's score on this variable was the sum of the number of years served in various *cargos* multiplied by the value given to those *cargos*. For example, a person who served three years as *fiscal* and seven years as a *carguero* would receive a score of 16. Scores on this variable ranged from a low of 0 (shared by eighteen people who had never held a *cargo*) to a high of 38. The mean score was 7.8, and the standard deviation was 9.8.

There is a moderate correlation ($r = .32$) between these two variables, indicating that people who serve *cargos* in the local community also tend to be fairly religious in terms of participation in the ceremonies of the Catholic church. However, the correlation is sufficiently low to indicate that not all churchgoing Catholics participate actively in the *cargo* system (or vice versa).

Relationships between religious variables and adaptive strategies

Weber (1930), Nash (1971), and many others have investigated the relationship between religion and economic development. Their research, along with my comments concerning the time and money spent in religious activities, lead one to suspect that Catholic religiosity and *cargo*

Table 8.3. *Correlations of the adaptive strategies with religiosity and cargo system participation*

	Religiosity	*Cargo* system participation
Forage production	.07	−.18
Animal improvement	−.06	−.19
Tractor use	−.08	−.03
Fertilizer use	.09	−.01
Subsistence agriculture	.00	.20

Note: * indicates $p < .05$ and ** indicates $p < .01$.

system participation should be negatively related to adoption of the new adaptive strategies.

Table 8.3, however, shows that neither religiosity nor *cargo* system participation is significantly correlated with any of the adaptive strategies. There is some tendency for *cargo* system participation to be negatively correlated with forage production and animal improvement, both of which require considerable capital to implement. It is also somewhat more likely that individuals who are high in *cargo* system participation will continue practicing subsistence agriculture rather than investing in any of the new adaptive strategies. On the whole, however, neither measure of religious participation appears to be significant in terms of inhibiting or encouraging the adoption of any of the adaptive strategies.

Correlations between religious variables and other independent variables

The *cargo* system has been discussed primarily in the context of Indian communities. Because the *ejido* of Puerto de las Piedras is a mixed *mestizo* and Mazahua Indian community, I expected to find a high positive correlation between Indian language ability and *cargo* system participation. The correlation between these two variables confirms this hypothesis, as we can see in Table 8.4. The "more *mestizo*" a person is, the less likely he or she is to participate in the *cargo* system. It is also interesting to note that Indian language ability is also positively correlated with religiosity. Not only do people who are "more Indian" participate more often in the *cargo* system, but they also tend to participate more often in the rites of the Catholic church.

Table 8.4. *Correlations of independent variables and the religious measures*

	Religiosity	Cargo system participation
Land quantity–quality	−.12	−.24*
Distance from land	.11	.16
Wealth ratings	−.02	−.28*
Material style of life	−.37**	−.31*
Cash value of animals	−.16	−.17
Value of agricultural equipment	.02	−.09
Income from other pursuits	−.30*	−.29*
Ejido leadership	.05	.00
Community leadership	−.09	−.12
Alcohol use	−.05	.09
Education	−.01	−.22
Political knowledge	.23	.23
Mass media exposure	−.07	−.14
Change agent contact	.00	−.01
Cosmopolitanism	−.23*	−.26*
Age	.05	.24*
No. of people in house	−.12	−.20
Indian language ability	.34**	.53**
Times worked elsewhere	.08	.10

Note: * indicates $p < .05$ and ** indicates $p < .01$.

I have also pointed out that the *cargo* system has been called an economic "leveling mechanism" (Nash 1971). That is, the system requires substantial expenditures of capital and time and thus may act to reduce inequalities among individuals in the community. Presumably, those who accumulate wealth will be pressured into serving in the more expensive positions, where they will spend their money and again become poor like everyone else. It is obvious from the large wealth differentials that exist that Puerto de las Piedras is not a community in which there is shared poverty (see Chapter 6). However, it may be that *cargo* system participation is taking substantial resources away from some individuals. If this is indeed the case, *cargo* system participation should be negatively related to the various measures of wealth. Table 8.4 indicates that this relationship may exist. *Cargo* system participation is negatively related to all five measures of wealth; and the correlations with wealth ratings, material style of life, and income from other pursuits are statistically significant. These findings suggest that there is some tendency for people who participate frequently in the *cargo* system to be poorer.

The data could be interpreted in a different way, however. I have already pointed out that people with more Indian language ability tend to participate more frequently in the *cargo* system. I have also reported that Indians tend to be poorer than *mestizos* (see Chapter 6). It is then appropriate to ask whether individuals are poorer because they participate in the *cargo* system or because Indians (who tend to be poorer) are most likely to take on *cargos*.

This question can be addressed with the assistance of path analysis (see Duncan 1966; Hadden and DeWalt 1974). Path analysis is a flexible, multivariate statistical technique that allows the researcher to evaluate the effects of several independent variables on one or more dependent variables. In order to apply path techniques, the researcher must be able to make explicit the causal ordering of variables in a model and should also be able to specify whether the relationship between variables will be positive or negative. Path analysis has the advantages of (*a*) making assumptions more explicit than is possible with more discursive studies, and (*b*) permitting more systematic examination of the effects of intervening variables (Hadden and DeWalt, 1974: 106).

In the present case, I was interested in determining how much of an effect *cargo* system participation and Indian language ability had on the wealth ratings. Expressed another way, how much is poverty related to ethnicity as opposed to participation in the *cargo* system? The path analysis (Table 8.5) shows that Indian language ability has a greater direct effect (path coefficient) on the wealth rating than does *cargo* system participation. In addition, part of the correlation that was observed between *cargo* system participation and the wealth ratings ($r = -.28$) was due to the relationship of Indian language ability to both of those variables (i.e., the joint effect shown in Table 8.5). Thus the most important determinant of wealth is the individual's ethnic status rather than his or her participation in the *cargo* system.

Another relationship that I wanted to explore was between *cargo* system participation and other types of leadership positions. As I have pointed out, in many Mesoamerican communities, civil and religious leadership is linked in a single hierarchy. Although the *cargo* system in Puerto de las Piedras is now almost completely religious, it may once have had a civil portion as well. If so, some overlap might remain between individuals who fill religious and political leadership positions. This appears to have been the case in Amatenango, for example, until recently (J. Nash 1970: 327). Table 8.4, however, indicates that such overlap has not existed in Puerto de las Piedras. *Cargo* system participa-

Table 8.5. *Path diagram of the interrelationships among cargo system participation, wealth ratings, and Indian language ability*

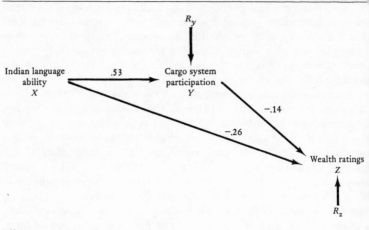

Effects on wealth ratings	Effects
Indian language ability	
Direct effect[a] (p_{zx})	-.26
Indirect effect[b] through *cargo* system part $(p_{zy}p_{yx})$	-.07
Correlation (r_{zx})	-.34
Cargo system participation	
Direct effect (p_{zy})	-.14
Joint effect[c] due to common cause of Indian language ability $(p_{yx}p_{zx})$	-.14
Correlation (r_{zy})	-.28

[a] A direct effect is the effect on any variable of an immediately prior variable in the causal model. This effect is represented by a single causal arrow or path in a path diagram. The magnitude of the direct effect is given by the path coefficient (e.g., p_{zx}).

[b] An indirect effect is the effect of variable X on variable Z through one or more intervening variables (Y in this case), when there exists a direct effect from X to Y and a direct effect from Y to Z. This effect is represented by a sequence of causal arrows or paths in a path diagram. The magnitude of the indirect effect is given by the product of the corresponding direct effects (e.g., $p_{zy}p_{yx}$).

[c] A joint effect is any effect not classifiable as direct or indirect. There are two types: (1) correlational joint effects, which involve one or more unanalyzed correlations, and (2) concomitant joint effects in which a single causally prior variable

tion is not related to either *ejido* leadership or community leadership, which indicates that there is now a de facto separation in the two spheres of leadership as well as the de jure separation required by state and federal laws.

Among the other correlations reported in Table 8.4, a few deserve at least some comment. Cosmopolitanism is negatively related to both religiosity and *cargo* system participation. It is tempting to say that both types of religious participation reflect a traditional orientation and that these individuals are not likely to be interested in trips to cities. Other correlations do not support this interpretation, however. For example, both types of religious participation are positively related to political knowledge, another indicator of exposure to the modern world. Religiosity, like *cargo* system participation, is negatively related to material style of life and income from other pursuits, indicating that these individuals are less likely to purchase consumer goods or work in nonagricultural pursuits than are people with a more secular orientation.

Summary

The religious system that exists in Puerto de las Piedras has undergone some significant changes in the past century. *Oratorios*, which once were widespread in El Puerto and Las Piedras, now have been reduced to a handful. The *cargo* system also is different from its counterparts in other Mesoamerican communities and appears to have changed considerably. The period of service for *cargueros* now is indefinite, and procedures for changing officials are very informal and unclear. In the recent past, *cargos* lasted for a year, as is true in most Mesoamerican communities. In addition, although there is a definite hierarchy of responsibility and decision making in the *cargo* system, there is no requirement that individuals pass through lower-level *cargos* before moving on to positions of more responsibility.

Despite the changes that have taken place, religion does play a very important role in the life of the community. In the *cargo* system alone, substantial amounts of money are spent each year. I have estimated the total amount spent by the *cargueros, mayordomos,* and *fiscales* to be about $885 each year. This figure neither includes the value of the food

---

xerts direct or indirect effects on two subsequent variables, thereby causing the subsequent variables to vary concomitantly (i.e., to be correlated). The latter applies in this case because X has direct and indirect effects on both Y and Z. More information on these different types of effects can be found in Hadden and DeWalt 1974.)

that is contributed nor the donations collected from households or from visitors to the *fiestas*.

Regardless of the money spent for *fiestas* and in other religious activities, religious participation is not significantly related to any of the adaptive strategies. Those who participate in the *cargo* system or who score high on religiosity are no more or less likely to adopt any of the adaptive strategies.

There did appear to be some tendency for individuals who scored high on the *cargo* system participation variable to score lower on the various measures of wealth. However, this pattern appears to be due more to the fact that those who participate in the system are Indians (who tend to be poorer) than to *cargo* service itself.

9

Alcohol use: causes and consequences

A substantial amount of literature on alcohol use in Mesoamerican communities shows the important role this behavior has in the social and ritual lives of the people. For this reason, it is important to demonstrate how the patterns of alcohol use in the *ejido* of Puerto de las Piedras are similar to, and different from, those reported for other communities. To facilitate comparison, I have included considerably more background and descriptive information on this aspect of life than I have in some other chapters. The ultimate objective of my discussion, however, is to determine how drinking behavior is related to decisions about which adaptive strategies are adopted.

A separate chapter concerning the relationship between alcohol use and the adaptive strategies was dictated by the oft-repeated claims by development agents and *ejidatarios* alike that drunkenness is endemic in the region. Many of these individuals also reported that heavy alcohol consumption is a major obstacle impeding economic development in the Valley of Temascalcingo. Several change agents, for example, told me that the peasants spent considerable sums of money on alcohol and that they often chose to get drunk instead of working on their fields. In contrast with these views, this chapter demonstrates that the relationship of alcohol use to the adaptive strategies is not completely negative and is more complex than might at first be imagined.

The reader who is simply interested in how drinking behavior affects the adoption of adaptive strategies may skip directly to the section entitled "Measuring alcohol use." Those who have a stronger interest in patterns of alcohol use are directed to the historical and comparative portions of the chapter as well.

Historical and ethnographic introduction

Intoxicating liquor was known to the indigenous peoples of Mesoamerica prior to the Spanish conquest. *Pulque*, fermented from the juice of the *maguey* plant, was a sacred beverage to the Aztecs. Apparently alcohol abuse as a social problem was not widespread. According to the Madsens,

Pulque was regarded as a divine gift from the goddess Mayahuel. To drink *pulque* was to honor the gods. Being holy and blessed, *pulque* was not to be abused. People were expected to become intoxicated on certain holy days, but otherwise public intoxication was forbidden and punished. The penalties ranged from public disgrace to death by stoning or beating. Drunkenness in secular contexts was rare except among the aged who were exempt from social sanctions prohibiting public intoxication. Excessive drinking was attributed to the misfortune of being born with the fate of becoming a drunkard. (1974:439)

This situation rapidly changed after the Conquest and the imposition of colonial government. Drunkenness among the Indian population became widespread, and the Spanish took a number of steps to try to curb the problem. Taverns and *pulquerías* (places that sell *pulque*) were prohibited in towns, the sale of liquor to Indians was forbidden, and harsh punishments were imposed on drunkards (Gibson 1964:150), all apparently without much success.

The severity of the problem of drunkenness during the entire colonial period cannot be overemphasized. Gibson, for example, concludes his classic work on *Aztecs Under Spanish Rule* as follows:

Indians in general yielded to Spanish demands, protesting only in rare instances of community resistance. The civilization became infused with Hispanic traits at many points, but it retained an essential Indian character, partly through the conviction of its members, partly because it was depressed to a social status so low that it was given no opportunities for change. One of the earliest and most persistent individual responses was drink. If our sources may be believed, few peoples in the whole of history were more prone to drunkenness than the Indians of the Spanish colony. (1964: 409)

One of the most consistent patterns to emerge from the ethnographic literature about village life in Mesoamerica is the very important role assumed by alcohol in ritual behavior. Alcohol in the ritual context has been described by ethnographers who have studied villages in all areas of Mesoamerica (e.g., Parsons 1936:203-4; Romney and Romney 1966: 68-70; Bunzel 1967:256; Nutini 1968:65; Vogt 1969:395-6; Pozas 1971; Kearney 1972:98; and Madsen and Madsen 1974:443). Vogt reports that in Zinacantán, "Just as the most important communication or transaction among the people . . . is accompanied by the drinking of rum, so must transactions between men and their supernaturals be accompanied by the proper consumption of this liquor" (1969:395-6). The Madsens claim that in Tecospa, "ritualized drinking within the

community performs an integrative function by reinforcing group solidarity and corporate identity" (1974:445). Drunkenness in these contexts was neither condemned nor ridiculed.

There is considerably less agreement about alcohol use and drunkenness outside the context of these ceremonial occasions. The Romneys,
in their study of Juxtlahuaca, state that "outside of the *fiesta* context,
the *barrio* men almost never drink *aguardiente* or other alcoholic beverages" (1966:69–70). The Madsens report finding much the same pattern in Tecospa and hold that drinking as a deviant behavior "simply
does not exist" (1974:443).

The situation in these villages contrasts markedly with other views of
the rural Mesoamerican scene. Fromm and Maccoby state that "alcoholism is a critical problem for the village" (1970:156); and Kearney's
analysis leads him to say that "as in much, if not most, of rural Mexico,
drunkenness is endemic in Ixtepeji" (1972:96). Bunzel shows how outsiders used the drunkenness of Indians in Chichicastenango to gain control over them in order to exploit their labor on plantations (1967:258–
9). Given the large amount of liquor consumed in ritual contexts, it is
difficult to believe that alcoholism does not become a problem. Ricardo
Pozas' moving account of *Juan, the Chamula* is an illustration of the
dilemma faced by a man who has served many *cargos* in his village and
sells liquor to help finance his obligations:

> My friends come to my house every day to buy *aguardiente*, and
> they always give me a drink. My son Lorenzo and my wife Do-
> minga keep telling me to stop drinking, but I can't. Sometimes I
> don't eat anything all day long. That's how my father died, from
> not eating.
>   But I don't want to die. I want to live. (1971:108)

The Madsens have attempted to cope with this diversity through an
analysis of drinking in *mestizo* communities versus that found in Indian
communities. Their general point is that drinking patterns change along
with the more general societal changes that take place during the process of acculturation. Thus "loss of community and identity opens the
door to drinking problems" (1974:449). This view does not seem to account for the apparent lack of problems with alcohol abuse in Tecospa
and Juxtlahuaca. Tecospa is only an hour's drive from Mexico City, and
most of the inhabitants are bilingual. The *barrio* studied by the Romneys
is actually part of a larger community composed primarily of Spanish-
speaking individuals. These communities, following the Madsen's hypothesis, should also be experiencing difficulties with drinking problems.

In part, some of the disagreement about the role of alcohol outside
the *fiesta* context may result from the kinds of observations made by

ethnographers, all of whom may have different research styles. For example, the ethnographer who spends quite a large portion of the evening gathering information from the local gang at the most popular bar in town will have quite different views on the prevalence of alcohol use than the ethnographer who spends every evening diligently typing notes.

There is no doubt that in addition to whatever integrative functions it may perform, drinking is associated with considerable friction and violence in many parts of Mexico (as well as elsewhere). All recent homicides in the *municipio* of Temascalcingo, for example, were preceded by drinking bouts. Romanucci Ross (1973:136–8), too, felt that drinking was involved in many of the acts of violence in the community that she studied. In addition to its role in violence, alcoholism also has some very serious effects on health. A recent Mexican report showed that alcoholism, malnutrition, and death from cirrhosis of the liver are all linked and are a serious problem. The alcohol is apparently not only damaging in itself but also satisfies the individual's appetite. The resulting malnutrition increases the danger of cirrhosis (*Excelsior* 8 June 1973:19A).

The drinking behavior of people in the *ejido* of Puerto de las Piedras and the Temascalcingo region will be described in the following sections. I will try to emphasize both the positive, integrative functions that might be served by consuming alcohol as well as its more negative, disruptive aspects.

Types of alcohol consumed

By far the most popular alcoholic beverage consumed in the Temascalcingo region and in the *ejido* is *pulque*. *Pulque* is fermented from the juice (*agua miel* or honey water) of the *maguey* (Agave). This beverage can be made easily by any of the inhabitants of the community who own or can buy a plant that is ready to be tapped. Just before the *maguey* is to flower (when it is seven to ten years old), the heart of the plant is cut open and cleaned. Then, for a period of several weeks, a hollow gourd can be inserted into the opening and the *agua miel* sucked out. The juice is then put into a barrel and allowed to ferment for several days.

A considerable amount of mythology has grown up about *pulque* among the people of the region. A number of the *ejidatarios* in El Puerto told me that carrying along a quantity of *pulque* enabled them to stand up well to the rigors of hard work in the fields. They reported that they could work all day without eating as long as they had a little

pulque. Informants also told me that *pulque* is one of the recommended foods for nursing mothers; a glass with every meal will help to ensure
that the mother has enough milk for the baby. *Pulque* is also reported
to be a "hot" food in the folk categorization of foods. Although hot
and cold foods are supposed to be kept in balance, in Temascalcingo
hot foods are not considered to be as potentially dangerous as cold
ones. Finally, one of the schoolteachers in Temascalcingo stated, only
half-jokingly, that *pulque* was responsible for the large number of
children in Mexican families. He reported that he had not fathered a
child in four or five years, a fact he attributed to a lessening of sexual
interest. When he began having a glass of *pulque* in the evening before
going to bed, he reported that his sexual activity increased, and soon his
wife had another child.

There are many houses in El Puerto, Las Piedras and El Jardín where
pulque can be bought. Some of these are established businesses (*pulquerías*) that almost always have *pulque* and that pay taxes to the *municipio* and the state. Other individuals often have *pulque* to sell illegally,
and yet others will only sell *pulque* when they have a *maguey* plant that
has reached the age when it will bear its precious liquid. In communities
farther from Temascalcingo, the usual means of advertising that a house
has *pulque* for sale is to fly a white handkerchief on a tall pole or stick.
I never saw this method of advertising used in El Puerto, Las Piedras, or
El Jardín, however. I attribute this fact to the communities' locations
close to Temascalcingo, for those selling the *pulque* illicitly would be
easy to catch and prosecute.

Because the majority of places that sell *pulque* are doing so illegally,
it is difficult to get an accurate count of all of the places in which the
beverage can be bought. In El Puerto alone, I heard of six *pulquerías*
during the course of my research, probably only a small fraction of the
real total. These ranged from some aboveboard, legal operations to an
old widow who made and sold *pulque* sporadically as one means of supporting herself. The price of *pulque* was a fairly uniform 1.20 *pesos* per
liter (about ten cents) in 1973.

Beer is becoming more popular in some settings. Small stores (*tiendas* or *miscelaneas*) in each community sell beer. The cheaper beers sell
for as little as 1.50 *pesos* for a small (approximately eight-ounce) bottle.
Temascalcingo now has two beer distributors who market the produce
of two of the largest breweries in the country. In addition, distributors
of other brands also send weekly shipments to Temascalcingo.

Beer has not come close to supplanting *pulque* as the favorite beverage of the *ejidatarios*. Some *ejidatarios* will drink a beer or two if they

happen to be in one of the *tiendas* or when they pass by a bar in Temascalcingo. However, at least one *ejidataria* preferred a beer or two with eggs for breakfast.

Brandy, rum, and tequila are the most popular hard liquors consumed in the region. However, consumption of these is limited almost exclusively to people in Temascalcingo. Occasionally one of the *ejidatarios* will drink one of these types of liquor in a bar in Temascalcingo, but few have probably ever purchased a bottle.

Places in which alcohol is consumed

Most of the *pulque* consumed in Puerto de las Piedras is drunk in the home. Little children can often be seen on the paths of the community, carrying pottery jars containing *pulque*. Many families drink *pulque* with every meal, much as wine is a part of the meal in some European countries. Consumption is usually limited to a liter or two for the adults. Children may or may not drink a little. Some individuals, however, do drink to the point of inebriation at home. Others who have begun a drinking bout elsewhere continue to drink when they reach home.

Some individuals carry *pulque* along with them as they go to work in the fields or the quarry, and various informants reported that the *pulque* not only quenches their thirst but also gives them the sustenance they need to work hard all day without food. Harvest time is a period of very heavy *pulque* consumption. Whole families go out to harvest the corn, and many of them carry food and large jars of *pulque* with them for picnics in the fields. The prospect of newly harvested corn and perhaps a little extra cash make these gay occasions. The *remolques* that haul corn from the fields to the houses are also useful for carrying inebriated men and women home from the fields. Persons who have become too drunk to walk can occasionally be seen tied to one of these carts.

Women's drinking is confined almost exclusively to the home, except during the harvest season. Some women may drink to the point of inebriation within the home; but they are still expected to be able to care for the children, animals, and food preparation tasks. Although I never heard any specific cultural rule prohibiting women from drinking outside the context of the home, this seemed to be the norm. The norm apparently does not apply to old women and widows, however. Some of the women who sell *tortillas* in the Temascalcingo plaza each day, for example, can occasionally be seen staggering toward home with jugs of *pulque* in their hands. Heavy drinking among these older women who are unburdened by the many duties of younger women, is not criticized.

Males often go together to drink in the *pulquerías*. In fact, I had difficulty interviewing a number of males because they rarely were home. They might go off to work in the fields, stop at home to drop off their tools, and then not appear at home again until late at night. Occasionally, a few men will go into Temascalcingo to drink in a bar or *pulquería*. Drinking groups in a bar or *pulquería* may be quite large. It is rare, however, to see more than two or three men walking home together. I never saw large groups of inebriated men walking the streets or paths.

Sunday, market day in Temascalcingo, is a favorite occasion for drinking among the people of Puerto de las Piedras and the other communities in the region. The triple problem of widespread drunkenness, crime, and violence on Sunday market days prompted the government of the state of Mexico to enact a law in 1973 requiring that bars and *pulquerías* be closed from late Saturday until Monday morning. In radio broadcasts, the reasons for closing the bars and *pulquerías* were elaborated: (1) many acts of violence and crime occurred as a result of the widespread drunkenness on Sundays; and (2) the *campesinos* and other poor in the state could thereby be discouraged from wasting their very limited resources in drinking sprees. Carloads of state police patrolling different communities ensured that local authorities were enforcing the law.

Coupled with levying very high taxes on bars and *pulquerías* (600 *pesos* a month for bars), the new law immediately resulted in the closing of one very popular bar in town as well as a number of *pulquerías*. The owners of these establishments reported that they could no longer make a profit for the greater part of their business had been on Sundays. In addition, the five or more vendors of *pulque* who set up in the market on Sundays also were put out of business.

Despite the closing of bars and *pulquerías* and the ban against selling alcohol on Sundays, there is still a considerable amount of drunkenness on market day. One informant reported that *pulque* now was just a little bit more difficult to find. A number of establishments in Temascalcingo set up back rooms where they continued to sell *pulque*. After a number of very stiff fines against offending establishments, however, most of these back rooms also closed down, except perhaps for preferred and trusted customers. The result has been an upsurge in business for entrepreneurial *pulquería* owners in the *barrios* and outlying communities who are willing to take the risk and sell illegally on Sundays. Because they are situated a little farther away from the authorities in Temascalcingo, they may remain successful for a while. The current *municipio* government, however, has enforced the law vigorously. In any event, the decentralization of drinking has undoubtedly contributed to a decrease in fights and other violence in the region. Municipal authorities reported that they have had fewer problems with drunks since the law was passed.

The other favorite occasions for drinking remain untouched by the new law. During *fiestas,* individuals from surrounding communities pour into the community holding the celebration to join in the festivities. There is always plenty of *pulque* and beer available. An important part of the market associated with the *fiestas* involves individuals who set up large awnings to house a bar. In the larger *fiestas,* some of these portable bars even set up tables and chairs and have *mariachis* (bands) to entertain the patrons. In the largest *fiesta* of the year in Temascalcingo, the beer distributors themselves have the largest and most elaborate stands to sell their products. Those who sell *pulque* are more modest in their efforts: the stand may consist of nothing more than a barrel of *pulque* and a number of *jarritos* (mugs).

Liquor, as I indicated earlier in this chapter, plays an important ritual role in the *fiestas* of most rural Mexican communities; but this is not the case with celebrations that take place in Puerto de las Piedras. On one hand, liquor is not permitted in the church or at the ceremonial meals during the *fiestas.* On the other hand, other nearby communities such as San Martín do serve *pulque* with the ceremonial meals. Inebriation of the *cargueros* is common at these times.

Much drinking certainly occurs during the *fiestas* in El Puerto. This drinking, however, takes place within the context of the more secular aspects of the festivities and plays no role in the ritual. Despite the bar on drinking in the church, abstinence from alcohol is neither prescribed for nor practiced by the *cargueros.*

Alcohol is also consumed during *fiestas* attending major life events - baptisms, confirmations, marriages, housewarmings, and so forth. Wealthier families even in Puerto de las Piedras may serve beer, and perhaps brandy and rum, along with *pulque* to heighten the spirits of those helping to celebrate these occasions. Poorer families usually limit their liquor expenditures to *pulque.* Considerable sums of money are often spent on these occasions. In addition to liquor, a *mole* (turkey and/o chicken in a chocolate and chile sauce) is almost always part of a family celebration.

In summary, liquor consumption is not limited to *fiestas* and market days, as Bunzel (1940) reports is the case in Chichicastenango. That is although a definite cultural pattern encourages drinking during *fiestas* market days, and family celebrations, drunkenness also takes place apart from these occasions. Also, unlike Chichicastenango, drinking is not limited to public occasions in the company of others but also may occur in the solitude of individual homes. Liquor is not a part of the ritual carried out in Puerto de las Piedras and, in fact, is explicitly excluded from religious occasions. Perhaps as a result, the formalities that are observed even in secular drinking by the people of Chamula (Bunzel 1940) do not exist among the *ejidatarios* of Puerto de las Piedras. However, there is much more raising of glasses and offering of toasts, especially during family celebrations, than occurs at a cocktail party in the United States.

Behavior exhibited during alcohol use

It is very difficult to generalize about the behavior exhibited by individuals who are inebriated. Instead of offering generalizations, I will describe certain behavior patterns that, although not typical, do give an idea of the behavior range of people who become drunk in Puerto de las Piedras.

Some anthropologists have placed considerable emphasis upon the socially integrative function of drinking in Mesoamerican communities (Bunzel 1940; Romney and Romney 1966; and Madsen and Madsen 1974). In Chamula, the *barrio* of Juxtlahuaca, and Tecospa, drinking within prescribed social contexts is supposedly valued in the culture and is not negatively defined. In Puerto de las Piedras, although drinking does have some role in terms of social integration, many of my informants indicated that it was also the cause of many problems. Several of the *ejidatarios* and most of the change agents told me that widespread drunkenness was one of the primary reasons for the lack of economic development in the region. One younger *ejidatario* told me: "For this [drunkenness] many *ejidatarios* never make any progress and they stay poor. They get drunk and sell their corn. They gather their harvest and go to get drunk; they feel they no longer have to work and so do nothing but drink *pulque.*"

Drunkenness was often cited as the reason why some of the *ejidatarios* rent their lands. One man reported that he could rent a hectare of land from some individuals for as little as one hundred *pesos* (eight dollars) if they needed money to continue a drinking spree. In talking with some informants, I sometimes got the impression that the majority of the *ejidatarios* were drunkards who were renting their land. When I pressed for specific names and instances, it turned out that very few individuals exhibited this behavior. Some individuals are drunkards who rent their lands; it is not a prevalent practice but does exist.

Inebriated persons also may become involved in fights. Occasionally a murder results from these fights. I heard of very few instances o fighting among the *ejidatarios* of Puerto de las Piedras, however, an never received a report of homicide committed by an *ejidatario*. Surli ness among drunks was more prevalent in Temascalcingo. Some *ejidata rios* were more demanding and stubborn when drunk, however. On individual began to stop by my house frequently when he was drunk and would demand loans, handouts, and more alcohol. If any of his de mands were not met, he would become very unruly. I expressed my concern to other members of the community, who promised that they would talk with this person when he was sober and "could understand." When he was subjected to this sort of informal social pressure, he im mediately stopped coming to the house when he was drunk.

As in our own culture, certain individuals use alcohol as a lubricant for social interaction. One *ejidatario* was very friendly but shy in an swering my questions. One evening, quite unexpectedly, he and a friend dropped by my house after a drinking spree. In contrast with the surli ness of the individual just mentioned, these two men were very friend ly. The man who had previously been quite shy told me that he wanted to sing some songs for me. While I taped, he sang a number of songs, in cluding two in Otomí that his father had taught him. A few days later he apologized for his behavior even though it was very friendly and had been appreciated.

An antisocial behavior that occasionally results from the excessive use of alcohol is wife beating. I heard reports of a number of cases in which a man beat his wife. Sometimes this behavior resulted in the man being imprisoned in Temascalcingo for a few days. Apparently, such in cidents do not lead to the dissolution of the marriage. One woman whose husband beat her regularly reported that she also believed that he had given her children *mal de ojo* (evil eye), which accounted for so many of them dying. Even though her husband drank heavily, beat her, and in her eyes was responsible for the deaths of some of her children, there was no danger of the marriage dissolving.

Wife beating by drunk husbands was by no means universal in the villages. Most men never physically abused their wives when drunk. A number of my informants, in fact, stated that only cowards beat their wives. Another informant said that he believed that those men who regularly drank heavily were less likely to hit their spouse. He said that these men could handle the alcohol, in contrast with the men who got drunk only occasionally and might have a tendency toward violence on those few occasions when they were inebriated.

One of the more common results of drunken sprees was the loss of work days. Monday mornings were especially likely to be lost by those who woke up *crudo* (hungover). The men who worked in the quarry institutionalized the Monday morning hangover and simply defined it as a day on which they would not work. On one occasion during 1973, an important *ejidal* meeting was called for 10:00 A.M. Monday morning. At the appointed hour, only six *ejidatarios* were present. The meeting did not start until 1:00 P.M. when enough *ejidatarios* (about thirty) had finally arrived.

The loss of work days by significant numbers of the population must be put into cultural and economic perspective, however. In an agricultural society such as that of Puerto de las Piedras, it is not necessary to work in the fields every day. Estimates of work days per year by individuals in the region were made by Plan Lerma. According to their figures, the agriculturalists spent only 156 days per year cultivating their fields. The quarry workers also have schedules that allow considerable leisure for drinking. They work on a contract basis. Thus as long as they meet their obligations for delivering the stone (which they seem to do successfully), the hours they spend working in the quarry can be relatively flexible.

Those individuals who work for merchants in Temascalcingo or in other wage labor have schedules that are less flexible than those of the agriculturalists and the stoneworkers. Although these men do sometimes miss a day or two of work because of drinking, I never heard of a villager losing a job because of frequent absence from work. Quite possibly, there is a selection process taking place. Individuals who are able to keep their drinking and work schedules from overlapping maintain their employment. Those who don't control their drinking lose their jobs and have to seek some employment that does not require a fixed schedule.

These findings should not be interpreted as meaning that there are no social and economic costs incurred because of alcohol use in Puerto de las Piedras. Many families drink a liter or two of *pulque* with their meals. A liter cost 1.20 *pesos* (about ten cents) in 1973. If a family bought only two liters of *pulque* per day, the total cost for the week would be 16.80 *pesos* ($1.35). Weekly costs for many families are, of course, much higher, for a person might drink six to eight liters when getting drunk. However, even the 16.80-*peso* figure can give us some idea of the economic impact of drinking. Data collected by Kathleen DeWalt indicate that the median amount of money spent on food per week by the families of *ejidatarios* is 53.75 *pesos* ($4.30). Thus many families spend from 20 to 25 percent as much on *pulque* as they do on food and other beverages. (See Table 6.8 for estimates of *pulque* costs in relation to other expenditures for two families.)

Because *pulque* consumption is so ubiquitous and can comprise such a large proportion of the family food budget, it is interesting to see how much of a nutritional contribution *pulque* makes. Table 9.1 gives the approximate nutritional contents of one-*peso* worth of *pulque* compared to one-*peso* worth of various other common foods. The total of the various nutrients that a normal male would need each day are given at the bottom of the table. It is easy to see that the major contribution that *pulque* makes to the diet is vitamin C. Only one-*peso* worth of *pulque* supplies all the vitamin C that a person would need in a day. Aside from vitamin C, one-*peso* worth of the other foods listed in the table seem to be a much better buy from a nutritional standpoint. *Pulque* does provide a fairly large number of calories (385) for one *peso*, a fact that probably accounts for the *ejidatarios'* observation that they can work long hours in the fields with only *pulque* to sustain them. Even in the case of calories, though, both *tortillas* and beans provide more value per *peso*.

Measuring alcohol use

The measurement of alcohol use among the *ejidatarios* was impossible to accomplish with questions on an interview schedule. Like Fromm and Maccoby (1970:158), I found that the *ejidatarios* and their spouses were markedly unreliable in their reports about the amount of alcohol consumed. Almost all of the families reported drinking moderate quantities of *pulque* (usually one, two, or three liters per day) at meals, but responses to questions about total quantity consumed during an average week or the frequency of drunkenness were not as candid. Fromm and Maccoby, apparently in consultation with older villagers (1970:159), divided the 209 males of the village they studied into five categories based upon the frequency of drinking. They felt that they had enough participant observation in the village to perform these ratings, including the classification of thirty men as "alcoholics."

The procedure that I used for measuring alcohol use was similar to that used for measuring wealth (Chapter 6). Cards containing the names of the *ejidatarios* were presented to three informants. They were asked to compare each individual to every other individual in terms of the frequency of alcohol use. In practice, this procedure results in informants sorting individuals into a number of categories. The number of categories are determined by the informants, as are the criteria for the sorting

Table 9.1. *Nutritional value per peso of various common foods and beverages*

Food	Money	Quantity	Calories	Protein	Calcium	Iron	Thiamine	Riboflavin	Niacin	Vitamin C	Vitamin A
Pulque	1 *peso* (1.20/l.)*	.833 l.	358.2	3.33	99.96	5.83	.17	.17	3.33	50.0	0.00
Tortillas	1 *peso* (1.50/kg.)	.667 kg.	1,507.4	39.35	720.36	16.81	1.13	.53	6.00	0.0	10.67
Beans	1 *peso* (7/kg.)	.143 kg.	477.6	27.46	326.04	7.92	.89	.20	2.43	0.0	0.00
Milk (boiled)	1 *peso* (1.20/l.)	455 l.	286.0	15.93	514.15	1.41	.18	.41	.46	0.0	75.99
Tomatoes	1 *peso* (4/kg.)	.250 kg.	27.5	1.50	147.50	.90	.18	.13	2.00	42.5	1,266.75
Beef (lean)	1 *peso* (20/kg.)	.050 kg.	56.5	10.70	8.00	2.00	.04	.10	1.45	0.0	0.00
Male requirements per day (65 kg. weight)			2,750.0	83.00	500.00	10.00	1.40	1.70	24.80	50.0	1,000.00

Note: All food values in this table are taken from *Valor Nutritivo de los Alimentos Mexicanos* (Hernandez, Chávez, and Bourges 1974). The values were all converted to reflect what one *peso* could buy in the Temascalcingo market in 1973. Calories, proteins, etc. are all calculated to show the amount in one-*peso* worth of that food or drink.

*The numbers in parentheses refer to the average price of a commodity in Temascalcingo in 1973. Thus *pulque* was about 1.20 *pesos* per liter, lean beef was about 20 *pesos* per kilogram, and so on.

Table 9.2. *Informant ratings of alcohol use*

Pedro		Vicente		Felipe	
Classification	Number	Classification	Number	Classification	Number
Drunkards	15	Drunkards	15	Drunkards	1
Drunk once a week	16			Heavier drinkers	37
Occasional drunks	10	Occasional drunks	9		
		Meal-time drinkers	18	Light drinkers	24
Abstainers	20	Abstainers	19		

Note: Approximate correspondence among the categories is indicated by line position.

operation. The three informants who rated the other *ejidatarios* in terms of alcohol use were the same three who performed the wealth ratings (see Chapter 6 for descriptive information about the informants).

Pedro sorted individuals into four categories on the frequency of alcohol use (see Table 9.2). He identified twenty male and female *ejidatarios* as rarely drinking. He noted that some of these "abstainers" drank a glass or two of *pulque* at mealtimes but rarely or never became inebriated. Ten individuals were put into a category that Pedro defined as "occasional drunks." These individuals, like most others in the community, drank *pulque* with meals; but they also sometimes became drunk, especially during festive occasions. Pedro characterized the sixteen individuals in the third category as "drunk once a week." These were primarily individuals who would become inebriated only on Sundays and during *fiestas*. According to Pedro, those in the fourth group were the "drunkards"; these individuals became inebriated whenever they had the money or the opportunity. He indicated that the fifteen individuals in this category would rather drink than eat; and, in fact, he reported that they often did so. He cited two *ejidatarios* who had died in the previous three months from alcohol-related physical problems.

Although he also used four categories, the basis of Vicente's ratings of alcohol use differed somewhat from Pedro's. Vicente's first and fourth categories corresponded closely with Pedro's. In the lowest category were those individuals who almost never drank, the "abstainers." Vicente put nineteen people in this category. He also characterized as "drunkards" the fifteen people he put into the fourth category. Vicente's second category was reserved for individuals he reported as drinking only with meals and rarely, if ever, becoming inebriated. There were eighteen

Table 9.3. *Gamma correlations among the informant ratings of alcohol use*

	Pedro's ratings	Vicente's ratings
Vicente's ratings	.85	
Felipe's ratings	.88	.82

people whose drinking habits corresponded to this description. The third category used by Vicente was reserved for people who might not drink with meals but, most importantly, became inebriated every once in a while (*a vez en cuando*). Nine individuals fit this description.

Felipe's ratings of alcohol use included only three categories. The third category included two notorious drunkards (only one of whom was in the sample used here). Otherwise, Felipe made a very simple distinction between those who occasionally became inebriated and those who rarely or never drank to the point of intoxication. He reported that twenty-four individuals were "light drinkers" or abstained completely and that thirty-seven individuals were "heavier drinkers."

I have indicated in Table 9.2 the approximate correspondence among the classifications that the three informants used. I did not attempt to use this ordering in constructing the final "alcohol use" score, however. Instead, I simply treated each of the informant classification systems as a scale – Pedro and Vicente used a four-point scale; Felipe used a three-point scale. Despite this arbitrary procedure, the correlations among the informant ratings are fairly high. Table 9.3 shows that the gamma correlations range from .82 (between Vicente and Felipe) to .88 (between Pedro and Felipe). I feel that this level of agreement is acceptable.

The final alcohol use score for all of the individuals in the sample was created by simply adding all three informant ratings. The scores on this variable ranged from a low of 3, which indicated very little use of alcohol, to a high of 11, indicating very heavy drinking behavior. The mean of this variable was 6.39, and the standard deviation was 2.60. Thus despite the statements by some individuals to the effect that almost every *ejidatario* is a drunkard, we see that there is really considerable intracommunity variation in alcohol use.

Relationships between alcohol and the adaptive strategies

Serious drinking problems can easily lead to economic hardships for the family and/or debilitating illness. There is no question that drinking

Table 9.4. *Correlations of the adaptive strategies with alcohol use*

Adaptive strategies	Alcohol use
Forage production	.11
Animal improvement	−.28*
Tractor use	.46**
Fertilizer use	.18
Subsistence agriculture	−.22*

Note: * indicates $p < .05$ and ** indicates $p < .01$.

problems exist among some *ejidatarios*, although the problems are not as widespread as many people both within and outside the *ejido* believe.

Because of the drain on economic resources, I predicted that high alcohol use scores would be negatively associated with investment in the costly adaptive strategies of animal improvement and forage production. Corn can be grown with smaller capital investments and also permits frequent loss of time in the fields. I hypothesized that fertilizer use would be positively associated with alcohol use. The case with tractor use is more complicated. Although tractors can be used for valid reasons in hopes of increasing production, a tractor can also be hired to enable the drunkard to spend less time in the fields and more time in the *pulqueria*. Therefore, I predicted a small positive relationship between alcohol use and tractor use. Finally, I expected to find a positive relationship between alcohol use and the subsistence agriculture adaptive strategy. Individuals with high alcohol use scores probably would not be inclined to invest in any of the new adaptive strategies.

Table 9.4 shows the relationship between alcohol use and the five adaptive strategies. On the whole, the relationships reported in the table do not support the predictions that I made. Animal improvement is negatively related to alcohol use, as predicted. Fertilizer use is positively related to alcohol use, but the correlation is not statistically significant. Contrary to my expectations, there is a small positive correlation between the use of alcohol and forage production and a negative correlation with subsistence agriculture. Tractor use has a high positive correlation with alcohol use.

The finding that alcohol use is negatively associated with the animal improvement strategy is understandable for several reasons. First, individuals with a propensity to drink may be unable to accumulate the cash needed in order to buy animals. Second, animals are a fairly liquid form of investment. They are a form of savings account (see Chapter 6) that can be readily sold when the need arises. Heavy drinkers may recognize that they are apt to sell animals when they need money to continue a drinking spree and so do not invest cash to improve their livestock. Finally, unlike the fields, animals require daily care. They cannot be ignored for several days at a time while a person is drinking heavily or recovering from a drinking bout.

Apart from the tendency for alcohol use to be negatively associated with animal improvement, drinking behavior does not inhibit investment in the new adaptive strategies. This point is surprising in light of the complaints by development agents and others that most *ejidatarios* drink so much that they are not interested in the new opportunities now available. As Table 9.4 shows, people with high alcohol use scores are more likely than others to invest in forage production, tractor use, and fertilizer use and somewhat less likely to continue the subsistence agriculture adaptive strategy.

The fairly high positive correlation between alcohol use and tractor use has some interesting implications. Development agents have been vigorous in encouraging the use of tractors and other mechanical equipment to improve agriculture in the region. Those individuals who have been most likely to take advantage of these opportunities so far, however, have been the heavy drinkers. Although I believe that the direction of causation is such that heavier drinkers tend to use tractors, it is disturbing to think of what might happen if there is some feedback operating in this relationhip. That is, if those who use tractors then have more time to drink and begin doing so more heavily than before, the result of increasing mechanization could be to exacerbate alcohol-related problems in the community. I have no evidence that this feedback has occurred, and alcohol problems certainly preceded the introduction of tractors. However, I believe that the goal of mechanizing agriculture in this region should be reexamined for this and several other reasons. These will be discussed in the final chapter.

Alcohol use in relation to the other independent variables

Fromm and Maccoby found a number of interesting relationships with alcohol use in the Mexican village that they studied. One of their findings was that there was a higher incidence ($r = .29$) of drinking problems among older individuals of the community than among the young (1970:160). As we see in Table 9.5, this finding is also supported in the present study. The correlation is, like that found by Fromm and Maccoby, small but statistically significant. There is a greater likelihood that older individuals will drink more than younger people.[32]

Table 9.5. *Correlations of independent variables with alcohol use*

Independent variables	Alcohol use	Independent variables	Alcohol use
Land quantity–quality	.27*	*Cargo* system participation	.09
Distance from land	−.09	Education	−.31*
Wealth ratings	−.02	Political knowledge	−.09
Material style of life	.03	Mass media exposure	−.35**
Value of agric. equipment	−.05	Change agent contact	−.07
Cash value of animals	.06	Cosmopolitanism	−.18
Income from other pursuits	.05	Age	.25*
Ejido leadership	.02	Number of people in house	.16
Community leadership	.01	Indian language ability	.24*
Religion	.05	Times worked elsewhere	−.07

Note: * indicates $p < .05$ and ** indicates $p < .01$.

Fromm and Maccoby found only a small relationship ($r = -.15$) between alcohol use and education. Although their informants who were better educated were less likely to be heavy drinkers, the relationship was not found to be statistically significant. In Puerto de las Piedras, however, there is a stronger negative relationship between education and alcohol use. *Ejidatarios* who have had more education are less likely to be heavy drinkers.

Indian language ability is associated with high alcohol use. In other Mesoamerican communities this finding could be attributed to the Indians' greater participation in the *cargo* system, in which there is considerable ceremonial drinking. However, there is no ceremonial use of alcohol in Puerto de las Piedras. In fact, Table 9.5 shows that alcohol use and *cargo* system participation are only slightly related. Another possibility is that those who are "more Indian" are simply older members of the community. Because the age variable is related to heavy drinking, it is relevant to ask whether the relationship between Indian language ability and alcohol use disappears when we control for age. The first order partial shows that the relationship between Indian language ability and alcohol use is .23 ($p < .05$) even when controlling for age.[33] Thus neither *cargo* system participation nor age help to account for the correlation observed between Indian language ability and alcohol use.

One other possible explanation for this relationship is not testable with the data that I have collected. It may be that Indians drink more than *mestizos* because they are suffering from a "loss of community and identity," an idea advanced by the Madsens (1974:449). Although their hypothesis does not seem to account for intercommunity variability, it may have some validity for explaining differences within communities such as Puerto de las Piedras.

Heavy drinking may result in the expenditure of a significant portion of a family's income. Thus I expected that alcohol use would be negatively correlated with the various measures of wealth. Table 9.5, however, shows that there is no relationship between the wealth variables and drinking.

The finding that alcohol use is not negatively related to the wealth variables is surprising. This anomaly could be explained partially by one of the other correlations in Table 9.5, however. There is a positive correlation between land quality–quantity and alcohol use, which means that those individuals who have more or better land resources are able to drink more than those who have less land. This relationship is similar to a finding that Fromm and Maccoby also reported as surprising (1970: 175). They found that there was a much higher percentage of alcoholism among *ejidatarios* – those who had land and thus a fairly secure economic situation – than among the non-*ejidatarios* – those who had to seek wage labor opportunities. They concluded: "It now becomes clearer why the *ejidatario* is more vulnerable to alcoholism. It is not because his character structure is different from that of the non-*ejidatario*, but because the economic system offers a bait which appeals especially to those *ejidatarios* who are psychologically more vulnerable to alcoholism" (1970:177). The finding that individuals with more land tend to be heavier drinkers is limited only to *ejidatarios*. It would be interesting to determine whether non-*ejidatarios* in Puerto de las Piedras show this pattern of drinking less than the *ejidatarios*.

In any event, I would argue that the weight of the evidence supports the position that among the people of the community studied by Fromm and Maccoby and among the *ejidatarios* of Puerto de las Piedras, economic security has enabled those with a propensity to drink to do so. The previously reported finding that no relationship exists between the wealth variables and alcohol use may simply reflect the fact that heavy drinking is diminishing the wealth of people in spite of the fact that they have more and/or better land.

We can also investigate this hypothesis by using a path analysis (see Chapter 8). The simple three-variable path model (Table 9.6) shows that there is some support for this hypothesis. When land quantity–quality is a part of the model, the path coefficient between alcohol use and the wealth ratings is increased somewhat above the correlation coefficient. The summary of effects below the path model provides the

Table 9.6. *Path analysis of land quality, alcohol use, and wealth ratings*

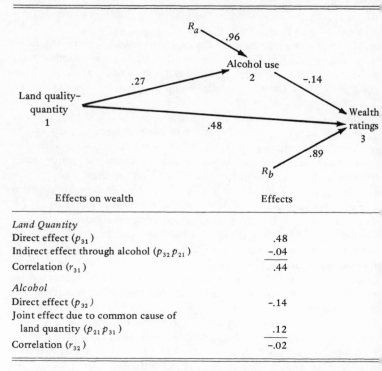

Effects on wealth	Effects
Land Quantity	
Direct effect (p_{31})	.48
Indirect effect through alcohol ($p_{32}p_{21}$)	−.04
Correlation (r_{31})	.44
Alcohol	
Direct effect (p_{32})	−.14
Joint effect due to common cause of land quantity ($p_{21}p_{31}$)	.12
Correlation (r_{32})	−.02

reason – there is a positive joint effect on the relationship between alcohol use and the wealth ratings due to the fact that land quantity–quality has a fairly high positive relationship with both. This joint effect is nearly equal in magnitude to the direct effect of alcohol use on the wealth ratings; thus the correlation is almost zero. In addition, the indirect effect of land quantity–quality through alcohol use is negative. What this all means is that heavy drinking behavior does inhibit the accumulation of wealth somewhat and slightly alters (in a downward direction) the fairly substantial positive relationship between land quantity–quality and the wealth ratings.

A number of empirical examples can be cited to illustrate the effects of this relationship. At least two grandsons of Naciano, the "founding father" of the *ejido*, received and continue to hold some very good parcels of land. Nevertheless, both of these men and their families are very poor. Other *ejidatarios* reported that because of their propensity to drink, these men have lost the fortune in animals that their grandfather and father had managed to accumulate. Another example is Guadalupe, who was also reported to be a heavy drinker. Now old, this man lives in a simple house with few material possessions, rents and gives his land *a medias*, and is constantly searching for odd jobs to support himself. One of my informants once shook his head and said that, at one time, Guadalupe's family was one of the wealthiest in the *ejido* and that they had owned a large herd of cattle.

I should not leave the reader with the impression that loss of family fortunes because of excessive drinking is epidemic. The path model in Table 9.6 suggests that it is not all that common. Nonetheless, the *ejidatarios* cite a number of prominent examples that suggest it is not a rare occurrence. The Mexican law that prohibits the sale of *ejido* lands has undoubtedly saved a number of *ejidatarios* from starvation. The fact that they retain their land irrespective of their drinking habits has made economic catastrophe less of a worry among the *ejidatarios* than would be the case in other cultural or social settings.

Finally, I should note that there is a statistically significant negative correlation between alcohol use and mass media exposure. Alcohol use is also negatively correlated with political knowledge, change agent contact, cosmopolitanism, and education. Although most of these correlations are not statistically significant, there seems to be a tendency for individuals who are more articulated to modern Mexico to be lighter drinkers.

Summary

Patterns of alcohol use were discussed in this chapter. Although change agents and some *ejidatarios* claimed that most individuals in the *ejido* were drunkards, a wide range of variation in alcohol use was found. Most of my expectations about correlates of alcohol use were not confirmed. Alcohol use was not, for example, negatively related to any of the new adaptive strategies except animal improvement. Otherwise, those who drank heavily seemed to be more likely to adopt adaptive strategies than those with low alcohol use scores. Those with high alcohol use scores are most likely to adopt the tractor use adaptive strategy. I suggested that mechanization of the region could be leading to greater use of alcohol, although at present it is more likely that those who drink choose to use tractors because of their drinking habits.

In my discussion of the correlations of alcohol use with the other independent variables, I found that those who are more educated, younger, and more articulated to modern Mexico tend not to drink as much. I also found that Indian language ability is positively correlated with alcohol use but was unable to provide a satisfactory explanation for this relationship. Finally, it also appears that those who have more and better land are more likely to be heavy drinkers. These individuals have their *ejido* lands as a secure economic base, and this fact may allow them to drink heavily without having to worry about economic catastrophe.

10

Information access

The importance of communication in the process of economic development cannot be overemphasized. The study of innovation diffusion explicitly emphasizes communication because it involves research on how certain items or ideas come to be passed from one group to another. Much of what has been called "modernization" has basically involved the passage of technology from the developed to the developing nations.

Communication has a number of different aspects, and in this chapter I will explore some of the most common means by which information is transmitted in the Temascalcingo region. I will begin with a discussion of education. This subject is important not only because of the specific bits of information it may pass along (e.g., about the way fertilizer works, good health practices, or the nutritional contents of foods) but also because it provides basic skills needed for the transmission of information in other ways. Knowing how to read provides individuals with access to magazines, newspapers, technical manuals, and other printed materials. Knowing how to write allows individuals to put down requests in writing or to communicate with people who may be inaccessible except through written messages. Being able to do basic arithmetic can help individuals to interact more knowledgeably in the marketplace and perhaps can lead to more informed decisions having to do with costs, benefits, and allocations of scarce resources.

Another avenue of access to information is through the mass media – radio, television, movies, newspapers, magazines, and so on. All of these types of media are present in the Temascalcingo region. The connection between mass media exposure and modernization is well established (Rogers 1969; Lerner 1958), but the causal sequence is in some doubt. Development leads to a growth in mass media and their spread over a wider area. Thus mass media expansion is certainly a result of modernization. The more relevant question for our purposes, however, is whether an exposure to mass media can in some way facilitate development in a rural region such as Temascalcingo. That is, do mass media communicate information that is useful in modernization; do they lead individuals to become more modern in their attitudes, beliefs, and methods of coping with their natural and social environments?

Access to information can also be direct; it can be communicated in face-to-face interaction. Because the Temascalcingo region has seen many development agents come and go, change agent contact should be an important variable associated with the modernization of some individuals. Although change agent contact has been studied in a number of modernizing situations, it has not been found to be as strongly associated with modernization as might be expected (Rogers 1969:180).

A final indicator of information access that I will investigate is cosmopolitanism, the degree to which an individual is oriented outside his social system (Rogers 1969:52). Cosmopolitanism, as measured by the number of trips to larger towns and cities, is an indirect method of learning new ideas. Towns and cities, especially in developing countries, are more modern than rural areas. Rural dwellers who go to the city come into contact with elements of modernity and might carry some of these back home with them. Some items of information or technology brought back from the city thus may be implemented in rural areas.

This chapter shows that individuals who have more access to information do tend to choose some of the adaptive strategies more frequently than others. Although this pattern suggests that information access is important, it is difficult to tell if a simple increase in knowledgeability is affecting people's decisions. Information access is shown to be part of a group of interrelated characteristics. These include wealth and leadership as well as knowledgeability.

Education

Formal educational opportunities in rural areas throughout Mexico have been expanding at a rapid rate. Nowhere is this trend better illustrated than in the Valley of Temascalcingo. Before 1970, the schools in the villages outside Temascalcingo rarely had all six primary grades. There was only one *secundaria* (grades 7 through 9), and that was situated in Temascalcingo. The facilities in this school were few, the building run-down (it was razed in 1973), and the teachers poorly paid.

Recently there have been dramatic changes. School construction has taken place in almost every community. Most of the villages now have schools with all six primary grades. The federal government provides the construction materials and a few skilled workers to oversee construction. The community in which the school is to be built then provides the rest of the labor needed.

The school in El Puerto had all six primary grades for the first time in 1973. Two brand new classroom buildings were built to replace the old one-room schoolhouse, which had served for many years. Like many of the rural schools, the one in El Puerto is staffed primarily by teachers who have only completed the *secundaria* but who spend vacations and weekends attending the normal school in Atlacomulco. After four years of this exhausting schedule, these teachers are fully certified (*titulado*) and receive a fairly decent salary ($200 a month).

Some of the teachers now staffing the rapidly expanding network of primary schools are recent graduates of the *secundaria* in Temascalcingo built by the federal government in the late 1960s. Although it still lacks some needed facilities, the *secundaria* contains slide projectors, microscopes, laboratories, and many other teaching aids. A second *secundaria*, funded by the state government, offers afternoon classes (held in the federal *secundaria*) for those who work or could not meet the entrance requirements for the federal school. Thirty *pesos* per month tuition is charged at the state school while the federal school is free except for books, uniforms, and supplies. In 1973, the federal *secundaria* graduated ninety-two students, most of whom were from Temascalcingo.

Many parents of students in the *secundaria* have been working to establish a *preparatoria* (grades 10 through 12). By late 1973, construction was already under way, and there were hopes that it would be completed and that the federal government would provide teachers for the school year beginning in September 1974. A few students from Temascalcingo were commuting to the *preparatoria* in Atlacomulco.

The expanding educational facilities offer some hope for children of people who live in El Puerto, Las Piedras, El Jardín, and similar communities. Even before the primary school in El Puerto had all six grades, many children finished primary school by attending the *primaria* in Temascalcingo. A few families have also begun sending their children to the *secundaria*. This is a considerable burden, for although it is a federal school, there are expenses for uniforms (about 200 *pesos* per year), books (about 170 *pesos* per year), and supplies. In addition, parents have had to pay about 160 *pesos* per year to help defray the cost of the land on which the school is built and the construction costs. Expenses of forty to fifty dollars a year are very difficult for peasant families to bear, without even considering the lost income and/or labor a teen-ager could provide.

Only the wealthiest *ejidatarios* have been able to send their children on to the *preparatoria* or to the normal school. A few of Juan's children, for example, have graduated from the normal school and are now teachers. His brother, Vicente, now has a son in the normal school and another in the *preparatoria*. Vicente reported that it costs him about one-thousand *pesos* per month (including room and board) to support the son in the *preparatoria*. As it becomes possible to acquire a higher level of education within the valley, children of some of the poorer *ejidatari-os* may be able to scrape together the resources that will open up new opportunities for them.

Although higher education for their children has been out of the reach of most families in Puerto de las Piedras, education is nonetheless highly valued. Many fathers and mothers with whom I talked repeatedly stated that they hoped their children could learn in school so that they would have a better life. A particularly poignant example was my twenty-four-year-old field assistant, Pedro, who had only had three years of education. He is able to do simple arithmetic and reads and writes, although with some difficulty. He reported that he wanted both of his sons to go to the university so that they would not end up "a burro like me."

Another indication that education is important to people in the region is the fact that factional disputes within communities frequently are reflected in the schools, and separate schools are sometimes established by the rival factions. This separation is made possible because there are two types of schools, those funded by the federal government and those funded by the state government. In 1973 at least three communities in the region (Ojo de Agua, La Purísima, and San Juanico) had both types of schools. These were attended by children whose parents were on different sides of the factional disputes (see also DeWalt, Bee, and Pelto 1973:61–2).

Because the growth of educational facilities has been a recent phenomenon, education among the sample of *ejidatarios* has been very limited. Two-thirds of the sample had fewer than three years of schooling, including one-third who had never attended school. Even among those who spent a few years going to school, I was often told, "Yes, I attended school, but in those days our families could not feed us well. I went to school with a dull mind and didn't learn anything." Some of those who were illiterate did learn to read and write a little in the course of a government-sponsored adult education program that took place during the 1950s. These classes apparently had some success, although other *ejidatarios* reported attending but learning nothing.

The few individuals who did attend school for four, five, or six years (the maximum anyone in the sample had completed) had gone to school in Temascalcingo, for the school in El Puerto has only had these grades in very recent years. Those who seem to have received the best educations attended the seminary in which priests were once trained. These individuals later dropped out but apparently received a very good basic education during their years in the seminary. In this sample of *ejidatarios*, the mean number of years of education was only 2.87; and the standard deviation was 2.05. This low level of education indicates that the great majority of *ejidatarios* lack the ability to read, write, and do simple arithmetic.

Political knowledge

Another important aspect of information access is "political knowledge." Individuals who understand how their government operates and who know the appropriate leaders to ask for aid are in a position to move toward modernization. If these individuals also use their knowledge for the benefit of others in the region in which they live, then community development may also result.

Political knowledge and awareness in rural areas of Mexico were stimulated greatly by the events following the Revolution. The most important event in Mexican history in terms of making rural people aware of national politics was the land redistribution. The national government and the national party (Party of the Institutional Revolution) have received the support of a generation of *campesinos* because they redistributed the lands of the great estates. In the Valley of Temascalcingo, as elsewhere in rural Mexico, Lazaro Cárdenas is particularly revered. It was under his administration during the 1930s that the most lands were redistributed.

The national government has remained the most important in terms of development. State and local governments have little money; thus all significant programs come directly from the national government. The Party of the Institutional Revolution (PRI), the only party that has been in power since the Revolution, has continued to encourage the populace's dependence on the national government. Although there is no doubt that the presidential candidate of the PRI will win the election, he undertakes a rigorous campaign that takes him to all parts of the nation. His name appears on billboards and posters everywhere; the mountains are even dotted with his name spelled out with painted rocks. The result is that by the time of his election, almost all Mexicans know the name of the man who will lead them for the next six years.

The *ejidatarios'* political knowledge was measured by asking whether each individual in the sample knew the name of the president of the *municipio*, the district's representative in the federal legislature, the governor of the state, the president of Mexico, the president of the United States, and the names of the political parties of Mexico. These items formed a very satisfactory Guttman scale (see Table 10.1). The coefficient of reproducibility was .96, an acceptable level for Guttman scales.

Table 10.1. *Guttman scale of political knowledge*

Case no.	Scale type	I	II	III	IV	V	VI
5	0						
16	1	X					
19	1	X					
53	1	X					
62	1	X					
20	2	X	X				
22	2	X	X				
26	2	X	X				
27	2	X	X				
36	2	X	X				
41	2	X	X				
55	2	X	X				
34	3	X	0	X			
59	3	X	0	X			
6	3	X	X	X			
7	3	X	X	X			
21	3	X	X	X			
24	3	X	X	X			
25	3	X	X	X			
30	3	X	X	X			
31	3	X	X	X			
32	3	X	X	X			
44	3	X	X	X			
48	3	X	X	X			
50	3	X	X	X			
51	3	X	X	X			
61	3	X	X	X			
49	3	X	X	X			X
11	4	X	X	X	X		
12	4	X	X	X	X.		
13	4	X	X	X	X		
14	4	X	X	X	X		
38	4	X	X	X	X		
40	4	X	X	X	X		
42	4	X	X	X	X		
43	4	X	X	X	X		
54	4	X	X	X	X		
1	5	X	X	X	0	X	
10	5	X	X	X	0	X	
15	5	X	X	X	0	X	
35	5	X	X	X	0	X	

Table 10.1. (*cont.*)

Case no.	Scale type	I	II	III	IV	V	VI
52	5	X	X	X	0	X	
3	5	X	X	X	X	X	
9	5	X	X	X	X	X	
17	5	X	X	X	X	X	
2	6	X	X	X	X	0	X
39	6	X	X	X	X	0	X
18	6	X	X	X	X	X	X
33	6	X	X	X	X	X	X
58	6	X	X	X	X	X	X

Items: I President of the *municipio* IV District federal representative
II President of Mexico V Names of political parties in Mexico
III Governor of the state of VI President of the United States
Mexico

Coefficient of reproducibility: $1 - \dfrac{10}{300} = .96$

The two best-known items were the names of the president of the *municipio* (96 percent) and the president of Mexico (84 percent). The least-known items were the name of the president of the United States (12 percent) and the name of at least one of the political parties of Mexico (22 percent). The two middle items were the name of the governor of the state (75 percent) and the federal representative (33 percent). These statistics indicate that there is very widespread knowledge of the most important leader at the local level (municipal president) and at the national level (president of the republic), with slightly less recognition of the governor of the state. The name of the district representative was known to very few of the respondents. Surprisingly, although there was a fairly good knowledge of the names of leaders, only a handful of the *ejidatarios* knew the party they represented. The small parties of Mexico (PAN and PPS) were known by even fewer informants. The small number of individuals who knew the name of the president of the United States indicates a lack of awareness of international events.

Political knowledge scores ranged from a low of 0 (individuals who did not know any of the items) to a high of 6 (individuals who knew all of the items). The mean score was 3.38, and the standard deviation was 1.56.

Mass media exposure

The advent of cheap, transistor radios has meant that news travels rapidly even into areas reached only by footpath. Everett Rogers relates that President Kennedy's death in 1963 was common knowledge in an isolated Colombian village only an hour or two after it took place in Dallas (1969:1). Similarly, during 1973, I was occasionally drawn into conversations with store owners in Temascalcingo about the possibility of President Nixon being impeached. Newspapers printed in Mexico City in the morning reached Temascalcingo in early afternoon carrying Watergate headlines.

Radio remains the main media by which *ejidatarios* from Puerto de las Piedras remain in touch with world events. Almost 60 percent have a radio. Most of them pay fleeting, if any, attention to news stories and are more interested in the *ranchero* music. Stories about natural disasters or other "big news" do, of course, attract attention. The floods in the Bajío and the large earthquake in Orizaba in 1973 were discussed in the community. Whether they listen to the news or not, the *ejidatarios* listen to radio stations from places they may never visit – Mexico City, Monterrey, Guanajuato, and Spanish language stations from Los Angeles rebroadcast in Mexico.

The radio stations nearest to the region are in Atlacomulco and El Oro, both about twenty miles from Temascalcingo. Both of these stations primarily play the *ranchero* music that is popular among rural Mexicans; but both also disseminate information from government agencies about vaccination programs, visits of important leaders to the area, and other useful items of local interest. In addition, both carry commercials for fertilizers, insecticides, and herbicides, as well as advertisements for druggists, furniture stores, hotels, clothiers, and other merchants. Some of the merchants from Temascalcingo advertise their wares through these radio stations.

It is by no means clear whether any of the informational or commercial messages have an impact on the population. Perhaps the main impact is to make individuals aware of goods, services, and places that exist. Like Rogers (1969:101) in his study of Colombian peasants, I must note that listening to the radio is an indicator of mass media exposure. It says nothing about influence or internalization of what is being heard.

Radio is only one of the sources of mass media exposure. Television is becoming increasingly popular in the Temascalcingo region. Antennas can be seen on many *adobe* houses in Temascalcingo and other communities. Only a few *ejidatarios* in Puerto de las Piedras have television sets. However, some of the individuals who have a set occasionally allow friends and neighbors to watch a program or two. A woman who lives next to the church in El Puerto opens her house to any of the villagers who wish to watch programs in the evening. She charges fifty *centavos* (four cents an hour). Usually she has very few individuals who wish to see a program. The exception is when there is a championship or other important boxing match. Many men with whom I talked had received their only exposure to television in this way. Other respondents reported that the only time they ever watched television was when they visited relatives in Mexico City. However, forty-two percent of the *ejidatarios* had seen television at least once during the past year, and five *ejidatarios* owned a television set.

Movies are another medium to which the *ejidatarios* of Puerto de las Piedras have access. Every Saturday and Sunday there are 4:00 and 8:00 P.M. shows at the movie house on the main street of Temascalcingo. A sound truck makes the rounds of the neighboring villages advertising the attraction of the week. For approximately a half hour before each show it parks in front of the theater and blares out popular songs, which can be heard throughout Temascalcingo. Attractions usually consist of Mexican westerns, romances, horror movies, or the Mexican version of *Superman* played by a masked former wrestler. The vast majority of the clientele for these movies are teen-agers, who have little other form of entertainment around Temascalcingo. Older individuals rarely go to the movies. Only three of the sixty-two *ejidatarios* in the sample had attended a movie in the past year.

The final two forms of mass media available in the region are magazines (including comic books and *novelas*) and newspapers. A few of the more literate *ejidatarios* read a newspaper about once a week, and some others receive a church magazine once a month. Otherwise, the only materials read in the community were comic books and *novelas*. The majority of *ejidatarios* rarely read anything.

The final "mass media exposure" score was obtained by combining five variables – frequency of listening to radio, watching television, attending movies, reading a magazine, and reading a newspaper or book. In order to give equal weight to each of these, an individual's score on a variable was divided by the maximum score on that variable and then multiplied by ten. In this way, each variable was converted to a ten-point scale; and then the five scales were summed. Final mass media exposure scores ranged from a low of 0 (held by twelve individuals who had no exposure to any of the five forms of mass media) to a high of 37 (held by one individual). The mean score was 10.5, and the standard deviation was 9.2.

Change agent contact

As I indicated in Chapter 2, there has been a succession of planned change programs in the Valley of Temascalcingo. The technical experts who accompany these projects can be a source of useful information: That, in fact, is their function – to communicate helpful information to the people in the region. The lack of success experienced by so many programs is due in part to the inability of the change agents – those promoting development projects – to communicate with people whose life styles, beliefs, attitudes, resources, and background are so different from their own.

Nevertheless, some of the *ejidatarios* have had considerable contact with change agents who have been in the region. Those who serve as officers in the *ejido*, for example, are often the intermediaries with whom the change agents deal. Some of the more educated *ejidatarios* may even seek out technical personnel when they have a problem. Thus it is worth considering whether change agent contact has had any effect on which adaptive strategies are chosen.

This variable was measured by assigning one point to each contact an *ejidatario* reported having with a different change agent. Because adaptive strategies are fairly recent introductions, I only asked the *ejidatarios* about contacts with development personnel who have recently been in the region. These included change agents from Hydraulic Resources, Plan Lerma, Plan Maíz, the Department of Agriculture and Livestock of the State of Mexico (DAGEM), and the Banco Agropecuaria (the bank financing the dairy cooperatives). Some *ejidatarios* reported contacts with other individuals who could be considered change agents. One man's son, for example, had gone to an agricultural school where he learned a little bit about agricultural practices and pruning fruit trees. A number of other men had gone directly to talk with the governor about some problems they were having with development programs. Such contacts were also included when assigning points to *ejidatarios* for "change agent contact."

No attempt was made to differentiate the actual amount of contact each person had with a change agent. There is considerable variation in this area. One man, for example, traveled almost constantly with the agricultural engineer who was in charge of Plan Maíz. He undoubtedly learned more than the man who asked a Plan Lerma agent how to cure his sick horse. It would have been very difficult to determine the amount of contact in each case, however.

Seventy-two percent of the *ejidatarios* in the sample had never had any contact with a change agent. Two individuals had had contact with four change agents (this was the highest score). The mean score for all *ejidatarios* was only 0.64, and the standard deviation 1.19. The *ejidatarios,* for the most part, have had little change agent contact.

Cosmopolitanism

The final measure of information access was "cosmopolitanism," the amount of contact with cities. Travel within Mexico is greatly facilitated by the bus routes that reach even the smallest communities. Temascalcingo has benefited greatly by the road built during the 1930s to link the community with the road between El Oro and Atlacomulco. Atlacomulco is situated on one of the main highway arteries in Mexico that connects the cities of Querétaro and Toluca. Soon after the completion of the road to Temascalcingo, bus service was established; and the community gained easy access to the rest of Mexico.

The road between Temascalcingo and Atlacomulco is now completely paved, and bus service has steadily grown. Between 5:00 A.M. and 10:00 P.M. there is hourly bus service to Mexico City from Temascalcingo. Many of these are clean, modern second class buses (not air-conditioned or express, but with the number of stops fairly limited and restricted to certain types of cargo). Third class *guileros* – older buses, which stop anywhere and carry any type of cargo, including *guilos* (turkeys) – run less frequently between Temascalcingo and El Oro. On Sundays, these *guileros* carry shoppers to Temascalcingo from the small towns of the valley.

In contrast with the period before the road and the buses, when only the wealthiest individuals traveled to Mexico City, now even the poorest peasants can make the trip. The fact that there is hourly bus service between Temascalcingo (a *municipio* of only 33,000) and Mexico City indicates that many do.

Trips to larger towns and cities provide many different types of ideas. One man who spent some time working in Mexico City began going to Protestant services with one of his relatives. He reported that he was impressed with the religion and found that he liked reading the Bible, something he said he was not encouraged to do by the Catholic church. Nevertheless, back in his home community, he has remained a Catholic and is now a *carguero*. Another man was working in Mexico City and saw a dance group called the *Concheros* (Stone 1975). He started a group in his own village, and they are currently the most frequently requested dancers at *fiestas* in the region. A third man worked for many years on a chicken farm near Toluca. Now back in the valley and working his *ejido*, he has dreams of starting his own farm. Because he has worked with modern methods of raising chickens, he feels that he will be able to be successful.

Although some people have received ideas for innovations during their travels, others may simply acquire a desire for the modern life style of the city. The city is a showcase of consumer goods. The wealthier merchants in Temascalcingo may be able to acquire these goods immediately; the *ejidatarios* may only acquire a desire for them.

The urban world can also lead the peasant to think about different occupations. His own community, while exhibiting some occupational specialization, does not offer the array that is found in the city. Many occupations in the city are available only to those who have had a good deal of schooling. This fact can be translated into a person placing a high value upon education for his or her children. Although the process by which cosmopolitanism leads to increased modernization is not well understood, a variety of researchers including Redfield (1941), Lerner (1958), and Rogers (1969) have shown that the two are related.

Cosmopolitanism was measured by an *ejidatario's* number of trips in the previous year to three urban centers – Mexico City, Toluca (the state capital), and Atlacomulco and/or El Oro. Obviously, the degree of cosmopolitanism in these centers is not equal; it probably varies with the size of the community. In order to take this factor into account, the number of trips made was multiplied by the distance from Temascalcingo to each of these centers. The distance is correlated somewhat with the size of the community; El Oro and Atlacomulco are only about twenty miles away and are fairly small (3,000 and 5,000 respectively), Toluca is about seventy-five miles away and has 115,000 people, and Mexico City is about one hundred miles away with a population of about 10 million.

Scores of "cosmopolitanism" ranged from a low of 0 (five individuals who had not left the *municipio* during the previous year) to a high of 7,275 (an individual who went to Mexico City about once a week and to Toluca and Atlacomulco frequently). The mean score was 747, and the standard deviation was 1,230.

Because these scores do not give much of an impression of the amount of travel actually taking place, I will include a few descriptive statistics on trips to the urban centers (see Table 10.2). Over 70 percent of the male *ejidatarios* (no data were collected for women on this variable) had been to Mexico City during the past year. Most of them have relatives whom they visit occasionally in Mexico City; others work there for varying periods during the year. The *ejidatarios* travel less frequently to Toluca (the state capital), El Oro (the district headquarters), and Atlacomulco (headquarters for a number of government agencies

Table 10.2. *Number of trips to cities by male ejidatarios (1973)*

Frequency of trips in past year	Number of respondents going to		
	Mexico City	Toluca	Atlacomulco or El Oro
Never	15	31	26
1 to 10 times	31	16	14
More than 10	7	6	13

and site of the *preparatoria* and normal school, as well as a market center) than they do to Mexico City.

Interrelationships among the information access variables

Because all of these variables – education, political knowledge, mass media exposure, change agent contact, and cosmopolitanism – measure various aspects of what I call information access, I expected that correlations among all of them would be positive. As we see in Table 10.3, this turns out to be true. Although not all of the correlations are statistically significant, they are all positive.

Mass media exposure is significantly correlated with each of the other four variables; change agent contact and political knowledge both have significant correlations with three of the other four variables. Education and cosmopolitanism have significant correlations with only two of the other four. It seems that one can conclude that all of these variables are measuring various aspects of what I call access to outside sources of information.

Relationships of information access variables to the adaptive strategies

I predicted that all of the information access variables would be positively correlated with the adoption of the forage production and the animal improvement strategies. Both of these strategies require more technical knowledge than either of the other two new strategies. Therefore, those who have had more access to outside information should be in a better position to adopt these adaptive strategies. Because neither fertilizer use nor tractor use require much technical knowledge, I predicted that they should have relationships of close to zero with the information access variables. Finally, I expected that people with high

Table 10.3. *Interrelationships of the information access variables*

	Education	Political knowledge	Mass media exposure	Change agent contact	Cosmopolitanism
Education	—				
Political knowledge	.28*	—			
Mass media exposure	.43**	.44**	—		
Change agent contact	.22	.44**	.26*	—	
Cosmopolitanism	.17	.10	.28*	.27*	—

Note: * indicates $p < .05$ and ** indicates $p < .01$.

Table 10.4. *Correlations of information access variables and adaptive strategies*

	Education	Political knowledge	Mass media exposure	Cosmopolitanism	Change agent contact
Forage production	.43**	.44**	.42**	.06	.39**
Animal improvement	.16	.23	.36**	.50**	.27*
Tractor use	-.23*	-.02	.03	.17	.07
Fertilizer use	-.07	-.02	-.04	.10	-.02
Subsistence agriculture	-.16	-.30*	-.38**	-.40**	-.35**

Note: * indicates $p < .05$ and ** indicates $p < .01$.

information access would adopt at least some of the new adaptive strategies, and thus the information access variables would be negatively correlated with subsistence agriculture.

In Table 10.4, these predictions are shown to be correct. There are positive relationships between adoption of both forage production and animal improvement and all of the access to information items. Only the correlation between cosmopolitanism and forage production is low and not statistically significant. Animal improvement does not have a significant correlation with either education or political knowledge. Mass media exposure has high positive correlations with both forage production and animal improvement. The same is true for change agent contact.

The prediction of no correlation between tractor use and fertilizer use is confirmed. Only the negative relationship between education and tractor use for which I can offer no explanation, is statistically significant. All of the other relationships are very close to zero. My prediction that all of the information access variables would be negatively correlated with subsistence agriculture is also confirmed: All of these relationships are statistically significant, except for the correlation with education.

I feel that these results support my belief that the animal improvement and forage production adaptive strategies require greater technological expertise. Those individuals who have had more access to outside information, or who have been willing to seek this information, are adopting forage production and various techniques for animal improvement. The use of tractors or fertilizer does not require much technical expertise, and so outside information has not been crucial in determining who will adopt these adaptive strategies. Because little expertise is needed for these strategies (especially in view of the fact that tractors are hired rather than operated by the *ejidatarios*), the demonstration effect and communications among the people of the region have probably been the most crucial factors in their spread.

Relationships with other independent variables

Table 10.5 shows the correlations between the information access variables and the other independent variables. I have already discussed many of the correlations in Chapters 4 through 9 and so here will only mention briefly some of the more interesting results.

We should first note the tendency for the information access items to be correlated with the wealth variables. Although some of the correlations are not statistically significant, all are positive. The wealth rat-

Table 10.5. *Correlations of independent variables with information access variables*

	Education	Political knowledge	Mass media exposure	Change agent contact	Cosmopolitanism
Land quantity-quality	.29*	.38**	.31*	.41**	.11
Distance from land	-.14	.03	-.19	.13	.42**
Wealth ratings	.40**	.37**	.41**	.46**	.27*
Material style of life	.19	.15	.54**	.40**	.29*
Value of agric. equip.	.34**	.38**	.33**	.64**	.06
Cash value of animals	.19	.15	.22	.16	.10
Income from other pursuits	.23*	.20	.41**	.34**	.52**
Ejido leadership	.16	.33**	.18	.70**	.09
Community leadership	.17	.23	.13	.44**	.10
Cargo system participation	-.22	-.15	-.14	-.02	-.26*
Religiosity	-.01	.23	-.07	.00	-.23*
Alcohol use	-.31*	-.09	-.35**	-.07	-.18
Age	-.10	-.23	-.30*	.14	.10
No. of people in house	-.22	-.27*	-.15	-.03	-.02
Indian language ability	-.25*	-.24*	-.33**	-.24*	-.44**

Note: * indicates $p < .05$ and ** indicates $p < .01$.

ings are positively correlated with all of the information access items. The same is true of value of agricultural equipment, except for the correlation with cosmopolitanism. The correlation between material style of life and mass media exposure is interesting, for this high correlation may mean that those who are exposed to the many commercial messages carried by the mass media buy more consumer goods. However, the material style of life scale includes items on owning a radio and a television set. Individuals who own these items should also have high scores on mass media exposure.

There are also positive correlations between the access to information variables and the two types of leadership – *ejido* and community. These correlations, however, are not as high as we might expect. Only change agent contact is correlated significantly with the two types of leadership. This finding, and the fact that change agent contact is correlated significantly with four of the five wealth variables, supports my general impression that change agents have dealt primarily with the wealthy and the leaders, who are usually the same individuals.

Indian language ability is negatively correlated with all of the information access variables. Those who are "more Indian" have lower levels of education, less mass media exposure, less political knowledge, less cosmopolitanism, and less change agent contact.

Finally, I should note that four of the five correlations between information access items and the "land quantity–quality" index are positive and statistically significant. This relationship is probably due to the tendency for individuals who are wealthy and leaders to accumulate land through questionable means (see Chapters 6 and 7). The results in Table 10.5 suggest that information access is one more element in the favor of these individuals.

Summary

The information access variables investigated in this chapter – education, political knowledge, mass media exposure, change agent contact, and cosmopolitanism – were all found to be positively related to one another and to have predictable relationships with other independent and dependent variables. Information access seems to be particularly important in determining whether people will choose to adopt the forage production and animal improvement adaptive strategies. There are positive correlations between these two adaptive strategies and all of the information access variables. Forage production and animal improvement both appear to require general knowledgeability, and this fact is reflected in the positive correlations that were found.

Those individuals who have high scores on the information access variables are much more likely to adopt one of the new adaptive strategies rather than continue to practice subsistence agriculture. In fact, there are negative correlations between all of the information access variables and subsistence agriculture.

Information access appears to be part of a general group of traits that includes wealth and leadership as well as knowledgeability. That is, individuals who have high information access are also likely to be wealthy, to be leaders, and to have high land quantity–quality scores. The causal linkages between these different sets of variables will be explored at greater length in Chapter 12. Finally, Indian language ability was found to be negatively related to all of the information access items.

11

Some other independent variables

have discussed several important aspects of life in Puerto de las Piedras n the preceding chapters. Although my primary purpose was to determine how these aspects of life affected the adaptive strategies identified n Chapter 4, these are topics that would be found in any traditional thnographic study. In this chapter, I will discuss a number of other variables that I felt were of potential importance in explaining the changes aking place in the *ejido*. However, unlike those discussed in preceding hapters, these do not fit easily under a single heading. Therefore, I ave chosen to present a potpourri in this chapter. The variables that re considered are "age," "household composition," "Indian language bility," and "number of times worked elsewhere."

Age

n many other studies of modernization, "age" has been found to be an mportant variable (e.g., Rogers 1969; Pollnac and Robbins 1972). In eneral, it has been found that older individuals tend to be much more onservative than those who are younger.

The mean age of the *ejidatarios* is forty-five years. This figure is high-r than the mean age of all the household heads in the villages. Many ndividuals who received land during the redistribution are still alive. 3ecause the number of people who have land rights in the *ejido* has re-nained fixed in accordance with agrarian reform laws, the only way ounger people can gain access to land is by inheriting it from a close elative or possibly by applying for lands left without an heir. The rapid opulation increase since the 1930s has far outstripped the number of jido plots, and so most young household heads do not have access to and. The result is that the *ejidatarios*, as a group, are older than the eneral population. *Ejidatarios* ranged in age from twenty-three to eventy-four.

I expected that there would be little correlation between age and the lifferent adaptive strategies. One factor that would help to eliminate lifferences in innovativeness between older and younger *ejidatarios* is hat many older landholders have sons who help them with their agri-

Table 11.1. *Correlations of the adaptive strategies with "other variables*

	Age	Number of people in house	Indian language ability	Times work elsewhere
Forage production	.07	.02	-.31**	-.03
Animal improvement	.01	.13	-.32**	-.03
Tractor use	.01	-.02	.03	-.08
Fertilizer use	.10	.05	.13	.26*
Subsistence agriculture	-.09	-.09	.24*	-.04

Note: * indicates $p < .05$ and ** indicates $p < .01$.

cultural tasks and decisions. That is, the *ejidatario* may not be the onl
(or even the primary) decision maker with regard to land use. Tabl
11.1 shows the correlations between age and the adaptive strategie
Age is not significantly related, either positively or negatively, to an
strategy.

Table 11.2 contains the correlations between age and the other inde
pendent variables. Although most of these have been discussed in prev
ous chapters, I will review some of the more interesting relationship
Age is positively correlated with *ejido* leadership, community leadershi
and *cargo* system participation. This pattern seems to indicate that, a
in other Mesoamerican communities, older people are important i
both civil and religious leadership positions. However, scores on th
leadership variables are based upon the total number of positions a pe
son has held throughout his life. Older individuals have been availabl
for service for a longer period of time and would be expected to hav
higher scores on the civil and religious leadership variables. If older pec
ple really were much more involved in leadership, we would expec
these correlations to be higher. In recent times, younger people increa
ingly have been selected for leadership positions. The *primer delegad*
of Las Piedras in 1973 was in his early twenties, and in 1970 the *prime
delegado* of El Puerto was only twenty-one. None of the officials in im
portant civil or religious posts in 1973 was over sixty.

Age is negatively correlated with two information access variable
mass media exposure and political knowledge. Although both of thes
correlations are fairly low, the relationships seem to be part of the pr
viously mentioned tendency for young people to have greater educatio
and greater knowledgeability about "more modern" things.

Older individuals also tend to drink more than do younger *ejidatar*

Table 11.2. *Correlations of independent variables with "other variables"*

	Age	Number of people in house	Indian language ability	Times worked elsewhere
Land quantity–quality	.05	−.07	−.18	.03
Distance from land	.22	.10	−.11	.24*
Wealth ratings	.11	.05	−.34**	.04
Material style of life	.05	.13	−.40**	−.15
Value of agric. equip.	.11	−.20	−.05	−.02
Cash value of animals	.06	−.04	−.22	−.11
Income from other pursuits	.01	.09	−.40**	.11
Ejido leadership	.28*	−.02	−.05	−.23*
Community leadership	.44**	−.02	−.24*	−.12
Cargo system participation	.24*	−.20	.53**	.10
Religiosity	.05	−.12	.34**	.08
Alcohol use	.25*	.16	.24*	−.07
Education	−.10	−.22	−.24*	−.12
Political knowledge	−.23	−.27*	−.27*	.01
Mass media exposure	−.30*	−.15	−.34**	.04
Change agent contact	.14	−.03	−.22	.02
Cosmopolitanism	.10	−.02	−.40**	.18
Age	—	−.01	.21	.01
No. of people in house		—	−.29*	.10
Indian language ability			—	−.03

Note: * indicates $p < .05$ and ** indicates $p < .01$.

use. There is a significant relationship between age and alcohol use; but, again, the magnitude of the correlation is not large. It may be that young people recognize the potentially negative effects of alcohol use and therefore drink less frequently than older *ejidatarios*. On the other hand, drinking may increase with age as individuals suffer more disappointments and frustrations and realize little improvement in their economic position.

Household composition

The household is the basic production and consumption unit among the *ejidatarios*. Nevertheless, there is considerable variation in household composition, as we see in Table 11.3. Twenty-nine percent of the

Table 11.3. *Household composition of ejidatarios*

Family type	No.	Percentage
Nuclear (husband, wife, unmarried children)	33	54
Matrifocal (woman and unmarried children)	5	8
Grand-matrifocal (grandmother and grandchildren)	2	3
Single persons living alone	4	6
Extended		
Patrilocal (married couple live with husband's parents)	6	10
Matrilocal (married couple live with wife's parents)	5	8
Stem (one or more parents of a spouse live with husband, wife, and their unmarried children)	5	8
Fraternal (male siblings live together with their wives and children)	2	3
Totals	62	100

households are comprised of some type of extended family. About th
same number of married couples live with the wife's family (matriloca
residence) as with the husband's family (patrilocal residence). Als
common are families that take in a parent of the husband or wife (usu
ally when they are widows or widowers). The nuclear family of hus
band, wife, and unmarried children is the most common arrangement
although only slightly more than half (54 percent) the households ar
of this type.

Household composition might be expected to affect the lives o
people in Puerto de las Piedras in a number of different ways. In farm
ing areas where large amounts of land are held, it is adaptive to hav
large families so that labor does not have to be purchased. The shift o
the majority of the population from rural to urban areas in the Unite
States was accompanied by a substantial decline in the number of chi
dren per family. In the city, the large family was not as economically
adaptive as it was on the farm. Alexander Chayanov, an economist, di
an intriguing analysis of the relationship in Russia between family siz
and age and the amount of land sown by that family. He showed that a
a family grew larger and began to have children reaching maturity, the
amount of land sown by the family became greater. As the large fami
lies broke up, creating a series of smaller families (i.e., the children be

an to marry and have families of their own), large farms gradually be-
ame smaller (Chayanov 1925:67-8, quoted in Kerblay 1971).

The situations in the United States and Russia were very different
rom one another and from that found in Mexico. The land base of
amily farms in the United States was obviously much larger than in the
jido of Puerto de las Piedras. Chayanov's analysis works best for areas
with low population densities; surplus land must be available for pur-
hase and cultivation. The Valley of Temascalcingo is densely popu-
ated, and land holdings are fixed by the dictates of the *ejido* system
although as I show in Chapter 5, some people have expanded their
ands). The little private land that is available is very expensive and out
•f reach of all but the wealthiest individuals. Nevertheless, it is impor-
ant to determine whether household composition is of major signifi-
:ance in the *ejido* of Puerto de las Piedras, especially in relation to the
daptive strategies.

The first variable that I used to reflect household composition was
he "number of people in the house." An average of 6.1 people live in
he *ejidatarios'* houses. A few households contained a single person,
whereas one house had 15 people living there. Because the amount of
and held by the *ejidatarios* is very small and does not require a large
amount of labor input, I did not expect the number of people in the
house to be important with regard to either cultivation techniques or
he adaptive strategies. Table 11.1 shows that this variable is not signifi-
:antly correlated with any of the adaptive strategies.

The relationship between number of people in the house and the
wealth variables was difficult to predict. On one hand, families with
many young children are obviously at a disadvantage, for they have
ew productive workers and many mouths to feed. On the other hand,
amilies with many grown children who still live in the house can improve their position if these children bring an income into the house.
The Temascalcingo region is notably short of employment opportunities,
however. Thus many children leave for Mexico City as soon as they are
ible. In fact, 72 percent of the households had at least one child living
n Mexico City. Some send money back home to their families, but
others do not. Although a comprehensive discussion of the many fac-
ors involved cannot be undertaken here, I predicted that there would
e no (or perhaps a slightly negative) relationship between family size
and the wealth variables. In Table 11.2, we see that there is no signifi-
:ant correlation between family size and the wealth variables – material
style of life, value of agricultural equipment, cash value of animals,
wealth ratings, and income from other pursuits.

The only significant correlations between number of people in the

house and other independent variables are somewhat surprising. Ther
is a negative relationship between family size and political knowledg
and also a smaller negative relationship with education. It might b
tempting to speculate that those who have more education and mor
political knowledge are making attempts to limit family size. I do no
believe that this is the case, but I have no alternative explanation

The other significant correlation is with Indian language ability
Those people who are "more Indian" have smaller households. Thi
relationship is also difficult to explain, but perhaps those household
that are "more Indian" have had a higher infant mortality rate.

I also wanted to investigate what the absence of a male household
head means to a family. The common pattern in the *ejido* is for land t
be passed on to the widow when a man dies. At present many widow
have *ejidal* land in Puerto de las Piedras. Some of these widows hav
children who cultivate the fields and give a portion of each year's cro
to their mother. Other women, however, cannot find anyone to tak
responsibility for the land. One woman, who is only in her forties, ha
taken over the cultivation of the land herself. Although she does no
produce a large amount of corn, she is supporting herself, an agin
mother, and three children. However, the most common pattern fo
widows who have no sons or sons-in-law to take responsibility for thei
fields is to enter into a sharecropping arrangement each year. Under thi
arrangement the proceeds are shared equally by the landowner and th
sharecroppper. Usually, sharecroppers are only interested in larger
more productive fields. Thus widows often have some small plots or les
fertile lands that remain uncultivated year after year. This land ha
sometimes been taken away by unscrupulous *ejido* leaders. Household
with female heads do have significantly lower land quality-quantit
scores (see Table 11.4).

Table 11.4 also includes several other comparisons between female
headed households and those households that have an adult male pres
ent. Female-headed households produce less than half as much corn a
households that have a male head. Part of this difference results becaus
widows are not able to get someone to cultivate all of their lands
Another reason is that sharecropped lands generally do not receive th
same quality of care; the sharecropper is interested in producing cor
but with a minimum of both capital and labor input.

Elderly widows have considerable trouble making ends meet an
most depend upon sons or daughters to help them along. Widows d
have various means of helping to support themselves. One woman get
her meals and five *pesos* (forty cents) a day for washing clothes for a
wealthy family. Others sell handmade *tortillas* door-to-door or in th

Table 11.4. *A comparison of female-headed households to male-headed households on selected variables*

	Household type	
	Female-headed households	Male-headed households
Land quantity–quality	$\overline{X}$ = 3.49	$\overline{X}$ = 5.29**
	s.d. = .98	s.d. = 2.46
Corn production	$\overline{X}$ = 33.50	$\overline{X}$ = 71.72**
	s.d. = 25.80	s.d. = 53.17
Wealth ratings	$\overline{X}$ = 5.37	$\overline{X}$ = 7.39
	s.d. = 3.34	s.d. = 2.75
Forage production	$\overline{X}$ = -.46	$\overline{X}$ = .07**
	s.d. = .11	s.d. = .95
Animal improvement	$\overline{X}$ = -.09	$\overline{X}$ = .01
	s.d. = 1.04	s.d. = .89
Tractor use	$\overline{X}$ = -.60	$\overline{X}$ = .09**
	s.d. = .13	s.d. = .94
Fertilizer use	$\overline{X}$ = -.31	$\overline{X}$ = .05
	s.d. = .79	s.d. = .78

Note: In this table $\overline{X}$ stands for the arithmetic mean, s.d. is the standard deviation, and ** indicates that the t-test of the difference between the means of female-headed households and male-headed households is statistically significant ($p < .01$).

market in Temascalcingo. One woman belongs to a wealthy family; and she has been able to establish a fairly large store where she sells beer, soda, corn, soap, cigarettes, candy, and other odds and ends. Although most of the *ejidatarios* are extremely poor (as indicated by their low mean scores on the wealth ratings), they are fortunate in having land from which they can obtain at least a major portion of their subsistence needs. A woman left without a husband and without land rights has an even more difficult life.

It was easy to predict that female-headed households would have lower scores than male-headed households on all of the new adaptive strategies (see Table 11.4). They are almost all poor, old, and do not have anyone to take responsibility for cultivating their land and caring for their animals. I believe that they primarily want to avoid the economic risks, the problems in obtaining credit, the uncertainty of planting new crops, and all of the other pitfalls involved in investing in the new opportunities. Their desire is simply to obtain enough corn to

Table 11.5. *Monolingual speakers of Indian languages in the municipio of Temascalcingo*

	1878*	1930*	1960†	197C
Total of Indian language speakers	4585	5872	3313	124
Otomí	?	728	298	21
Mazahua	?	5144	3015	103

*From Quezada 1972:19.
†Dirección General de Estadística 1963, 1971.

support themselves while they live out the remaining years of the lives.

Indian language ability

The Temascalcingo region is one of ethnic diversity, as I mentioned i Chapter 2. Otomí and Mazahua Indians are present along with *mestizo* who are the dominant and majority ethnic group.

Classifying a person as a member of one of these ethnic groups is nc an easy task, as is true in communities throughout Mesoamerica (see th discussion in De La Fuente 1968:76–96). Biological or somatic diffe. ences do not easily distinguish the Indian from the *mestizo* or Ladinc Usually we have to resort to cultural differences to define who is or i not an Indian. In some areas, a distinctive local costume identifies eth nic groups. In other areas, language differences seem to be the distir guishing feature. It is important to recognize, however, that people ca cross the ethnic barrier if they so desire. They may have to adopt a di ferent mode of dress, learn to speak fluent Spanish, and drop typicall Indian behaviors, but "passing" is fairly easy and is very common (D La Fuente 1968:82). In each generation, many Mexican Indians cros over into *mestizo* status; and the spread of Castillianization program into previously isolated rural regions will undoubtedly increase thi trend.

The Temascalcingo region provides a good illustration of the growin number of individuals who are born to Indian parents but become *mest. zos*. Table 11.5 contains census data for the *municipio* of Temascalcing on the numbers of people who speak only Otomí or Mazahua. Sinc 1930 there has been a rapid decline in the number of monolingua Indians despite the very large increase in total population.

Puerto de las Piedras illustrates quite clearly the kinds of changes that have been taking place throughout the region. Older informants report that around the time the *ejido* was formed (1933), El Puerto and Las Piedras were both "very Mazahua" communities. The women wore traditional *quexquemitls* (woolen capes) like those now seen in communities that have retained a stronger Indian tradition (e.g., Ojo de Agua, San Diego, and Santa Rosa). The men wore *calzones blancos* (white pants) and white shirts, the traditional peasant dress of much of Mexico. By 1973, clothing styles had changed completely. None of the men wore *calzones blancos,* and the only woman who wore a *quexquemitl* was the daughter of a wealthy *mestizo.*

Some traditional customs that are normally associated with (but not limited to) Indians still survive in the communities. Many individuals believe in the efficacy of herbs for curing; believe in witches; talk about such diseases as *bilis* (caused by excessive anger), *aire* (effects of bad air), and *susto* (fright); and participate in the *cargo* system. Mazahua is still spoken by many of the people; but except among a few elderly inhabitants, Spanish is the preferred language for daily interaction.

However, ethnic distinctions do play an important part in social and economic relationships both outside and within the community. A number of *mestizo* families have lived in El Puerto, for example, for many years. One man told me that his father had moved to El Puerto *"para hacer negocio con los indios"* (to do business with the Indians). Other *mestizo* families lived in communities associated with the *haciendas.* They worked for the *hacendado,* and one man served as a foreman for the workers on the great estate. When the *ejido* was formed, these individuals were among those who received land. Because they had such skills as fluency in Spanish and perhaps a little schooling, some of these people became leaders of the *ejido.* Many also continued to do business with the Indians.

Thus I felt that the amount of "Indian-ness" would be a potentially important variable. If *mestizos* had taken control of many of the economic activities within the *ejido* in the early days, then I felt that the social and economic advantages they acquired would probably be passed on to their sons and daughters. These would take the form of more schooling, more business connections, greater facility in economic wheeling and dealing, and greater inherited wealth. With these attributes, such individuals would still hold a great advantage over the Mazahua, who have only recently begun to become *mestizo.*

"Indian language ability" was measured solely by informants' reports about their own language capability and that of their parents. One point was given to each informant if he reported that he could under-

Table 11.6. *Proportions of scores on Indian language ability*

Indian language ability score	No.	Percentage
0	12	22.6
1	9	17.0
2	14	26.4
3	10	18.9
4	8	15.1

Note: $\overline{X} = 1.87$; s.d. = 1.37.

stand but not speak Mazahua, two points if he could speak Mazahua, three points if his mother or father spoke Mazahua, and four points if both parents spoke Mazahua.[34] Long-term *mestizos* (i.e., people who had no ability in Mazahua and whose parents also spoke only Spanish) received a score of zero on Indian language ability. Table 11.6 shows the proportions of individuals who received each of the scores on this scale. Although the scale reflects exposure to Indian language, I believe that it can be taken as a general indicator of "Indian-ness."

Because forage production and animal improvement require substantial capital as well as a fair degree of knowledge, I predicted that Indian language ability would be negatively associated with both of these adaptive strategies. I had no reason to expect that people with more Indian language ability would be more or less disposed to the adoption of fertilizer use or tractor use than other, "more *mestizo*" individuals. Thus no correlation was predicted. I did expect that Indians would be less oriented toward new adaptive strategies and predicted a positive correlation between Indian language ability and traditional subsistence agriculture. Table 11.1 shows that these predictions are confirmed. Indian language ability is negatively related to both forage production and animal improvement and is positively related to subsistence agriculture. As predicted, no significant correlation was found with tractor use or fertilizer use.

As I have just indicated, forage production and animal improvement both require capital and knowledge. One reason why I expected Indian language ability to be negatively correlated with these strategies was my impression that Indians have less capital and less "modern" knowledge. Table 11.2 shows that Indian language ability is negatively related to all of the wealth and information access variables. In particular, Indians score lower on wealth ratings, material style of life, income from other pursuits, education, political knowledge, mass media exposure, and cosmopolitanism.

These correlations indicate that there are clear differentials between Indians and *mestizos* in terms of wealth and access to information. *Mestizos* have exploited Indians both in Puerto de las Piedras and in Temascalcingo. I have mentioned that at least one *mestizo* family moved into El Puerto "to do business with Indians." One of the wealthier *mestizo ejidatarios* still does business with the Indians. He tries to buy animals cheaply and then sells them to butchers in Temascalcingo. Although this man will buy from other *mestizos* as well as Indians, he has his greatest success dealing with Indians. He takes advantage of their lack of knowledge concerning local and regional markets for products and, as middleman or broker, can often reap hefty profits.

One indication that Indians have sometimes been taken advantage of by the *mestizos* is the negative correlation between Indian language ability and land quantity–quality. Although this correlation is not statistically significant, it does suggest that land sometimes has been taken from Indians and has ended up in the hands of *mestizos*. My impression is that this pattern has only existed in recent years when *mestizos* have dominated *ejido* leadership positions (see Chapter 7).

Although Indians are not as likely to be filling community leadership positions, they are much more likely to participate in the *cargo* system. The *cargo* system is characteristic of Indian communities in Mexico, and it is not surprising that those with more Indian language ability tend to have higher scores on the *cargo* system participation variable. A bit more surprising is the fact that those who are "more Indian" are also more active in orthodox religious activities: Indian language ability is positively related to religiosity.

Indian language ability is also positively related to alcohol use, a fact that may result from Indians' frustration at being a minority in an area dominated by *mestizos*. As I have noted in Chapter 9, I do not see a direct connection between *cargo* system participation and heavy use of alcohol, as is true in other areas of Mexico (Cancian 1965: Pozas 1971). Alcohol use is not an institutionalized part of *cargo* activities in Puerto de las Piedras.

Finally, Indian language ability is negatively related to the number of people in the house. This relationship may result from two possible causes: (1) infant mortality has been higher among "more Indian" families, and (2) those who are "more Indian" are primarily older members of the population whose children are grown and have already left the house. There is some support for each explanation. K. DeWalt (n.d.) reports that there is a small positive correlation between Indian language

Table 11.7. *Number of times ejidatarios of Puerto de las Piedras worked elsewhere*

Times worked outside the valley	No.	Percentage
0	18	34.6
1	8	15.4
2	4	7.7
3	7	13.5
4	7	13.5
8 or more	8	15.4

ability and "proportion of children who have died." Table 11.2 shows that there is a small positive correlation between age and Indian language ability. Thus both a higher infant mortality rate and an older population among Indians may account for the observation that there are fewer people in "more Indian" households.

Migration in search of wage labor

In earlier chapters, I reported that many people in the Temascalcingo region have migrated, both temporarily and permanently, to other areas in search of work opportunities. Floods often made it necessary for the *ejidatarios* to find some source of extra income in the past; an improvement in life style still requires an income apart from agriculture for most people. A few men have made it standard procedure to sow their crops as soon as the weather permits and then leave for Mexico City to try to find a job, usually in construction. They return just before the harvest in November and usually stay with their families until their crops are sown again.

"Number of times worked elsewhere" is a measure of the extent of temporary migration among the *ejidatarios*. Table 11.7 shows that 65 percent of the male *ejidatarios* have migrated at least once in search of work. These data give some idea of the severity of the economic problems that plagued and, to a large extent, still plague the region. I should also point out that I am talking only about *ejidatarios*, those individuals who have land rights: The number of people who migrate (either temporarily or permanently) is greater still among those who do not have land. As I indicated previously, 72 percent of the *ejidatarios'* households had at least one child living in Mexico City. Another indication of the extent of migration is that over 70 percent of the male *ejidatarios* also had one or more brothers or sisters living in Mexico City.

Working outside the region, like cosmopolitanism, can expose individuals to new ideas and better methods of production. Although most of the men work in construction jobs, some have worked in jobs related to agriculture or livestock production. This is especially true of the few individuals who worked as *braceros* (agricultural workers) in the United States. In addition, wage labor can provide individuals with the money to invest in new techniques. Thus I expected that working outside the region would be associated with some of the adaptive strategies. However, as we see in Table 11.1, this is not the case. With the exception of a positive relationship between fertilizer use and number of times worked elsewhere, none of the adaptive strategies are significantly related to temporary migration.

I would interpret the positive relationship between fertilizer use and working outside the community in the following way. Individuals who leave the community to work outside the valley cannot perform all of the proper agricultural operations on their fields. One way in which they may be trying to compensate for the resulting decline in production is by applying fertilizer. The fertilizer is substituted for the proper labor input. Confirmation of this hypothesis would involve an analysis of the temporary migrants' behavior with regard to the use of fertilizer during the years when they migrate. I did not have sufficient data to enable me to test this hypothesis, but two *ejidatarios* told me that they applied fertilizer to their fields whenever they spent the summer working in construction in Mexico City.

In general, new ideas or techniques learned while working outside the community do not appear to provide any stimulus for investing in a new adaptive strategy. It also does not appear that working outside the community makes any difference as far as obtaining enough resources to invest in new strategies (i.e., number of times worked elsewhere is not significantly correlated with any of the wealth variables). Those who migrate may be led to do so precisely because they view agriculture, livestock production, and other economic activities within the region as being nonviable sources of income. Migration for them may be viewed as ultimately leading to a better life outside the region, if they manage to obtain a permanent job. Thus they do not invest in new adaptive strategies within the region.

Number of times worked elsewhere is significantly correlated with only two other independent variables (Table 11.2). Both of these relationships are revealing, however. First, working elsewhere is correlated positively with distance from land. That is, the farther the house site is from the land plots, the more inclination there is to migrate in search of wage labor. People who have a long walk to their fields may not be able to tend them as well, they are not able to watch them in order to keep out intruding animals or people, and they have a long way to transport their harvests. It appears that some of these people have decided that temporary migration, supplemented by the corn raised on poorly tended land, meets their needs better than attempting to get the most out of their fields.

Number of times worked elsewhere is also negatively correlated with *ejido* leadership. There is also a negative correlation with community leadership, although this figure is low and not statistically significant. People who migrate often in search of wage labor probably do not serve as *ejido* leaders because: (*a*) they are less interested in these posts, for service may interfere with their mobility; and (*b*) others may perceive their lack of commitment to the land and to the *ejido* and do not choose them as leaders.

Summary

Of the four independent variables introduced in this chapter (age, number of people in the house, Indian language ability, and number of times worked elsewhere), only Indian language ability has much of an impact on the choice of adaptive strategies. Those who are "more Indian" were less likely to invest in the forage production and animal improvement strategies and more likely to continue traditional subsistence agriculture. Indians are poorer than *mestizos* and have less access to information, and these factors probably limit their ability to adopt either forage production or animal improvement.

The number of times worked elsewhere was positively related to fertilizer use. I suggested that this relationship might arise because of inadequate care of fields when individuals migrate in search of wage labor. They apply fertilizer to try to make up (in production) for the lack of labor input.

Female-headed households were found to be much less likely to invest in any of the new adaptive strategies. Most of these women are poor, old, and have no able-bodied person to care for their fields. They are interested only in eking out a living from their corn crops and are understandably not willing to become involved in the problems of adopting new adaptive strategies.

12

Models of agricultural modernization in a Mexican *ejido*

In the preceding chapters, I have looked at the relationships among the five adaptive strategies and over twenty-five independent variables. In addition, I have considered the interrelationships among those independent variables. Some patterns consistently appear in the data (e.g., the interrelationships among the "wealth," "leadership," and "information access" variables and the "forage production" adaptive strategy); but all of the information that has been presented still needs to be put in order.

This chapter brings together much of the information scattered in preceding sections of this work. My first objective is to simplify or reduce the many different independent variables to a more manageable number. I accomplish this reduction by using the technique of factor analysis. The second objective is to create a causal model of the process of choosing the different adaptive strategies. The factors representing the independent variables are causally ordered and put into a predictive model for each of the five different adaptive strategies. These models are then utilized in the final chapter in: (*a*) talking about the processes involved in economic development in this *ejido;* and (*b*) making recommendations to change agents who will work in the Temascalcingo region in the future, as well as those who will work under similar situations in rural regions of the world.

Factor analysis for data reduction

I did not expect that all of the variables that I measured were tapping totally different domains of behavior. Chapter 6, for example, discussed several different indicators of an underlying dimension that I suggested reflect economic inequalities. Factor analysis is a technique that enables us to examine a large number of variables to see if their collective variations can be accounted for by a smaller set of underlying dimensions called factors (see Chapter 4). Factor analysis is best used when the researcher has some idea of what these underlying dimensions are. Although I was not able to formulate hypotheses about the factor analysis of the independent variables as detailed as those for the factor analysis of the innovation adoption items, I did have some expectations about possible patterns in the data. First, the five different measures of wealth (wealth ratings, material style of life, value of agricultural equipment, cash value of animals, and income from other pursuits), the five access to information variables (education, political knowledge, mass media exposure, cosmopolitanism, and change agent contact), the land quality–quantity index, and the community and *ejido* leadership scores are all part of the cluster that social scientists usually call socioeconomic status. Although all thirteen variables were not expected to load highly on only one factor, I believed that they would be distributed among two or three factors. Second, I felt that there would be a factor on which Indian language ability, *cargo* system participation, and religiosity would load highly. Finally, distance from land and alcohol use both seemed to be variables that might define factors by themselves.

Appendix A contains the correlation matrix that was factor analyzed. Some of the correlation coefficients presented there differ slightly from those presented in earlier chapters, for I limited my factor analysis to the fifty-three males in the random sample. There were considerable data missing for the nine females in the sample (see Chapter 3), and so they were eliminated from the analysis.

One other point about Appendix A should be noted. Three variables that were considered in other chapters – education, number of people in the house, and times worked elsewhere – are not included. Preliminary factor analysis showed that the communality of these variables – the total variance of a variable accounted for by the combination of all factors (Nie et al. 1975) – was very low. In addition, although these variables loaded on factors in somewhat predictable ways, the loadings were not high. Therefore, they were not retained for further analysis.

Tables 12.1 and 12.2 contain two different factor solutions. Table 12.1 presents an analysis based on principal factors with iterations and a varimax rotation. To reiterate, varimax rotation attempts to make the factors orthogonal (uncorrelated) with one another and to maximize the loading of variables on one factor, thus making loadings of a variable on all other factors as near zero as possible. The dimensions that emerge from this procedure are easy to interpret. Factor 2 indicates "Indian-ness," Factor 3 indicates "distance from land," and Factor 6 reflects "use of alcohol." Factors 1, 4, and 5 contain the variables that I felt were generally indicative of socioeconomic status. Although this solution is easy to interpret, it is unsatisfactory in terms of one of my expectations. I expected that the "wealth," "leadership," and "information access" variables would define a number of different factors (as they do in Table 12.1) but that these factors would be positively correlated. The factor analysis using varimax rotation forces a solution in which factors are uncorrelated with one another.

Table 12.1. *Orthogonal rotated factors of independent variables*

	Factor 1	Factor 2	Factor 3	Factor 4	Factor 5	Factor 6
Ejido leadership	*.69*[a]	.04	.04	*.42*	-.05	.08
Community leadership	*.79*	-.14	.07	.06	.11	.12
Wealth ratings	*.62*	-.02	-.04	.28	.33	.18
Value of agricultural equipment	*.75*	.10	.16	.33	.18	.11
Cash value of animals	*.64*	.16	.21	.15	.19	.09
Cargo system participation	-.33	*.68*	.01	.08	.04	.19
Indian language ability	-.12	*.62*	-.18	-.10	-.27	.31
Religiosity	.02	*.60*	.11	.09	.34	.27
Distance from land	-.15	.04	*.84*	.03	.08	.01
Age	.38	.22	.32	-.13	.01	*.56*
Alcohol use	-.05	.10	-.10	.10	.05	*.58*
Political knowledge	.23	-.02	.04	*.57*	.02	*-.40*
Change agent contact	*.52*	.02	.24	*.55*	.18	-.03
Land quantity–quality	.12	-.13	-.05	*.71*	.22	.18
Income from other pursuits	.18	-.20	.12	.10	*.69*	-.05
Mass media exposure	.13	-.03	-.16	.31	*.56*	*-.49*
Cosmopolitanism	.08	-.24	*.55*	.02	*.52*	-.12
Material style of life	.37	-.24	-.19	.18	*.63*	.04

Factor 1: Local leadership and wealth
Factor 2: Indian-ness
Factor 3: Distance from land

Factor 4: Sociopolitical manipulation
Factor 5: Extralocal orientation
Factor 6: Use of alcohol

Note: The six factors (all with eigenvalues more than 1.00) account for 75% of the variance in the data.

[a] Factor loadings more than ±.40 are in italics.

225

Table 12.2. Oblique primary factors of independent variables (factor pattern matrix – direct oblimin with Delta = 0)

	Factor 1	Factor 2	Factor 3	Factor 4	Factor 5	Factor 6	(Unrotated) Communalities
Ejido leadership	-.67[a]	.02	-.04	.06	-.38	.15	.76
Community leadership	-.81	-.12	-.07	.09	.02	.00	.68
Wealth ratings	-.54	.04	.05	-.16	-.19	-.29	.68
Value of agricultural equipment	-.68	.14	.17	-.12	-.25	-.13	.77
Cash value of animals	-.66	-.12	.22	-.10	.24	-.11	.58
Cargo system participation	.04	.74	-.01	.07	.08	-.11	.43
Indian language ability	.08	.62	.17	.20	.06	.16	.60
Religiosity	-.04	.54	-.09	-.40	-.12	.25	.45
Distance from land	.13	.01	-.84	-.06	-.05	.07	.54
Age	-.44	.25	-.34	.44	.17	.00	.57
Alcohol use	.04	.11	.08	.58	-.13	.06	.45
Political knowledge	-.13	-.06	-.02	-.35	-.56	.01	.55
Change agent contact	-.42	.03	-.23	-.01	-.50	-.12	.77
Land quantity–quality	.02	-.10	.04	.30	-.71	-.16	.53
Income from other pursuits	-.05	-.06	-.12	.04	-.01	-.71	.66

Mass media exposure	.05	.07	.19	-.39	-.23	*-.61*	.64
Cosmopolitanism	.01	-.16	*-.54*	-.08	.04	*-.52*	.61
Material style of life	-.24	-.12	.20	.15	-.08	*-.60*	.68

Factor 1: Local leadership and wealth   Factor 4: Use of alcohol
Factor 2: Indian-ness   Factor 5: Sociopolitical manipulation
Factor 3: Distance from land   Factor 6: Extralocal orientation

Note: The first six factors account for 75% of the variance in the data.

[a] Factor loadings more than ±.40 are in italics.

Thus I decided to do a factor analysis of the same variables but to use oblique rotation rather than varimax. In oblique rotation, the requirement of orthogonality among the factors is relaxed; and the factors are allowed to be correlated if such correlations exist in the data. In actual practice, a myriad number of oblique rotations can be done depending upon whether the researcher wants the solution to be more or less oblique (i.e., wants the factors to be more or less correlated). In addition, the factors that emerge and the correlations among the factors may make the solution uninterpretable, especially in cases where the researcher is unfamiliar with the data or has no idea of the patterning present in the data (for further discussion of oblique rotation, see Rummel 1970:395–422 and Appendix B).

In the real world, those sets of behavior that are measured by our factors are usually, of course, correlated with one another. Therefore, if the oblique factor solution is interpretable, it can provide the same information as the orthogonal rotation (identification of underlying factors); but in addition, it also provides us with information about the relationships among the factors (i.e., product moment correlations between the factor scores).

Tables 12.1 and 12.2 compare the results of the orthogonal and the oblique rotations. Although the loadings differ somewhat and the factors appear in a different order, the same factors are identified using either oblique or orthogonal rotation. Those variables with a loading (correlation of the variable with the factor) of .40 or higher are in italics in both tables and can be taken as indicators of the factors.[35] I have named these factors as follows (factor numbers refer to the oblique solution).

Factor 1: *local leadership and wealth.* This factor contains a composite of "community leadership," "value of agricultural equipment," "*ejido* leadership," "cash value of animals," "wealth ratings," "age," and "change agent contact."

Factor 2: *Indian-ness.* This factor is composed of the variables "*cargo* system participation," "Indian language ability," and "religiosity."

Factor 3: *distance from land.* The two variables that have high loadings on this factor are "distance from land" and "cosmopolitanism."

Factor 4 (Factor 6 on the orthogonal rotation): *use of alcohol.* "Alcohol use," "age," and religiosity" (negatively) are the variables that load most highly on this factor.

Factor 5 (Factor 4 on the orthogonal rotation): *sociopolitical mani-*

pulation. This factor is defined by the variables "land quantity–quality," "political knowledge," and "change agent contact."

Factor 6 (Factor 5 on the orthogonal rotation): *extralocal orientation.* This factor is a composite of the variables "income from other pursuits," "mass media exposure," "material style of life," and "cosmopolitanism."

These six factors were very close to my predictions. I expected the "Indian-ness," "distance from land," and "use of alcohol" factors to emerge. I also expected one or more socioeconomic status factors to emerge; and "local leadership and wealth," "sociopolitical manipulation," and "extralocal orientation" contain the variables that I had discussed. Because of my prediction, I expected that these last three factors would be positively correlated.

The advantage of oblique rotation is that a hypothesis about correlations among factors can be tested; the oblique rotation allows for correlations among the factors. Table 12.3 contains the correlation matrix of the obliquely rotated factors. As predicted, there are positive correlations among the three factors. Factor 1 (local leadership and wealth) has a correlation coefficient of .35 with both Factor 5 (sociopolitical manipulation) and Factor 6 (extralocal orientation). There is a correlation of .27 between sociopolitical manipulation and an extralocal orientation.

One other correlation among the factor scores should be noted here. There is a strong negative correlation between Indian-ness and an extralocal orientation. Individuals who are "more Indian" are less likely to be oriented toward the outside world. This tendency does not seem to be due to economic factors alone, for Indian-ness is not significantly correlated with either sociopolitical manipulation or local leadership and wealth. Thus it appears that the relative lack of wealth and information access among Indians noted earlier (see Chapter 11) may be limited to one area of socioeconomic well-being, that measured by extralocal orientation.

Correlations of factor scores with the adaptive strategies

The next step in the analysis is the correlation of the factor scores of the independent variables with the dependent variables, the different adaptive strategies.[36] These correlations are contained in Table 12.4. I will briefly summarize these relationships from the perspective of the independent factors.

Local leadership and wealth is, as I expected, positively correlated

Table 12.3. *Correlation matrix of the obliquely rotated factors*

	Local leadership and wealth	Indian-ness	Distance from land	Use of alcohol	Sociopolitical manipulation	Extralocal orientation
Local leadership and wealth	—					
Indian-ness	-.03	—				
Distance from land	-.01	.02	—			
Use of alcohol	.02	.16	.07	—		
Sociopolitical manipulation	.35**	-.01	.00	-.18	—	
Extralocal orientation	.35**	-.49**	.01	-.16	.27*	—

Note: * indicates $p < .05$ and ** indicates $p < .01$.

Table 12.4. *Correlations of the adaptive strategies with the factor scores*

	Local leadership and wealth	Indian-ness	Distance from land	Use of alcohol	Sociopolitical manipulation	Extralocal orientation
Forage production	.41**	-.14	-.16	-.16	.52**	.34**
Animal improvement	.25*	-.21	.23*	-.33**	.12	.37**
Tractor use	-.21	.02	.00	.26*	.20	.13
Fertilizer use	-.05	.15	.11	.10	-.10	.04
Subsistence agriculture	-.20	.10	-.08	.07	-.38**	-.44**

Note: * indicates $p < .05$ and ** indicates $p < .01$.

with both the forage production and the animal improvement strategies. This pattern follows that of many of the variables that load highly on this factor (see Chapters 6 and 7). This factor is also negatively correlated to some extent with tractor use and subsistence agriculture.

Indian-ness is not highly correlated with any of the adaptive strategies. The highest relationship is a negative correlation with animal improvement, but even this is not statistically significant. Although there does seem to be a slight tendency for those who are "more Indian" to adopt subsistence agriculture and fertilizer use rather than the more expensive animal improvement and forage production strategies, none of these correlations are high or statistically significant.

Distance from land seems to slightly inhibit investment in forage production and is positively associated with animal improvement. This relationship seems to be perfectly logical: Animal raising can be done close to one's house site, whereas the other adaptive strategies in one way or another involve the agricultural lands (see Chapter 5). This factor has little correlation with the other three adaptive strategies.

Use of alcohol is negatively correlated with the two adaptive strategies that require the most capital investment, animal improvement and forage production. However, there is a fairly high positive correlation with tractor use, a pattern noted in Chapter 9. There are small and nonsignificant positive correlations of this factor with fertilizer use and subsistence agriculture.

Sociopolitical manipulation has the highest positive correlation with forage production. In addition, there are small nonsignificant positive correlations with animal improvement and tractor use. There is a fairly high negative correlation with subsistence agriculture and a smaller one with fertilizer use. The high negative relationship with subsistence agriculture indicates that, as we would expect, those who are manipulators are usually found to be investing in some new strategy rather than standing pat with traditional crops and techniques. The new strategy they are most likely to adopt is forage production.

Extralocal orientation has statistically significant positive correlations with forage production and animal improvement, the two most expensive strategies to adopt. This factor also has the highest negative correlation with subsistence agriculture. Those with high scores on this factor are clearly interested in investing in new adaptive strategies. In fact, this factor is the only one that has positive correlations with all four new adaptive strategies, although the relationships with tractor use and fertilizer use are quite weak and not statistically significant.

Path analysis of the independent variables

The correlations between the factor scores for the independent variables and the adaptive strategies are interesting and convey substantial information. However, many questions remain. For example, three factors – local leadership and wealth, sociopolitical manipulation, and extra-local orientation – are all highly correlated with forage production. Does each factor contribute a unique proportion of the variance to the explanation of who will adopt forage production? Or do the high correlations arise partially or wholly because of the intercorrelations among the three independent factors? In brief, it is useful to know how each factor is related to the different adaptive strategies when other factors are considered.

A causal model can give us some tentative answers to these questions. In addition, however, these models can also give us some idea of the processes that may be involved in the choice of particular adaptive strategies. Path analysis is especially appropriate for testing hypotheses about relationships among the variables.[37]

The first task of the researcher who uses path analysis (assuming that the sampling, linearity, and other assumptions necessary for the use of correlation and regression procedures have been met) is to posit a causal model that includes a temporal–causal ordering of the variables as well as predictions about the sign (positive or negative) of relationships among the variables (see my discussion in Chapter 8). Figure 12.1 shows my hypothesized causal ordering of the independent variables. I will now attempt to justify this ordering of variables.

In my view, three particular variables are temporally antecedent to all of the other variables. These are Indian-ness, distance from land, and use of alcohol. Indian-ness is a status that is more ascribed than achieved. That is, although it is possible to change one's identity from Indian to *mestizo* (see Chapter 11), enculturation and sociocultural norms make it unlikely that there will be a complete and rapid shift to *mestizo*-ness. Thus ethnic status should be more or less fixed at birth and will be little affected by other variables in the model.

In the same way, for most individuals in the *ejido*, residence site is relatively fixed, although a few individuals have moved in order to be closer to their fields (see Chapter 5). I did not see distance from land as being affected by changes in the other variables in the model.

Finally, use of alcohol was also thought to be antecedent to other variables in the model. Although a number of studies have shown a relationship between ethnic status and drinking behavior or between socio-

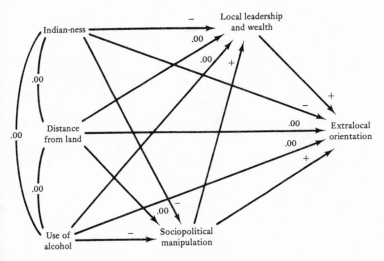

Figure 12.1 Hypothesized path model of the interrelationships among the independent variables

economic status and drinking behavior, I decided to treat drinking behavior in Puerto de las Piedras as independent of these factors.[38]

I hypothesized that sociopolitical manipulation would be dependent upon two of the three factors just discussed and would be an independent variable with regard to local leadership and wealth, extralocal orientation, and the five adaptive strategies. I predicted that those who are "more Indian" and are high users of alcohol would not be sociopolitical manipulators (i.e., negative paths were predicted). Distance from land was not expected to be related to this factor (i.e., a path close to .00 was predicted).

Local leadership and wealth is the next factor variable in the model. I hypothesized that it would be determined by a negative path from Indian-ness and a high positive path from sociopolitical manipulation. Near-zero paths from distance from land and use of alcohol were also predicted.

In the real world, I would expect that there is a definite feedback loop from local leadership and wealth to sociopolitical manipulation. That is, leadership positions are especially useful for manipulative purposes with regard to acquiring more land (see Chapter 7). However, I feel that the primary causal path leads from sociopolitical manipulation to local leadership and wealth. Some wealth, and with it a greater advantage in securing leadership positions, has certainly been inherited by a number of *ejidatarios*. However, I believe that the local scene is a relatively open one in which people who have or can acquire manipulative skills are able to go on to accumulate wealth and political power. A good case could be made for the primary causal effect to run from either variable to the other. It is in cases like this that a provision for feedback in the model would be desirable.

Extralocal orientation was expected to be the final dependent variable among the set of independent factors. Although there is little question that the problem of feedback already discussed also applies to the relationships between this variable and both local leadership and wealth and sociopolitical manipulation, again I feel that the primary causal path is in the direction indicated in Figure 12.1. In fact, the ordering of these three variables corresponds to what seems to be a very common pattern in modernization. That is, those individuals who are able to acquire and utilize information (i.e., sociopolitical manipulators) often maneuver themselves into positions of economic and political power in the local scene (i.e., local leadership and wealth). From these bases in the local scene, individuals sometimes expand their horizons and their life styles toward the outside world (i.e., extralocal orientation). Thus I predicted very strong positive paths from local leadership and wealth and from sociopolitical manipulation to extralocal orientation. Furthermore, I expected a negative path from Indian-ness and negligible paths from distance from land and use of alcohol to extralocal orientation.

In sum, all of these predictions make up the model that is presented in Figure 12.1, with the symbols +, −, and .00 filled in on the appropriate paths. Figure 12.2 is the same path model but with the path coefficients now indicated. Comparison of Figure 12.2 to Figure 12.1 in effect constitutes a test of the proposed model.

Some predictions about specific paths were not correct. However, the majority of the predictions were confirmed, and so discussion here will be limited to those paths that did not turn out as hypothesized. First, although there was a near-zero correlation expected between Indianness and use of alcohol, actually a .16 correlation coefficient exists. This correlation is not very large, however, and it is not statistically significant. Second, a negative path was expected between Indian-ness and sociopolitical manipulation. A near-zero path was observed, however. Finally, Indian-ness was expected to be negatively related to local leadership and wealth. Although the path is in fact negative, the magnitude is much smaller than I had expected.

It is interesting that all three incorrect predictions involved Indianness. Indians were found to have slightly more use of alcohol than had

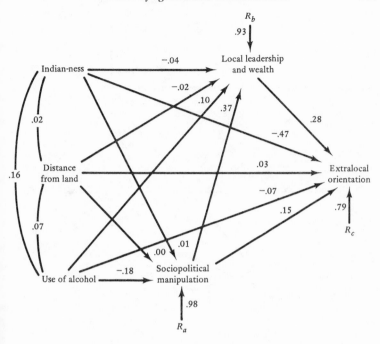

Figure 12.2 Path model of the interrelationships among the independent variables

been expected. In addition, it appears that Indians do not differ significantly from *mestizos* on either sociopolitical manipulation or local leadership and wealth. There are no ethnic differences in the scores on these two variables. This finding is all the more interesting when we see the very strong negative relationship between Indian-ness and extralocal orientation. It appears then that Indians are just as likely to "make it" on the local scene but are more reluctant or less able than *mestizos* to expand their interests and orientations to the world outside.

Although theoretically any model that does not completely confirm all predictions may be thrown out, the deviations from expectation in this model do not appear to be important enough to invalidate the entire model. That is, the predictions not confirmed were all due to a relationship appearing that was not predicted or to expected relationships that failed to show up. None of the errors had to do with a path being of the opposite sign (e.g., predicted to be positive and yet actually negative). Thus I will go on to discuss the model further, this time with par-

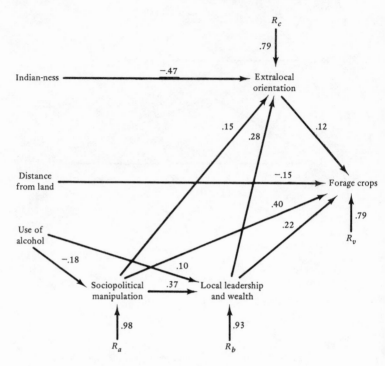

Figure 12.3   Paths leading to the adoption of forage crops

ticular emphasis upon the ultimate dependent variables, the five different adaptive strategies.[39]

Predictors of forage production

Figure 12.3 is the path model of predictors of forage production adoption. The most powerful predictor is sociopolitical manipulation. Because one of the variables that loads highly on this manipulation factor is land quantity–quality, it should be expected that these individuals have been able to sow a portion of their lands with *pradera*.

A smaller positive path was observed from local leadership and wealth to forage production.[40] Table 12.5 also shows that the indirect effects (i.e., through other variables or concomitantly with other variables) that local leadership and wealth exerts on forage production are fairly large. Those individuals who have high local leadership and wealth

Table 12.5. *Total, direct, and indirect effects of independent variables on adaptive strategies*

	Indian-ness	Distance from land	Use of alcohol	Sociopolitical manipulation	Local leadership and wealth	Extralocal orientation
Forage production						
Total[a]	-.14	-.16	-.16	.52	.41	.34
Direct[b]	-.05	-.15	-.05	.40**	.22	.12
Indirect[c]	-.09	-.01	-.11	.12	.19	.22
Animal improvement						
Total	-.21	.23	-.33	.12	.25	.37
Direct	-.04	.26*	-.31*	-.08	.20	.25
Indirect	-.17	-.03	-.02	.20	.05	.12
Tractor use						
Total	.02	.00	.26	.20	-.21	.13
Direct	.11	-.03	.37**	.34*	-.45**	.31
Indirect	-.09	.03	-.11	-.14	.24	-.18
Fertilizer use						
Total	-.05	.11	.10	-.10	-.05	.04
Direct	.25	.10	.07	-.11	-.08	.24
Indirect	-.10	.01	.03	.01	.03	-.20

Table 12.5. (cont.)

	Indian-ness	Distance from land	Use of alcohol	Sociopolitical manipulation	Local leadership and wealth	Extralocal orientation
Subsistence agriculture						
Total	-.10	-.08	.07	-.38	-.20	-.44
Direct	-.11	-.07	-.04	-.29*	.05	-.44**
Indirect	.21	-.01	.11	-.09	-.25	.00

Note: The only significance levels indicated in this table are for the path coefficients (direct effects) for each dependent variable. Next to the path coefficients, I have indicated those that are statistically significant. As in all previous tables, * indicates $p < .05$; ** indicates $p < .01$. Statistical significance was determined by the F ratio for 46 degrees of freedom (number of cases minus the number of variables minus one).

[a] The total effect is the Pearson correlation coefficient.

[b] The direct effect is the path coefficient (beta weight).

[c] The indirect effect is the difference between the total effect and the direct effect.

scores are very likely to adopt forage production, either because they are wealthy leaders (the direct effect) or because they also have other characteristics (indirect effects) that favor the adoption of this adaptive strategy.

There is a very small path between extralocal orientation and forage production. This relationship indicates that individuals who are successful in nonlocal activities are not unusually interested in investing in forage crops. It may be that these individuals have decided that agriculture, even when it offers potential economic benefits, does not hold the key to success. I should note that there is a fairly high indirect effect of extralocal orientation on forage production, indicating that people with an extralocal orientation often have other characteristics (e.g., are manipulators, wealthy, and leaders) that do encourage or enable investment in forage crop production.

The other predictors of forage production are fairly small (see Table 12.5). Both Indian-ness and use of alcohol have small negative path coefficients. Neither ethnicity nor heavy drinking seem to make much difference (when controlling for the other variables) in predicting which individuals will invest in this new adaptive strategy. Distance from land has a larger negative path, indicating that there is some tendency for individuals who live far away from their lands not to invest in forage production. This tendency has been noted earlier (see Chapter 5). People probably do not want to invest considerable sums of money to plant *pradera* in fields that cannot be kept under relatively close surveillance.

A composite picture of an individual who is likely to become involved in the forage production adaptive strategy can now be formed. This individual is likely to be wealthy, a leader, a sociopolitical manipulator, and to live relatively close to the *ejido*.

Predictors of animal improvement

Figure 12.4 is the path model for predictors of animal improvement. The largest path is a negative one between use of alcohol and animal improvement. Those individuals who are heavy drinkers are unlikely to be investing in this adaptive strategy. I think the explanation of this relationship lies in the fact that animals are a very liquid form of investment (see also Chapter 6). That is, because animals can be readily bought and sold, it is unlikely that those who have a propensity to drink will accumulate or hold on to their animals for very long. These individuals are likely to sell any animals they have in order to start or prolong a drinking spree. As a result, these *ejidatarios* probably feel that improving the condition of their animals is an unwise investment. Vaccinations, feeding the animals good foods, and bathing animals are prac-

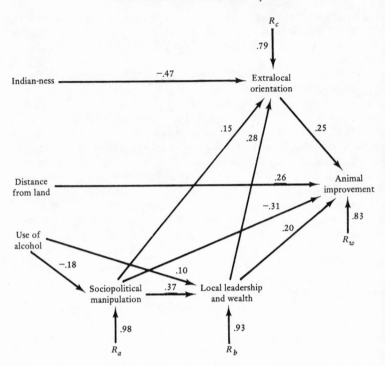

Figure 12.4   Paths leading to the adoption of animal improvement

tices that are adopted by people who are interested in long-term pay-offs. They are not adopted by individuals who have a drinking problem and who are likely to possess animals for only a short time.

In contrast with the effect that it had on the adoption of forage production, distance from land is positively related to animal improvement. Because animals are generally kept at the house rather than in the fields, they can be watched. Thus cash invested in vaccinations and other animal improvement items can be protected. It may be that individuals who were reluctant to invest in forage production because they lived far away from the fields are investing in animal improvement instead.

Local leadership and wealth and extralocal orientation are both positively associated with animal improvement. This adaptive strategy does require a fairly large capital investment, and it is not surprising that wealthy leaders are adopting it. The path coefficient with extralocal orientation again can be explained with reference to the proximity of the *ejidatarios'* houses. Even though these individuals may lack interest in agriculture because they are becoming oriented toward the outside world, they have cash resources and may be willing to invest them in animals that are always close at hand. In addition, animals are easily sold and thus are a ready source of cash should a need or other investment opportunity arise.

Indian-ness and sociopolitical manipulation both have small negative relationships with this adaptive strategy. However, both have fairly large indirect effects, as we see in Table 12.5. Indian-ness has a negative indirect effect upon animal improvement, for people who are "more Indian" also have other characteristics that are not conducive to investment in this adaptive strategy. However, controlling for other variables, it is again impressive how little ethnicity has to do with whether or not individuals will adopt animal improvement. Sociopolitical manipulation has a fairly large positive indirect effect on animal improvement even though its direct effect is negative. This pattern results from the relationship of sociopolitical manipulation to the other independent variables. All other things being equal, however, it seems that those who have high scores on this variable are more interested in investing in strategies that make use of the land rather than in animal improvement.

Thus individuals who are likely to adopt this strategy are wealthy leaders who are extralocally oriented, live far away from the land, and are not heavy drinkers. Although some of the conditions or characteristics that favor the adoption of animal improvement are similar to those that favor the adoption of forage production, there are also some very clear differences.

Predictors of tractor use

Figure 12.5 is the path model for predictors of tractor use. The independent variable with the strongest path coefficient is local leadership and wealth, which is negatively related to the use of tractors. This relationship is not surprising when we consider that one of the items that loads highly on this factor score is the value of agricultural equipment. Thus those individuals with money invested in nonmechanized equipment are less likely to adopt the use of tractors on their land. The negative path coefficient between local leadership and wealth and tractor use is much larger than the correlation coefficient, for local leadership and wealth has some positive indirect effects on tractor use.

Use of alcohol is positively associated with tractor use. This tendency was noted in Chapter 9 and indicates that individuals who drink frequently may find it necessary to hire tractors. The use of tractors elimi-

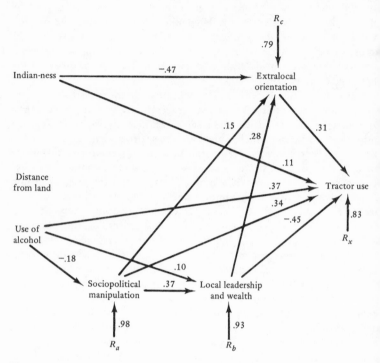

Figure 12.5 Paths leading to the adoption of tractor use

nates much of the work in cultivation and allows more time for drinking. It is interesting that a negative personality trait such as heavy drinking may actually encourage the use of certain forms of new technology
– in this case, tractors.

Sociopolitical manipulation and extralocal orientation are both positively associated with tractor use. The first of these has as one of its
items land quantity–quality. We would expect that those individuals
who have managed to accumulate more than normal amounts of land
would be interested in utilizing tractors, and this is the case. With respect to extralocal orientation, mechanizing agricultural operations
would allow these individuals more time to devote to nonagricultural
jobs and pursuits. In effect, these individuals can have the best of two
worlds. Mechanizing makes it possible for them to derive some production from their fields while not taking up their time and labor; this time
and labor can be allocated to other extralocal activities.

I should note that although sociopolitical manipulation and extra-local orientation are positively associated with tractor use, both have negative indirect effects on this adaptive strategy. These indirect effects are caused by the interaction of these variables with other independent variables in the model. Controlling for the other variables increases the positive relationships of these two variables with tractor use.

There is a small positive path between Indian-ness and tractor use. Once again, there is not much of an association between ethnicity and adoption of a new adaptive strategy. In this case, all other things being equal, Indians are somewhat more likely to be using tractors than are *mestizos*. Finally, distance from land only has a very small negative relationship with tractor use. There is no difference in use of tractors between those who live close to the *ejido* and those who live farther away.

Thus those individuals who are likely to adopt this adaptive strategy are people who drink heavily, are sociopolitical manipulators, and have an extralocal orientation. In addition, these individuals are not likely to be local, wealthy leaders.

On the basis of the evidence presented here, it might be wise to re-evaluate the development agents' heavy emphasis upon mechanization of the Temascalcingo region. Those who are most likely to adopt this form of mechanization are heavy drinkers and appear not to be very interested in agriculture except perhaps as a supplement to other economic activities. Two important goals of development in the region are: (1) to increase production, and (2) to expand employment opportunities. The pattern of mechanization discussed here seems antithetical to both goals. That is, if heavy drinkers and people with a nonagricultural orientation are the ones most likely to mechanize, then increased production is likely to be minimal. These individuals are attempting to minimize effort, not to maximize output. With regard to the objective of expanding employment opportunities, those people with extra-*ejidal* employment are in essence filling two spots in the employment picture. Increased use of tractors is only likely to lead to an increase in the number of *ejidatarios* with free time who are looking for other employment. Thus tractors may be exacerbating the underemployment and unemployment in the region.

Predictors of fertilizer use

The picture with regard to adoption of fertilizer use is not very clear. As we see in Figure 12.6, the residual, R_Y, is very large (.96), which indicates that only a very small part of the variance in fertilizer adoption has been explained. The only two paths that are fairly high in this

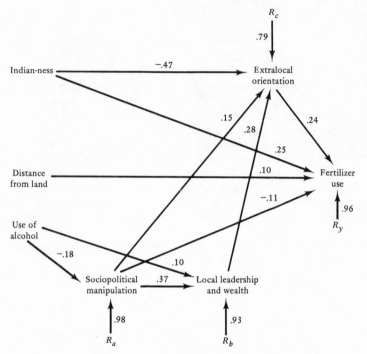

Figure 12.6   Paths leading to the adoption of fertilizer use

model are those with Indian-ness and an extralocal orientation. Indians are more likely to use fertilizer for growing corn than are *mestizos*. Those with an orientation toward the outside world also have adopted use of fertilizer. The explanation for this pattern may be much like that noted with regard to use of tractors; i.e., those not interested in agriculture adopt innovations that help them to achieve a minimal, viable level of production while minimizing their labor inputs. They may then invest their time in potentially more productive activities.

Local leadership and wealth and sociopolitical manipulation both have small negative relationships with use of fertilizer. Distance from land and use of alcohol both have small positive path coefficients.

I would tentatively suggest that the reason why such a small proportion of the variance (8 percent) in fertilizer adoption can be explained is that there is little pattern to the use of this item. That is, there appears to be a more or less random assortment of individuals who have

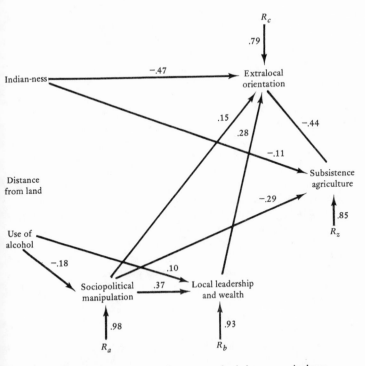

Figure 12.7 Paths leading to the maintenance of subsistence agriculture

chosen this adaptive strategy. Another explanation would be that no patterns emerge because of the variables selected for measurement. Psychological variables or some other set of social variables may be involved here. However, I have no hypotheses about other variables that might potentially prove relevant.

Predictors of subsistence agriculture

The final model to be presented deals with the predictors of those who have maintained the traditional adaptive strategy, subsistence corn cultivation.[41] Figure 12.7 is a path model of the predictors for this adaptive strategy.

The variable most highly associated with subsistence agriculture is extralocal orientation. Those individuals who are oriented toward the outside world are unwilling to cling to the traditional techniques of corn cultivation and are investing in the new adaptive strategies. Even though many of these people are successful, in the extralocal scene, they are still interested in economic profit from their agricultural and livestock activities within the valley.

Sociopolitical manipulation is also negatively associated with subsistence agriculture. We would not expect these "wheelers and dealers" to be sitting still, and they are not. They also are investing in the new adaptive strategies.

Path coefficients with the other independent variables are not very high. One surprising result is that Indian-ness has a slight negative relationship with subsistence agriculture. Indian-ness has a high positive indirect effect on subsistence agriculture. This fact accounts for the positive correlation coefficient ($r = .10$) that was observed between these variables. The important point, however, is that when we control for the other variables, Indians tend to be less likely to cling to traditional subsistence agriculture. This fact suggests that there is nothing inherent in being an Indian that predisposes individuals to be conservative and not to adopt new adaptive strategies. These data indicate that if Indians are given the same resources and access to power and information, they are just as willing as *mestizos* (and perhaps even more willing) to invest in new opportunities.

Another surprising result is that local leadership and wealth has a small positive path coefficient with subsistence agriculture. This relationship indicates that when all other factors are equal, we have little idea whether local, wealthy leaders will be investing in new adaptive strategies or not. I expected that these individuals would reject the old strategy and would invest in the new opportunities. Local leadership and wealth has a fairly large negative indirect effect on subsistence agriculture. The effects of local leadership and wealth through the other variables are negative, as we would expect. However, when controlling for these other variables, local leadership and wealth is not associated with adoption of new adaptive strategies.

In summary, those individuals who are sociopolitical manipulators or are oriented toward the outside world are most likely to be adopting new adaptive strategies. They are most likely to take risks and thus do not continue to practice traditional subsistence agriculture.

Summary and discussion

Analysis of the predictors for adoption of the various adaptive strategies has shown that the same variables are clearly not associated in the same way with all five different adaptive strategies. I will provide a gen-

Table 12.6. *Summary of direct effects associated with the different adaptive strategies*

Causal factors	Forage production	Animal improvement	Tractor use	Fertilizer use	Subsistence agriculture
Indian-ness	0	0	0	+	0
Distance from land	–	+	0	0	0
Use of alcohol	0	–	+	0	0
Sociopolitical manipulation	+	0	+	0	–
Local leadership and wealth	+	+	–	0	0
Extralocal orientation	0	+	+	+	–
R^2	38%	30%	30%	8%	28%

Note: In this table, a + indicates a path coefficient of more than .15; a – indicates a path coefficient of less than -.15; a 0 indicates path coefficients of less than plus or minus .15. R^2 indicates the amount of variance in the adaptive strategies accounted for by the independent variables.

eral discussion of these relationships in the next chapter. Table 12.6 provides a convenient summary of the most important relationships found in this chapter. This table shows the relationship of each independent variable to each of the adaptive strategies. Path coefficients above .15 are indicated with the symbol +; path coefficients greater than −.15 are shown as −; and all path coefficients less than plus or minus .15 are shown as 0. Also included in the table is the amount of variance in the adaptive strategies accounted for by all of the independent variables.

13

Economic development in a Mexican *ejido*: conclusions, predictions, and recommendations

The first order of business in this final chapter is to provide answers to the three general questions that were posed in Chapter 1: (1) how homogeneous are the people in this Mexican *ejido;* (2) is there only one dimension of agricultural modernization, or can others be identified; and (3) what are the predictors of modernizing behavior? The answers to these questions provide a summary of the more general implications of the preceding chapters.

The next portion of the chapter is devoted to an evaluation of the development projects that have been carried out in the region, predictions about the future of the *ejido* of Puerto de las Piedras, and recommendations to development agents. Although these recommendations are specifically concerned with the situation in the Temascalcingo region, I also discuss the more general implications of this case and make suggestions that are more widely applicable.

The concluding section of this work is a theoretical and methodological discussion about the ways in which economic development can be studied most fruitfully. I believe that the model of analysis I have used is more widely applicable and should be utilized by other investigators.

The extent of homogeneity in the ejido

The first major focus of my research was to investigate the extent of homogeneity or heterogeneity in various characteristics of the *ejidatarios.* As I showed in Chapter 1, homogeneity of attitudes, personalities, and behaviors has often been assumed in research among Mexican villagers and other peasants around the world.

Although I purposely chose to study a population of *ejidatarios,* who would be expected to be more homogeneous than the general population of the villages studied, significant variability was found in all behaviors and attributes that were measured. There was even a wide range of variation in the amount of land held, even though the amount to which each *ejidatario* is legally entitled is fixed at 2.38 hectares. One man controlled over 80 hectares of land, according to some informants.

248

Wealth was another area in which there was significant variability. Some researchers have minimized the differences in wealth among the people of Mexican villages and have claimed that a kind of "shared poverty" exists. However, I found that there were large differentials in wealth among the *ejidatarios* of Puerto de las Piedras and that these were perceived by the people themselves. Key informants from the community easily sorted individuals into a number of categories that reflected wealth differences. My own measurements of cash value of animals, value of agricultural equipment, material style of life, and income from other pursuits also showed considerable variability. Some *ejidatarios* had only the barest essentials for survival while others controlled capital of well over 100,000 *pesos* ($8,000).

Because similar variability was found in all other attributes measured, I feel that it is not valid to assume homogeneity among rural Mexican villagers or any other population. Any study purporting to describe a "typical peasant" will be susceptible to as much error as a study of a "typical American" or a "typical industrial worker." The differences within populations will be more pronounced than the similarities.

Although I did not focus on personality attributes or cognitive orientations in this study, I have no reason to suspect that there should be greater homogeneity in these than in the areas that I considered. If researchers actually tried to measure the image of the limited good, fatalism, amoral familism, or other traits often attributed to peasants, I believe that similar heterogeneity would be discovered. A study by Miller (1974) is indicative, I believe, of what would be found. Miller investigated Banfield's notion of "amoral familism" to determine: (*a*) if the ethos of Southern Italian villages really is amoral familism, and (*b*) whether this ethos explains much important social behavior (as Banfield suggested). Miller found in his study of fifty male southern Italian villagers that amoralism and familism were not, in fact, related to one another. In addition, he found that there was a large range of variation among the villagers on both the amoralism scale and the familism scale. Miller concludes:

> If "amoral familism" is a label that can only be legitimately applied to men who have proven themselves to be such by the responses that they have given to the tests which have been devised to detect this characteristic in this study, then only about one-quarter of the sample deserves to be described as such. (1974:532)

When subjected to careful study, the heterogeneity among peasants is much more striking than their homogeneity. If some researchers paid more attention to operationalizing and measuring the concepts they use, our understanding of people would be considerably advanced. Although our explanations of behavior would necessarily have to become more complex, there would be a distinct improvement in our theoretical models and a welcome decline in the vague, homogeneous stereotypes now often applied to populations.

The number of dimensions of modernization

In the past, research on modernization has often been carried out as though there were a single continuum, running from traditional to modern, along which people could be placed. Modern behaviors or attributes were assumed to replace the traditional. Recently, a number of writers from different disciplines have begun to challenge this assumption (Bendix 1967; Gusfield 1967; Armer and Schnaiberg 1972; and Robbins and Thompson 1974). Robbins and Thompson state that:

> many studies devoted to differentiating modern man from traditional man suggest that modern behavior and attitude patterns replace traditional patterns, and that modernization itself is a *unilinear additive process.* In so doing, they fail to account for the widely recognized fact that it is often the same individual who participates in both modern and traditional institutions and who on different occasions may express and manifest either modern or traditional attitudes and behavior. (1974:289, my emphasis)

Researchers who have used adoption of innovations as an index of modernization are also becoming cognizant of the fact that their domain of study is more complex than was originally thought. In the past, most studies used the adoption of an innovation as indicative of modernization. When comparing the results of such studies, however, it was often found that the predictors of the adoption of one innovation were not associated (or were negatively associated) with the adoption of another innovation. In my view, some of the apparently incongruous results that have been obtained in innovation studies can be explained by the failure to take into account the variations in types of items used as the dependent variables in such analyses. Fliegel and Kivlin (1966: 236) make the same point: "Failure to take into account similarities and differences among innovations makes it problematical at best to generalize from the known determinants of a given innovation to a second or third innovation." Perhaps this point can be summarized best with a simple illustration. If we were to use the following items as dependent variables in studies of the adoption of innovations among male members of any community in the United States – a motorcycle jacket more effective in insulation against the wind and cold, improved sup-

>ort hose, and a new type of electronic calculator – could we expect :he same individuals to be adopting them? I think it is clear that the >ocial and psychological characteristics of the adopters of each one of :hese innovations would be quite different.

If the *ejidatarios* of Puerto de las Piedras were simply moving along :he continuum from traditionality to modernity, a simple count of the 1umber of innovations they had adopted would have been sufficient for 4se as the dependent variable in this study. However, as I showed in Chapter 4, it seemed that there was a more complex set of choices >eing made about which innovations to adopt. That is, the *ejidatarios* ✓ere not simply deciding between becoming modern or staying tradi-:ional. Instead, they were choosing to adopt sets of items that would >enefit them. Because they could not afford (or did not want) all of :he items of new technology, they made the perfectly rational decision :o concentrate their resources in groups of items that logically fit to-gether. They did not simply randomly select from among the items 4vailable. These sets of items defined what I called adaptive strategies – 'the patterns formed by the many separate adjustments that people devise in order to obtain and use resources and to solve the immediate problems confronting them" (Bennett 1969:14).[42]

This method of looking at modernization has advantages that are 10t common to other methods of study. First, the identification of 4daptive strategies makes clear that modernization may expand the 4lternatives available to the people of a region. It has been recognized in aggregate-level analyses that one of the concomitants of moderni-zation is increasing occupational specialization; the few roles that can >e adopted in traditional societies increase rapidly with modernization. Those studies that consider modernization as a unidimensional pheno-menon (i.e., as a choice between modernization and traditionalism) give the impression that one limited set of roles is being exchanged for a similarly limited set. The adaptive strategies that I identified make it clear that there is an expansion of alternatives and that people are choosing from among these alternatives.

Second, because of the identification of adaptive strategies, it is pos-sible to specify more precisely the behavioral characteristics associated with the adoption of particular strategies. That is, my analysis has not been limited simply to looking at the general correlates of moderniza-tion. Instead, I have looked at those variables that are associated with the adoption of forage production, animal improvement, tractor use, fertilizer use, and subsistence agriculture. Variables associated with the decision to adopt one of the strategies were not associated with the

other strategies in the same way. Thus more specific information ha
been gathered than could have been in a study focused upon moderni
zation in general.

Finally, the adaptive strategies indicate that these peasants seem t
be making rational choices with regard to modernization. The new
items are not adopted at random; rather, there is a careful selection o
items that enable individuals to maximize their chances for improvin
one aspect of their productive activities. This selection may enable th
ejidatarios to increase forage or livestock production; or the decisio
may be to use tractors in order to allow more time for productive activ
ities other than agriculture. The important point is that peasants are no
simply clinging irrationally to their traditions but are changing thei
behavior in ways that they believe will make them better adapted t
environmental conditions.

Predictors of modernization in the ejido

The third and perhaps the most important focus of this study was upon
the predictors of modernizing behavior in this Mexican region. The pre
dictors of modernization are really quite different for each of the fiv
different adaptive strategies. Although I identified these predictors in
Chapter 12, I will provide a brief summary of them here.

Forage production is the most costly and at present the most poten
tially profitable adaptive strategy. The cash investment for seed, fencing
and a cart for transportation of the crop is considerable. It was not sur
prising to find that the variables (factor scores) sociopolitical manipula
tion and local leadership and wealth were most highly associated with
the adoption of forage production. The former is indicative of wealth in
land, while the latter is indicative of wealth in general. Having lots o
land and cash are both obviously important for the adoption of forage
production. The only relatively poor individual I knew who had adopt
ed forage production was a young married man whose father-in-law
loaned him the money to sow the forage crops.

Animal improvement is also a relatively expensive adaptive strategy
Vaccine, processed foods, and other items are fairly expensive when
used in the quantitites and frequencies recommended. The largest in
vestment, of course, is in the animals. Use of alcohol is negatively related
to adoption of animal improvement. There are two probable reasons for
this. First, those people who drink heavily are likely to sell animals at
inopportune times, especially when money is needed to start or prolong
a drinking spree. Second, the care of animals is a daily chore. Unlike
types of agriculture in which there is a relatively flexible working sched

le (e.g., plowing can take place any time within a span of a few weeks), keeping livestock healthy requires that their needs for food and water be met daily. This schedule does not allow for frequent drunken binges. For these reasons, it would be impractical for people who are heavy drinkers to invest money in improving and protecting their animals.

People who live a long way from their fields are likely to invest in animal improvement. Animals are kept at the house, and so there is no need to keep a vigil over the fields. In contrast, the other adaptive strategies are investments in agriculture. It makes sense that those who live farthest from their lands are investing in animals rather than in agriculture. The same explanation could be applied to why people with an extralocal orientation are investing in animal improvement. These individuals have other, nonagricultural means of support. Thus it might be expected that they would be investing in animals that are always close by the house rather than in agricultural pursuits.

Local leadership and wealth is also positively associated with animal improvement. This relationship reflects the need for cash and some knowledgeability among individuals who invest in animal improvement.

Tractor use is not significantly more expensive than traditional techniques for preparing the land. However, individuals who already have the implements needed (people with high scores on local leadership and wealth) are not likely to adopt the use of tractors. Those individuals who drink a lot, in contrast, are willing to use tractors. These individuals may realize their problem and hire tractors as a concession to their probable inability to put in the needed labor in the fields.

Tractor use is also adopted by people who have a lot of land (as indicated by sociopolitical manipulation). Tractors can perform the necessary agricultural work in a fraction of the time that it takes a team of animals. *Ejidatarios* who work in other occupations (as indicated by extralocal orientation) also adopt the use of tractors. As with those who drink heavily, this practice may result from their realization that they will not have sufficient time to devote to the preparation of the fields.

Very little is known about those who are likely to adopt the use of fertilizer. Indians do seem to adopt the use of fertilizer more often than *mestizos*. Those with an extralocal orientation also tend to be likely to adopt fertilizer use. Only a very small amount of the variance in this adaptive strategy is accounted for, however.

Subsistence agriculture is the variable that indicates the degree to which *ejidatarios* have not adopted any of these adaptive strategies. If they have not adopted any of the new adaptive strategies, then their subsistence agriculture score is high. Individuals who are sociopolitical manipulators or are extralocally oriented are least likely to continue subsistence agriculture. These individuals are clearly trying to improve their positions and are investing in some of the new opportunities.

The modernization that is occurring in this Mexican *ejido* is not a unidimensional phenomenon, and individuals with quite different characteristics are investing in the five adaptive strategies. The same individuals are not consistently adopting all of the new items available. The most encouraging feature about the patterns of adoption that I found is that they are easily explainable and make good sense upon close scrutiny of the various social, economic, and cultural factors affecting individual decisions. These patterns suggest that rational, calculating, logical, selective decisions are being made by the *ejidatarios*.

The answers that I have provided to the three general questions are theoretically useful. However, in addition to the value of this research for constructing theories about modernization or investigating peasant societies, it was also designed to be pragmatically useful for development efforts being made in the Temascalcingo region. Thus I will now turn my attention from these wider issues in order to: (*a*) evaluate the development projects that have been carried out in Puerto de las Piedras (*b*) make some predictions about the future of the *ejido*, and (*c*) make recommendations to change agents who may work in the region in the future.

An evaluation of modernization in the ejido

Development agents who have attempted to modernize the economy of the Temascalcingo region have been frustrated and discouraged. They see very few people mechanizing their operations, vaccinating their animals, planting forage crops, or using fertilizer, hybrid seed, or other modern techniques of cultivation. Perhaps their greatest frustration has come because the *ejidatarios* and other people in the region have shown no inclination to form the cooperatives that most development agents feel are necessary for modernization. As a result, the development agents and others have characterized the people as recalcitrant, conservative, apathetic, and uncooperative.

As I indicated in Chapter 2, much of the comparative failure of development efforts has been due to problems with the programs themselves. No one would have much confidence in change agents if they had seen programs in which so-called superior breeds of animals died, hybrid seeds failed to produce as much as the indigenous varieties, people were overcharged because previously made payments were embezzled by corrupt officials, or only a few individuals became rich from cooperatives that were formed to benefit the whole community. It is obvious that well planned, honestly run development efforts are a prime requisite for significant socioeconomic change.

In spite of all of the problems, the majority of people I encountered were quite aware of and desirous of improved technology. *Ejidatarios* in Puerto de las Piedras, for example, have seen fields of corn with two or three large ears on each plant, fat cows with full udders, healthy animals grazing on plots of lush green clover and alfalfa, and tractors manicuring fields in a few short hours. The demonstration effect provided by the farms of the few private landowners in the region has convinced them of the value of new forms of technology. Why, then, don't all *ejidatarios* willingly cooperate with change agents and adopt these new techniques?

Perhaps the greatest problem is that new technology is expensive. To be sure, the development agents have made loans available; but in most cases, the *ejidatarios* must form cooperatives in order to qualify for the loans. However, these people have had experience with this form of organization in the past, and invariably these ventures have failed. Most are adamantly opposed to the idea of cooperatives because, they say, in the past cooperative ventures have resulted in the labor of many being used for the benefit of a few.

As a result, the *ejidatarios* are faced with a situation in which many new items of technology are available; but there are only minimal resources they can allocate to investment. Thus the *ejidatarios* are forced to choose certain items for adoption from among all of those available. As I indicated earlier, the emergence of patterns in the ways in which these scarce resources are allocated means that the *ejidatarios* are not randomly selecting from among the items of technology. Instead, they are choosing sets of items to help them modernize one area of their operations.

Thus I believe that the development agents have succeeded in opening up new alternatives for the *ejidatarios*. However, the changes that are taking place are what I would characterize as evolutionary rather than revolutionary (see also Myrdal 1968:1910). That is, regardless of change agents' hopes, no sudden socioeconomic transformation of the region or the *ejido* has taken place. Instead, the *ejidatarios* are now only dabbling in new technology. They increase their investments as their previous efforts begin to pay off and/or their resources and expertise increase. As individuals accumulate more investments in one area, different modernizing adaptive strategies are slowly emerging.

The evolutionary form of change has many advantages over a quick revolutionary transition to a totally different economic base. The changes now taking place certainly minimize risk. Every *ejidatario*, withou exception, has continued to plant corn. Thus there is still an opportu nity to return completely to the adaptive strategy that has proved itsel over the centuries. While they are experimenting with new technolog and new economic enterprises, the *ejidatarios* are maintaining a hedg in case the new, unproved, and insecure adaptive strategies do not pa off. As investments continue and the new adaptive strategies are foun to be viable, I believe that a more rapid decline in the planting of corr purely for subsistence purposes will take place. Some individuals wil undoubtedly continue to cultivate corn, although with the clear goal o producing a surplus for sale instead of for self-consumption.

Another aspect of risk minimization is that this form of change doe not require the formation of cooperatives. Each individual *ejidataric* rises or falls on the basis of his/her own effort. There is no need to de pend upon or worry about other members of a cooperative.

Evolutionary change also means that the exchange of goods can stil take place on the local scene. That is, a surplus of forage, animals, o corn can still be sold to other *ejidatarios* or to individuals in Temascal cingo or other surrounding communities. The relatively slow growth ir the use of tractors means that individuals who depend upon wage labor in agriculture are slowly being displaced rather than immediately being rendered obsolete. Thus although the new opportunities are disrupting traditional economic patterns, the slow rate of change means that many "fine tuning" adjustments can be made. These minor adjustments however, cause little disruption when compared to the major disloca tions that would result from revolutionary changes. For example, a sud den switch by everyone (or even a large number of *ejidatarios*) to forage crops or to livestock production would entail finding outside markets for these products. The regional economy would not be able to handle the greatly increased output. Although outside markets for cattle, milk, forage, and other products exist, the *ejidatarios* would almost surely then come to depend upon middlemen. Means of transportation and storage would also have to be developed. All of these would require considerable capital and expertise. The need for efficient managers would be imperative.

I am not suggesting that Mexican peasants are incapable of develop ing the skills and knowledge necessary for modern entrepreneuria activities. They are. The point is that if production grows slowly, knowl edge, capital, expertise, and the necessary marketing facilities can evolv as the need for them is created. Currently, considerable dependenc upon nonlocal people would be needed if a large-scale socioeconomic transformation took place. The potential for exploitation of the *ejida tarios* by these outsiders is obvious.

As I showed in Chapter 12, the normal pattern for *ejidatarios* who achieve some success in their agricultural activities is to look increasingly toward the outside, more modern world. Those individuals who are manipulators (sociopolitical manipulation) become local-level, wealthy leaders. Many of these leaders (local leadership and wealth) then begin to turn toward the outside world (extralocal orientation). An extralocal orientation does not necessarily mean that these individuals leave the region or even desire to leave the region. It simply means that they become knowledgeable and experienced in the ways of the outside world and perhaps acquire a job outside of agriculture. My view is that these individuals are already beginning to bridge the kinds of gaps that will need to be closed if people in the *ejido* are to become more assimilated into the national economic picture. They are acquiring the "middlemen" skills.

Finally, I should note that the increasing diversification of adaptive strategies among the *ejidatarios* can also lead to a healthy generalization of the region's economy. That is, as the regional economy becomes less dependent upon one crop, it becomes less susceptible to the vagaries of market conditions, insect plagues, the weather, and other factors. There are many examples of regions that have suffered catastrophic declines because they were too dependent upon one crop or industry. United States examples that come readily to mind include the areas that suffered because they were dependent upon cotton, mining, or the shoe industry.

A generalized economic system also has the advantage of flexibility. Thus as the potential for profits in an area increases, there may be a possibility that some land or other productive resource can be converted quickly in order to take advantage of the new opportunity. For example, for many years the region has suffered because corn prices have remained fairly low; but because there were no other possibilities for production, corn continued to be produced even though surpluses were of little economic value. In a generalized economy, it might be possible for some individuals to plant forage crops when there is great demand for them, switch back to corn if prices increase, or begin to raise animals if meat prices should rise.

Thus my evaluation of the results of the development programs is not nearly as negative as evaluations by the change agents themselves. There is no denying that a better job could have been done in promoting the socioeconomic modernization of the *ejido* and the region. However, new opportunities have been established and are being adopted by some *ejidatarios*. I would now like to summarize the changes that have taken place and give some of my views about the future of the *ejido* of Puerto de las Piedras.

Changing adaptive strategies in the ejido:
past and future trends

Until the establishment of the *ejido* in the early 1930s, the people of
Puerto de las Piedras had only one adaptive strategy open to them –
wage labor for the *hacendado* or wealthy individuals from Temascalcingo supplemented by some hillside cultivation. With the redistribution of
land, the *ejidatarios* were able to engage in the production of corn as a
subsistence crop and the cultivation of wheat as a cash crop.[43] This new
adaptive strategy, which was made possible by the formation of the *ejido*, led to a marked increase in the economic position of most of the
people. This period of prosperity lasted only until about 1940; then
flooding began because of improper maintenance of the river control
system constructed by the former owners of the *haciendas* in the valley.

Of necessity, two new adaptive strategies arose at this time (see Figure 13.1). These were migration (temporary and permanent) and wage
labor. Many people abandoned their lands because of the flooding and
left in order to try to find permanent jobs in the city. Some continued
to cultivate their fields but supplemented their incomes by migrating
for varying periods of time to hold temporary jobs in the city. Some
ejidatarios were able to find jobs in and around Temascalcingo and supplemented their variable crop yields with earnings from wage labor.

These were the only alternatives available to the *ejidatarios* until the
late 1960s, although a few unsuccessful development schemes took
place before that time. Two major developments took place in the 1960s.
The first of these was the government project to construct flood control and irrigation facilities along the Lerma River. Second, coupled
with the technological input were a number of socioeconomic development programs. As I have shown in earlier chapters, these have had the
effect of increasing the number of possible alternative strategies available in the region. The new adaptive strategies of forage production,
animal improvement, tractor use, and fertilizer use have developed. The
old adaptive strategies of subsistence agriculture, wage labor, and temporary migration have continued (see Figure 13.1).

In earlier chapters, I suggested some possible future trends. I would
now like to make these more explicit and to offer some predictions
about future adaptive strategies within the *ejido* of Puerto de las Piedras.

First, wage labor and migration will continue to be attractive alternative adaptive strategies. They will continue to be necessities for sons
of *ejidatarios* and others who are not able to gain access to *ejido* lands.
Some of those who do have access to land will probably still continue
to migrate temporarily and/or engage in wage labor, especially if they

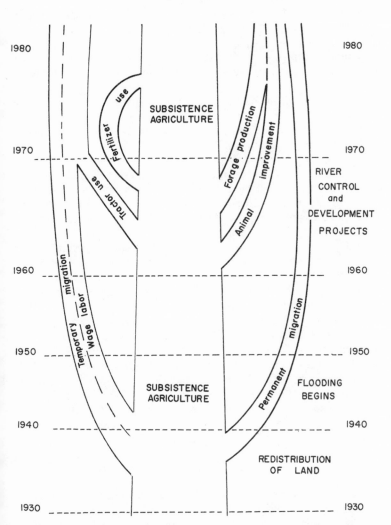

Figure 13.1 Changing adaptive strategies in the *ejido* of Puerto de las Piedras

have developed some skill which allows them to earn a decent salary. The vagaries of agriculture, despite the river control, will encourage these individuals to limit their cultivation to a part-time basis.

Second, as soil fertility continues to decline and as new opportunities are proven viable, the production of corn purely for subsistence purposes will decline. I believe that many individuals will cease to cultivate corn at all and will rely upon cash crops. Those people who continue to grow corn will gradually begin to use more fertilizer, improved varieties of seed, insecticides, herbicides, and other energy-intensive methods. Thus fertilizer use will combine with (or replace) subsistence agriculture.

Third, there will be some convergence of adaptive strategies, at least among some individuals. I believe that before long many individuals will be combining the forage production and animal improvement strategies. Although some individuals will continue to specialize in one or the other, the two are logically connected. As people accumulate resources from their previous investments in one or the other of these two production areas, they will generalize their activities to include both cultivating forage crops and raising animals. I have indicated the convergence of these two adaptive strategies in the "tree diagram" (Figure 13.1) by joining the two branches.

Another convergence that is already taking place is the combination of tractor use with wage labor and/or temporary migration. That is, people who devote only part of their time to cultivation are increasingly turning to the use of tractors as one means of cutting down on the amount of labor that they need to put into their land.

Finally, new adaptive strategies will arise. Even in 1973, a few individuals were already experimenting with new crops and ideas. Barley and wheat were grown by a few individuals, and one *ejidatario* was growing lettuce on one of his fields. In other *ejidos* in the valley, individuals were attempting to grow tomatoes, onions, and other vegetables. Although all of the efforts that I followed turned out to be failures for various reasons, it is possible to grow these crops in the region. As the *ejidatarios* acquire expertise with these other cultigens, some will prove to be profitable; and new adaptive strategies will develop.

Recommendations

I believe that the *ejidatarios* have benefited and will continue to benefit from the new opportunities becoming available. Although modernization has not progressed as rapidly as some people would wish, the different adaptive strategies that are evolving do seem to have potential for effecting the eventual socioeconomic development of the region.

However, in order to encourage future success, I feel that the efforts of the change agents should be modified in several ways. I would like to offer some recommendations that I believe would greatly aid in continuing the progress that has already been made. I enter the area of making suggestions with some trepidation, but I share Belshaw's views on anthropology and public policy. He states that: "Our responsibility, if we decide to enter this world, is to use our knowledge, give our advice, generate ideas, but never pretend that they have the kind of authority that can be provided in certain circumstances, in other fields, by physicists or engineers" (1976:275). Thus the following recommendations are based upon what I have learned about the Temascalcingo region. Although they are aimed specifically toward change agents within that region, I also believe that these suggestions are more widely applicable to other parts of the developing world.

1. *Identify and encourage the diversification of adaptive strategies.* In any modernizing situation in which people have some element of choice (i.e., where new productive techniques are not imposed by a central government), they will have different ideas about the kinds of activities in which they would like to be engaged. Thus I believe that different adaptive strategies can always be identified and that these will be important in understanding the dynamics of change in any region. Development agents should pay more attention to the efforts that individuals are making toward modernizing their productive activities. Once these are identified, the next step would be to determine which (if any) might be viable. Development personnel can then play the role of agents of cultural selection; they can provide more information and assistance to people with potentially viable ideas. Those individuals with ideas that are not as feasible should be encouraged (by demonstrating other alternatives, withholding credit, etc.) to reorient their adaptive choices. Development agencies usually have ample suggestions about new adaptive strategies that can be entered into the pool of possibilities. These, of course, should be adequately conceptualized, planned, and demonstrated.

The aim of development agents should not be to convert everyone in a region to a single adaptive strategy. As Belshaw states: "a key to development is *not* everybody doing exactly what everybody else is doing. It is precisely in specialized differentiation – once known as division of labor" (1976:236). I have already mentioned several cases in which areas dependent upon a single industry or crop go into a rapid decline when their specialty fails.

Another reason for encouraging diversity relates to energy problems. When fuel was cheap and plentiful, regional specialization costs were low even in cases where the final consumers were a considerable distance from the producers. Now that fuel supplies are declining and prices are rising, it is becoming increasingly apparent that the more self-sufficient regions are, the better off they will be. I believe it is quite valid to question any development scheme that makes communities more "de-localized" – that is, that increases their dependence upon outside energy and resources (see Pelto and Pelto 1976:476–81).

A simpler reason for being attuned to the existence of different adaptive strategies is that people often have good reasons for choosing one over another. I have already shown in Chapter 12 that people who live far away from their fields are not willing to invest money in expensive forage production. This fact was related to their inability to keep a close watch on these fields. These individuals are, however, willing to invest in the animal improvement strategy because animals are kept near the house where they can be watched closely. Development agents should be aware that people who live close to their fields and people who live far away from them are just as willing to invest in new strategies. Not much success, however, can be expected if development agents try to force forage production on people who live a considerable distance from their fields.

Suggesting that the diversity of adaptive strategies be identified and encouraged would mean that there would have to be much greater contact between development agents and the modernizing population. Such contact is always theoretically desirable but almost impossible to achieve in practice. The number of villages that need technical assistance is very large in comparison to the number of change agents. However, a tremendous amount of time and money has already been expended in the Temascalcingo region in development efforts that have achieved only minimal success. I believe that if one village in a region was selected for intensive change agent assistance along the lines that I have suggested, a development project with unquestioned success could result. The diverse adaptive strategies that prove viable could then serve as a model for people in other villages. These would spread through a region because of the demonstration effect. Change agents would still be necessary to assist individuals; but on the basis of an initial success, trust and confidence might grow between the two groups. Thus villagers would be more likely to seek out development personnel, and the task of communicating ideas would be greatly simplified.

2. *Make credit available to individuals and small groups.* Mexico is a country in which capitalism and individualism predominate, even among rural people such as those in the Temascalcingo region. Thus it seems foolish to try to force individuals to form cooperatives when the larger societal structure does not emphasize these organizations. Although cooperatives have obvious advantages in terms of economies of scale, they have not proved to be workable in the Valley of Temascalcingo. I feel that entrepreneurial efforts should be encouraged with

loans to individuals and small groups. Some groups could be encouraged for such purposes as plowing the land or buying seeds, fertilizers, and other materials in bulk. However, these groups need not be formalized or long lasting.

Although the banks and the government agree that making loans to individuals is risky, experience in the Temascalcingo region seems to indicate that making loans to cooperatives is at least as risky, if not more so. The formation of cooperatives, as far as I can tell, has basically shifted the onus of collecting loans from the banks and the government to the leader of the cooperative. This arrangement has not meant that loan repayments are made; instead, it simply seems that conflict has resulted among members of the cooperatives. The head of the cooperative reports that the members do not pay their money; the members report that they have paid but that the head has stolen the money.

Another common complaint about cooperatives is that some individuals end up doing all the work while others simply sit back waiting to collect the profits. Loans to individuals would alleviate this problem and would also make each individual's success or failure depend upon his or her abilities.

The problem of cooperatives is also related to the point about different adaptive strategies. Cooperatives are usually encouraged because the explicit aim of a development agency is to get everyone in a community doing the same thing. Were more emphasis placed on encouraging a diversity of strategies, there would also be a concomitant decline in the emphasis on cooperatives as forms of organization for development purposes.

3. *Whenever possible, encourage the use of appropriate technology rather than energy-intensive forms.* In recent years, there has been increasing concern that energy-intensive forms of cultivation practiced in the United States may not be appropriate for developing areas of the world (Schumacher 1973; Harris 1975). The rapidly rising costs of fertilizer, insecticides, and herbicides, many of which are manufactured from petroleum, are one aspect of the problem. Steinhart and Steinhart (1974:312) estimated that if United States methods of food production were used to feed the whole world, about 80 percent of the current annual expenditure for energy would be needed just to produce food.

A further problem is that these energy-intensive forms of food production automatically favor those farmers who are already better off and have the resources to adopt these expensive technological items (Franke 1973; Griffin 1974). Thus the result of this agricultural system could be an increase in inequalities that already exist (see also recommendation #5).

Finally, I should note that the adoption of mechanized agriculture also holds a number of dangers for developing areas of the world. Mechanization can exacerbate the problems of underemployment and unemployment that already exist. The greatest resource of these countries is the labor supply. In the desire to emulate the developed nations, countries that emphasize technology that eliminates the need for labor are further "marginalizing" a large segment of the population (see also DeWalt 1978).

The Temascalcingo region is one in which development agents have attempted the "technological fix." Green Revolution technology in the form of chemical fertilizers, insecticides, herbicides, hybrid seeds, and tractors have been advocated for improving the corn crop. Plan Maíz, one of the development projects mentioned earlier, was specifically designed to apply the techniques learned in the Puebla Project (CIMMYT 1969) to the *ejidos* in the Temascalcingo region. There is no denying that some of this technology (such as fertilizer to counteract the effects of monocultivation of corn) is badly needed. However, other inputs may not be as necessary. It is generally recognized, for example, that hybrid seeds require even more technology in the form of more fertilizer, more insecticides, more herbicides, and more irrigation. For small farmers with limited resources, and in an increasingly energy-scarce world, the eventual costs of this technology may outweigh the benefits.

I have also discussed how little tractors are needed in the region. The small and fragmented landholdings make it pragmatically impossible to utilize these machines efficiently. Tractors would be useful if cooperatives were formed; but as I mentioned earlier, these forms of organization have not been successful in the region. The individuals who are utilizing tractors now also indicate that mechanization of agricultural operations should be reexamined. Those who are using these implements are heavy drinkers, are working in occupations outside of the *ejido*, and/or have managed to accumulate more land than is legally allowed. Thus instead of increasing production and attachment to the land, as intended by development agents, tractors are simply allowing those with only a marginal interest in their lands to continue cultivation.

I believe that local resources should be utilized as much as possible, with doses of outside technology applied only when absolutely necessary. Implements drawn by animals may look primitive (see Photograph 5); but they provide useful, gainful employment for the people behind them (see also DeWalt 1978).

4. *Encourage the unification of scattered plots of land.* The scattered plots of land make cultivation difficult. Small, distant plots of land may

5. An *ejidatario* from Puerto de las Piedras cultivating among young corn plants.
Animal-drawn implements are used for all major agricultural operations, although
many individuals now rent tractors for the initial plowing.

receive only minimal care even though they are of good quality; it is simply too much trouble to perform the labor needed in order to produce good crops on them (see Chapter 5). The variation in the quality of the land and the flooding caused by minor variations in the topography of the fields would make the unification of plots very difficult, but some government intervention in the form of leveling the land and perhaps even actually implementing the reallocation of parcels might have to take place. There is a desire among most *ejidatarios* to have their lands unified, but there is also the fear that some individuals would manipulate this redistribution to acquire the best land and perhaps even more land. Precedents for such actions have occurred in the past (see Chapter 5). Care would have to be taken to insure that unification of fields takes place in an equitable manner.

One immediate payoff of unification might be to encourage more people to plant forage crops. Currently, many people are unwilling to invest money in planting *pradera* because their lands lie in locations where they would not be able to irrigate as often as necessary, because it would be too expensive to fence in the property, because it is too expensive to sow only a small piece of property with *pradera*, or because of a combination of these considerations. Unifying the parcels would not solve everyone's problems, but it would encourage many more people to plant forage crops.

5. *Make a special effort to contact individuals who are not wealthy and/or leaders.* In Chapters 6 and 7, I reported that people who are wealthy and/or leaders are often the ones who are contacted by the development agents. This practice gives these individuals an edge over others in taking advantage of new opportunities, which in turn can lead to increasing social stratification. In order to avoid this potentially disruptive pattern, those who are poor and are not leaders should have special efforts directed at them. They should be given special consideration for loans that will make them able to adopt new adaptive strategies as frequently as those who have more resources.

Making a special effort to contact the poor depends, of course, upon recognizing inequalities that exist within the community. I believe that no matter how homogeneous a community may look in terms of wealth, socioeconomic inequalities will always be found, and the "wealthy" will be the most likely to adopt new opportunities. This fact should be recognized, and steps should be taken to insure that others who are in poorer economic circumstances also have the possibility of modernizing their productive activities.

Development agents have a difficult task in this regard. Their job requires them to produce results in the form of people who will accept the program they are advocating. Just as the wealthier, more educated people of the community are more likely to accept them and their ideas, they are more likely to talk with the wealthy and the educated. The problem of growing inequalities is recognized by most development agencies, at least in theory. However, the impact of change programs must be continuously monitored if the unwanted effects of increasing stratification are to be avoided.

Those individuals in the *ejido* of Puerto de las Piedras who have begun to invest in the forage production and animal improvement strategies are the leaders, the wealthy, the more knowledgeable. These are the two strategies that are the most expensive to adopt and, at the same time, are the two most potentially profitable areas of endeavor. The common situation of the rich getting richer thus applies. Unless development agents make special efforts to contact poorer people and provide credit for them, inequalities in the community will only become more pronounced.

6. *Pay attention to subsistence needs as well as to commercial agriculture.* Most development projects give little attention to the subsistence crops grown in a region unless they view these as potentially profitable cash crops. Fortunately, in the Valley of Temascalcingo, major efforts have been made to improve corn production. Change agents reported, however, that increasing corn production was seen as an intermediate step; the hope was that people would invest in other cash crops after they had made a small profit from their corn.

Corn is not seen as having much potential as a cash crop. Even the *ejidatarios* realized this. Many of them told me that "corn is not business" (*maíz no es negocio*) and that a person would have to switch to another crop in order to make money. The fertilizer and other techniques that have been introduced do increase production. However, as I showed in my analysis of some of these data, the average increment was only twenty-four dollars for a hectare of corn on which fertilizer was used versus one on which no fertilizer was applied (DeWalt 1975:161). This finding may partially explain why I was able to account for so little of the variation in fertilizer use.

This point does not mean that development agents should turn their attention away from improving corn production. Corn is extremely important because it is the staple of the peasant diet. In my 1975 analysis, I suggested that those who are using fertilizer are simply trying to increase their corn production to the point at which their subsistence needs are met. Once they do not have to purchase corn in order to meet the minimal needs of their family, there is little incentive to produce much more. Money for fertilizer can be invested in some other potentially more profitable endeavor.

I believe that development agents should be cognizant of the *ejidatarios'* desire to meet their own subsistence needs. One of the keys to the relative success (in terms of managing to survive) of most peasant communities is their independent subsistence. Whenever there have been perturbations in the larger social system, peasant communities have usually been very successful in turning in on themselves and becoming relatively autonomous (see Greenwood 1974:7). Thus it is wise to attempt to insure the people's subsistence needs before, or in addition to, introducing cash-cropping possibilities.

Adaptive dynamics and the study of economic development

This work was written to address three major areas of scholarly endeavor. It was designed to fit into the literature on (*a*) Mesoamerican community studies, (*b*) economic development and sociocultural change, and (*c*) theory and methods for studying human behavior. The first two have received adequate emphasis, and so in this final section I will focus on the third of these. I will briefly review the theoretical and methodological tenets of my work and will argue that these can be fruitfully applied in other social scientific studies.

In the first chapter, I discussed a number of key elements that I stated were necessary for getting at the processes involved in modernization. Among these were a focus on intracultural variation, investigating the constraints and incentives affecting people's adaptive decisions through use of multivariate techniques, and combining quantitative and qualitative analyses. Recently, John Bennett has outlined a perspective that can be reconciled with the basic premises used in this work. He advocates an approach that looks at what he calls adaptive dynamics – behavior designed to attain goals and satisfy needs and wants, and the consequences of this behavior for the individual, society, and the environment" (1976:270). This perspective holds great promise because, used properly, such analyses can go beyond the simplistic, descriptive nature of most social scientific research and can begin to get at the dynamic process of human behavior.

One aspect of adaptive dynamics looks at the "actions by individuals designed to accomplish ends or effect change in the instrumental contexts of life" (Bennett 1976:270). Bennett puts proper emphasis on the crucial role of human choice in adaptation. He assumes that some choices are better than others, that some are mistakes, and that choices are generally made for the benefit of the individual rather than for the good of society.

From my perspective, the most important adaptive decisions that an individual has to make are those relating to the most basic of human needs – the provisioning of self and the household. This point is what led me to focus on the changes and lack of change taking place in productive techniques among the *ejidatarios* of Puerto de las Piedras. The intracultural variation in adaptive strategies of production among these people constitutes, in effect, "a pool of behavioral possibilities" (Pelto and Pelto 1975:14). Some of these possibilities will beome more widespread in years to come, others will disappear completely, and still others will continue to attract a minority of adherents.

The identification of adaptive strategies is one of the most important elements in the study of adaptive dynamics. There are some problems in this regard. At one extreme, every individual can be said to be pursuing a different adaptive strategy; no two people make the same choices with regard to what it is that they are maximizing or satisfying. At the other extreme, adaptive strategies can be identified at too general a level. Hunting and gathering, horticulture, pastoralism, or peasantry are commonly used terms in the literature on cultural evolutionism that can be seen as adaptive strategies. Ultimately, the investigator decides the level of generality to be encompassed by the term. However, it is my opinion that adaptive strategies as part of the study of adaptive dynamics should have the individual and his/her decision-making process as a referent. The choices that humans make should lie at the heart of this type of analysis.

Once adaptive strategies are identified, there are at least three possible courses of action for the investigator. First, the characteristics of the adaptive strategies themselves can be investigated in terms of profit, risk, necessary capital, type of social organization required, and so on. Bennett (1969) did this in his study of farmers, ranchers, Hutterites, and Indians in Canada. Greenwood has performed a similar analysis among the Basques he studied in Spain. He not only compared the strategies of gardening and cattle raising but also compared families with different levels of operation within the same community (Greenwood 1976).

A second possible course of action is to focus on the consequences of particular adaptive strategies. This can be done from ecological, social, economic, political, cultural, and/or other perspectives. Bennett, for example, looked at the ecological implications of the exploitative techniques being employed by the groups he studied. Several of the economists and economic anthropologists mentioned in Chapter 1 have explored the economic benefits and costs of following different adaptive strategies (e.g., Hill 1970; Greenwood 1976).

Finally, the researcher can explore the reasons why different individuals within a community or region choose to follow different adaptive strategies. This area, of course, has been the primary focus of this work, although some data in the preceding two areas were also included. I looked at the many factors that I (or others) believed were important in determining whether individuals would adopt new adaptive strategies.

I hypothesized from the outset that there would be intracultural variability in all areas considered and that determining modernizing behavior would require multivariate analyses. As a result, this study is much more quantitatively oriented than most anthropological research. I did not use these techniques because of any particular fondness for numerical gadgetry but because of an awareness that we need much more complexity in the models that we use (see Greenwood 1976:209 for a similar view).

Factor analysis and path analysis are not the only techniques that can be used to build more complicated models, and I would not suggest that other investigators have to use these methods of analysis. It is my general mode of analysis that I would like to see adopted. That is, more research should be done that focuses on intracultural variation, that carefully operationalizes variables, and that assumes human behavior is the result of a complex, multifaceted series of causes.

The use of these perspectives for the study of modernization should have been demonstrated. The simplistic assumption that some people are more modern than others was replaced by a picture of people following different adaptive strategies. Furthermore, their choice of strategies was shown to be due to a variety of understandable constraints and incentives. That is, their decision making was not seen as an irrational clinging to tradition but rather as their best attempt to cope with their social and environmental circumstances. As I have suggested, while some of their attempts are ill-fated given present conditions, others hold more hope for the future.

Every analysis has deficiencies, and there are at least two areas that can be improved upon in future studies of this type. First, more comprehensive economic data on the various adaptive strategies should have been collected. Part of my failure in this regard can be traced to the fact that I had only hypotheses about the adaptive strategies when I returned from the field (see Chapter 4). Another problem is the difficulty involved in getting relatively complete financial information from informants. Accounts, such as those reported by Greenwood for six Basque families (1976:161–207), require a substantial investment in terms of research time. They do, however, contain invaluable information for evaluating factors such as opportunity costs (see Bennett 1976:276).

The second area of improvement lies in getting people's own ideas about the adaptive strategies they are following. I identified strategies on the basis of the *ejidatarios'* reports about new productive techniques they had adopted. I did not systematically try to determine whether they recognized these as something akin to adaptive strategies. Expressed differently, I did not determine whether the peasant's emically recognized the same strategies that I identified etically (see Chapter 1). Here again, part of the problem is that the adaptive strategies were not completely identified until I returned from the field.

In conclusion, I believe that the methods I have utilized in this work have led to a theoretically useful delineation of the processes involved in modernization. The understanding that I have achieved of the modernization occurring among individuals in Puerto de las Piedras will have served well if it results in a diminution of the importance attributed to the homogeneity-oriented studies that emphasize the tradition-bound, conservative, irrational, apathetic, fatalistic nature of peasants such as these *ejidatarios*.

Despite the somewhat optimistic picture I have painted, the road ahead is not without obstacles for the people of Puerto de las Piedras. The problems of increasing population, declining soil fertility, and rapidly increasing prices of goods imported into the region are all very serious. However, the *ejidatarios* have not been passive in the face of adversity in the past, and there is no indication that they will be in the future. Since the redistribution of land in the 1930s, economic development has taken place in the region, albeit slowly. The direction of change has been established; and unless some unforeseen impediments arise, I believe that the people of Puerto de las Piedras will become increasingly articulated with the nation and will share in the benefits, costs, and responsibilities of that system.

Epilogue

I was able to spend three weeks in the Temascalcingo region in August 1977. This amount of time was enough only to gather some impressions and did not allow me to follow up on the predictions that I made in this work. I believe, however, that it would be worthwhile to discuss what has occurred since late 1973.

There were some outward changes in the appearance of the region. A new town hall had been constructed, and many buildings in Temascalcingo had been refurbished with the assistance of a government program. Power lines had been strung, and El Puerto was on the verge of getting electricity. Work was continuing to reinforce the banks of the river, but no new flooding had occurred. The main road running through the valley had been paved, making transportation easier and more rapid. Nevertheless, many of the problems that I identified earlier were still plaguing economic development efforts.

Forty to forty-five *ejidatarios* in Puerto de las Piedras were persuaded to join a cooperative to establish a dairy herd. They planted forage crops and began the construction of a stable for the cattle. As a temporary enterprise, about a year after the cooperative was established, 280 steers were brought in for fattening. Some of the steers disappeared; and when the rest were eventually sold, the leaders of the cooperative reported that there were no profits. The members were outraged, and many accusations were leveled concerning stolen steers and money. A further source of irritation was that welldrillers had been unable to find water on the hillside where the stable was being constructed. By 1977, after three years of effort, all but a handful of people had dropped out of the cooperative, leaving open the question of whether the stable would ever open and who would be responsible for the big debt incurred. In addition, *pradera* has to be cut in order to keep it healthy, and so many individuals were giving it away because they had no use for it themselves and no way to transport it to a buyer.

Other *ejidos* in the valley were successful in beginning the operation of their stables. However, the development agent with the most experience in the region told me that even though they are established, the effort has been a *"fracaso"* (disaster): the price that a private company was paying for their milk was not high enough to provide a profit. Some of the *ejidatarios* were benefiting because they were working for a daily wage for the stables, but there is little hope that these benefits will be spread more widely unless the stables are able to make a profit. And the banks will not continue to invest money to pay employees of an enterprise that is not profitable. The development agent was not sure what would be done, but he thought that one solution might be to increase the size of the stables and the herds. This, of course, would also increase the *ejidatarios'* debt.

The final irony is that the people of the Temascalcingo region are not benefiting from the milk that is being produced in the valley. All of the milk is shipped out of the area for pasteurization and sale elsewhere, and it is still impossible to buy pasteurized milk in Temascalcingo.

A new approach to development clearly seems to be in order.

Appendix A.

Correlation matrix used for the factor analysis

	Ejido leadership	Community leadership	Wealth ratings	Value of agric. equip.	Cash value of animals	Cargo system participation
Ejido leadership	—	.56	.47	.61	.35	.00
Community leadership	.56	—	.50	.57	.54	-.12
Wealth ratings	.47	.50	—	.71	.50	-.10
Value of agricultural equipment	.61	.57	.71	—	.52	-.05
Cash value of animals	.35	.54	.50	.52	—	-.13
Cargo system participation	.00	-.12	-.10	-.05	-.13	—
Indian language ability	.05	-.24	-.28	-.03	-.21	.48
Religiosity	.05	-.09	.00	.03	-.17	.37
Distance from land	.06	-.06	-.14	-.24	-.27	.07
Age	.28	.44	.11	.11	.06	.24
Alcohol use	.02	.01	-.15	-.07	.00	.21
Political knowledge	.33	.23	.37	.38	.15	-.15
Change agent contact	.70	.44	.46	.64	.16	-.02
Land quantity–quality	.35	.21	.41	.34	-.01	-.17
Income from other pursuits	.02	.32	.36	.30	.26	-.18
Mass media exposure	.18	.13	.41	.33	.22	-.14
Cosmopolitanism	.09	.10	.27	.06	.10	-.26
Material style of life	.36	.38	.46	.40	.36	-.20

	Indian language ability	Religiosity	Distance from land	Age	Alcohol use	Political knowledge
Ejido leadership	-.05	.05	-.06	.28	.02	.33
Community leadership	-.24	-.09	-.06	.44	.01	.23
Wealth ratings	-.28	.00	-.14	.11	-.15	.37
Value of agricultural equipment	-.03	.03	-.24	.11	-.07	.38
Cash value of animals	-.21	-.17	-.27	.06	.00	.15
Cargo system participation	.48	.37	.07	.24	.21	-.15
Indian language ability	–	.34	-.10	.21	.28	-.27
Religiosity	.34	–	.12	.05	-.09	.23
Distance from land	-.10	.12	–	.22	-.03	.03
Age	.21	.05	.22	–	.25	-.23
Alcohol use	.28	-.09	-.03	.25	–	-.09
Political knowledge	-.27	.23	.03	-.22	-.09	–
Change agent contact	-.22	.00	.13	.14	-.07	.44
Land quantity–quality	-.15	-.13	-.07	.05	.20	.38
Income from other pursuits	-.37	-.31	.01	.01	-.06	.20
Mass media exposure	-.34	-.07	-.19	-.30	-.35	.44
Cosmopolitanism	-.40	-.23	.42	.10	-.18	.10
Material style of life	-.40	-.37	-.30	.06	.01	.15

	Change agent contact	Land quantity–quality	Income from other pursuits	Mass media exposure	Cosmo-politanism	Material style of life
Ejido leadership	.70	.35	-.02	.18	.09	.36
Community leadership	.44	.21	.32	.13	.10	.38
Wealth ratings	.46	.41	.36	.41	.27	.46
Value of agricultural equipment	.64	.34	.30	.33	.06	.40
Cash value of animals	.16	-.01	.26	.22	.10	.36
Cargo system participation	-.02	-.17	-.18	-.14	-.26	-.20
Indian language ability	-.22	-.15	-.37	-.34	-.40	-.40
Religiosity	.00	-.13	-.31	-.07	-.23	-.37
Distance from land	.13	-.07	.01	-.19	.42	-.30
Age	.14	.05	.01	-.30	.10	.06
Alcohol use	-.07	.20	-.06	-.35	-.18	.01
Political knowledge	.44	.38	.20	.44	.10	.05
Change agent contact	—	.41	.34	.26	.27	.40
Land quantity–quality	.41	—	.27	.31	.11	.30
Income from other pursuits	.34	.27	—	.41	.52	.52
Mass media exposure	.26	.31	.41	—	.28	.54
Cosmopolitanism	.27	.20	.52	.28	—	.29
Material style of life	.40	.30	.52	.54	.29	—

Appendix B.

Discussion of the difference between orthogonal and oblique rotation

Figure B.1 illustrates the difference between orthogonal and oblique rotation of a factor analysis. "Orthogonal rotation involves moving the whole factor structure around the origin in a rigid frame (like the spokes of a wheel moving around a hub) until the best fit is obtained" (Rummel 1970:386). Figure B.1A illustrates the use of an orthogonal rotation in which the axes S^*_1 and S^*_2 move around the origin together (the angle between them always remaining 90°) until the best fit with the plots of variables is obtained. "Oblique rotation, however, individually rotates the factors until, in the simple structure case, each factor delineates a distinct variable cluster" (Rummel 1970:386). The axes S^*_1 and S^*_2 in Figure B.1B no longer define a 90° angle, which indicates that the variable clusters (factors) are correlated. If the variable clusters are in fact uncorrelated, then oblique rotation will result in orthogonal factors. Note in Figure B.1 that the oblique factor axes represent the clustering of the hypothetical variables more accurately than the orthogonal axes.

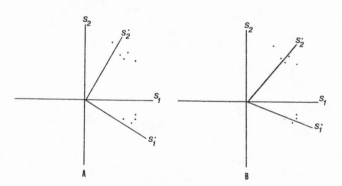

Figure B.1   Comparison of hypothetical two-factor orthogonal and oblique simple structure rotations (adapted from Rummel 1970:387)

Notes

1. GOVERNMENT OF THE STATE OF MEXICO
TEMASCALCINGO
Program to augment the production
of corn at the *ejido* level
Financed by: Government of the State of Mexico
Technical Assistance
Government of the State of Mexico
Secretary of Hydraulic Resources
Plan Lerma Technical Assistance

2. An *ejido* is the landholding group that was created when land was redistributed to the peasants after the Mexican Revolution. A minimum of twenty farmers had to organize into a group to petition for and receive the lands. There has been considerable diversity in the way that anthropologists and others have used the term *peasant* (Kroeber 1948:248; Firth 1956:87; Redfield 1960; Wolf 1966:12–17; and Foster 1967:6–11). Whereas there has always been some question concerning whether certain communities or types of peoples (e.g., potters or fishermen) fit into this descriptive category, there are also often people within what are clearly peasant communities who do not have many or all of the characteristics of a peasant. This is certainly true in the community that I have studied. I have decided to retain the use of the term for the purpose of comparison to other communities that have been described as "peasant." Most individuals do fit the traditional definition of the peasant: the basic unit of production is the family; the primary goal is the provisioning of the household; production techniques are rudimentary; and they have an asymmetrical structural relationship with a dominant group as part of a larger compound society.

3. The terms *modernization, development,* and *change* have been used interchangeably in this discussion, a practice that is in line with the use of these concepts in social science literature. However, there have been some recent attempts to be more precise in usage. Schneider, for example, defines development as "increase in productivity and wealth in general by whatever measure a people use," in contrast with change, which is "the shifting of ideas of what constitutes wealth and the structure of the economy to new forms" (1975:273). Modernization is usually used when talking about individuals; but Rogers uses the same definition for both modernization and development: "A widely participatory process of basic social structural change in a society, intended to bring about both social and material advancement of the majority of the people through means that

279

foster equality, freedom, and other valued qualities" (1975:358). Although some conceptual clarification is needed in regard to the use of these terms, in my review of the literature I will use all three terms, for other scholars have utilized them to talk about the same process. In Chapter 4, I will return to discuss the conceptual problems relating to modernization and elucidate my position on this problem.

4. Redfield's attempt to identify features common to peasant societies was only one of many such efforts. In his own work, he cited a number of other scholars who were all concerned with showing the "sameness" of peasant life everywhere (see Darling 1930; Porak 1943; Francis 1945; and Handlin 1951).

5. In fairness to Foster, it should be pointed out that he has taken individual differences into account in studying innovative behavior in Tzintzuntzan (1967: 293–310). Nevertheless, it is clear that he emphasizes the "image of the limited good" as an explanatory device for the lack of change in peasant societies.

6. Nash and others often note that economic inequalities do exist. However, they minimize the differences and state that these inequalities do not persist over generations. Rather, they believe that there is a shift of wealth through time because of the presence of leveling mechanisms (Nash 1961:190).

7. As I pointed out earlier (see note 3), Rogers recently has revised his definition to emphasize basic social structural change rather than technological change in societies. This shift indicates a growing realization by Rogers and others that "there are many alternative pathways to development" (Rogers 1975:356) and that traditional and modern systems are not mutually exclusive but may be combined in different ways.

8. Temascalcingo is the real name of the town and of the *municipio*. However, I have used pseudonyms for the other villages in the region, including Puerto de las Piedras.

9. All data on climate were obtained from the Department of Hydraulic Resources in Atlacomulco, state of Mexico.

10. Some households contained more than one individual with *ejidal* land rights, and some people with rights to land live outside of these communities. Thus the number of household heads in these three communities who have *ejido* land is only 120 rather than 146.

11. This definition is similar to that used by many social scientists in that it implicitly assumes that developing countries will follow paths similar to those followed by Western nations. Increased use of technology and industrialization are assumed to be the means by which a better way of life can be constructed. This view is coming under closer scrutiny (see Schumacher 1973; Rogers 1975; and DeWalt 1978), but it is still the dominant ideology among development planners. A less ethnocentrically biased reformulation of the concept is needed, but it is doubtful whether it would have any significant impact on the way change agents and the leaders of developing and developed countries operate.

12. Modernization has also been used to describe the process of change at the macroanalytic level (Chodak 1973). Its use at that level is also marked by a myriad number of definitions (Tipps 1973:199).

13. The problem is that people who acquire "modern" motivations, attitudes, or values will have little possibility of significantly changing their lives if socio-

economic conditions continue to block their efforts. Graves, for example, found in his study of Navajo migrants to Denver that individuals with high achievement motivation who met with little success in attaining their desires had higher rates of drunkenness than individuals with lower achievement motivation (1970:47–8). Their modernity only caused them problems because the constraints in the social system impeded their success.

14. See Table 6.3 for an example of a Guttman scale. These scales are best utilized when items are accumulated in a relatively fixed order. An item that, in the case of innovations, is adopted or possessed by nearly everyone would be the first item on the scale. The next item would be that next most frequently adopted, and so on. The last item would be that most infrequently adopted (i.e., the most difficult to acquire). The Guttman scale is perfect when any individual who has adopted an item has also adopted all of those before it and has not adopted any of the items that come after it.

15. Since I returned from the field, I have discovered a number of statements by people who also disagree with these views (e.g., Bendix 1967). Robbins and Thompson have pointed out that the same individual can manifest both modern and traditional attitudes and behavior (1974:289). Cancian (1974) has shown that the view that peasants are "non-economic men" and people in Western cultures are "economic men" is a false distinction.

16. The most widely accepted factoring method of principal factors with iteration, employing varimax rotation, was utilized. Those factors that had an eigenvalue of more than one on the unrotated matrix were kept for further analysis. Because varimax rotation was used, the factors were constrained to be orthogonal (i.e., uncorrelated) with one another (see Rummel 1970). In view of my expectations that the strategies would be more generalized, I also analyzed these data using oblique rotation (see Appendix B). This type of rotation, which allows factors to be correlated with one another, is sometimes difficult to interpret, as was the case when it was applied to the innovation adoption items. Thus I have only presented the varimax rotation here.

17. This method of computing factor scores is known as the "regression estimate" approach. These estimates are standardized so that each factor score mean will be zero and will have a standard deviation of approximately one.

18. For those who are interested in a composite measure of innovation adoption, this summation without the reversal of sign will yield this score. In future chapters, a reversal of the sign of correlation and path coefficients with "subsistence agriculture" will yield the relationship with innovation adoption.

19. This name is a pseudonym. I have used pseudonyms for other *ejidatarios* mentioned in the text in order to help preserve their anonymity.

20. The number of individuals in all of the communities who simply gave up their lands is fairly large. Over 25 percent of those in my sample, for example, reported that they had received their lands from an *ejidatario* who had abandoned the land in favor of other employment.

21. As I pointed out in Chapter 3, it is difficult to get accurate population estimates for the communities. Part of the problem is that the boundaries of the communities may sometimes be confused. A number of houses on the west side

of the bridge over the Lerma River, for example, are situated in El Puerto. These may have been included with the population of El Jardín in the Mexican Census. I have estimated the population of El Jardín as only 159 in 1973. However, my basis for saying that people have been moving into El Jardín is based on interviews with people who have moved in rather than on the census figures.

22. Soils in the United States are also often classified as sandy, clayey, and loamy (see Rodale 1971:16–17).

23. Informants were asked how many *costales* (bags) of corn they harvested from each *paraje* in which they had land. The *costal* is a very rough measure because the amount of corn a bag contains depends on the humidity present in the corn, the size of the cobs, the packing of the bag, and so on. Nevertheless, it represented the best estimate that my informants could give me of actual production, for they measured quantities only when buying or selling. A *costal* contains approximately fifty kilograms of shelled corn.

24. The best *paraje* in the *ejido* (Tecocote) produces about 2,160 kilograms of corn per hectare, whereas the poorest (La Chinqua) produces only 705 kilograms per hectare. The average yield for all fields from which I collected data was 1,569 kilograms. Average corn production in the United States during 1974 was 72 bushels per acre (Wittwer 1975:580). Assuming that a bushel of corn is equal to about 25.4 kilograms (Ennis, Dowler, and Klassen 1975:594), the yield would be approximately 4,515 kilograms per hectare. Nonhuman energy inputs into corn production in the United States (in the form of fertilizers, insecticides, herbicides, and machinery) are much larger and account for the substantially increased yields (Steinhart and Steinhart 1974). The yields from Puerto de las Piedras are higher than those obtained using traditional production techniques in the Puebla region of Mexico. The average production of plots without fertilizer in that area was under 1,000 kilograms (CIMMYT 1969:45).

25. The map of *ejido* lands done by Hydraulic Resources was invaluable to my research. The map was inaccurate as far as showing who owned what piece of land. However, with the aid of key informants, I was able to correct most of the inaccuracies. The land survey did make my task much easier. I thank the Department of Hydraulic Resources in Atlacomulco and its director, Servín de la Mora, for help in this and many other aspects of my research.

26. The other independent variables that are used in Table 5.6 are discussed and operationalized in subsequent chapters.

27. Nonetheless, as we have seen in Chapter 5, there are fairly large differences in the amount of land held by the *ejidatarios* as well as in the quality of that land.

28. The coefficient of reliability is simply one minus the number of errors divided by the total number of responses in the scale. The total number of responses is the total number of respondents multiplied by the number of items.

29. The animals that are included in the value of agricultural equipment were also included in the measure of cash value of animals. Thus these two variables were not measured independently of one another.

30. Note that Juan only had to pay 1.60 *pesos* for his corn, whereas Antonio had to pay 2 *pesos* per *cuartillo*. The difference results because Juan bought from a *compadre* while Antonio had to buy from a merchant in Temascalcingo.

31. Most wage labor does not pay anywhere near twenty *pesos* a day. As we saw, Juan paid workers on his fields fifteen *pesos,* and Antonio usually worked for a daily wage of only twelve *pesos.*

32. I should note that the correlation coefficient reported here is based only on the male members of the sample. All of the female members of the sample were fairly elderly widows. Among these widows, some were said to drink heavily, and others reportedly drank very little. Because of the bias toward elderly women in the sample, I do not wish to generalize about all *ejidatarios* but am confining my observations to males only. As I have indicated, however, I do think that there is a general tendency for older women to drink more than younger females.

33. In partial correlation, the values of the dependent and independent variables are adjusted in order to take into consideration the scores of the control variable (in this case, age). We pretend that the control variables are held constant (see Blalock 1960:330). A first-order partial correlation coefficient is one in which only one control variable is used.

34. Language ability was only measured for male respondents.

35. Factors 1, 3, 5, and 6 in Table 12.2 contain primarily negative factor loadings. In my interpretation of the factors and use of factor scores, I have converted the negative numbers to positive numbers for ease of discourse. For example, if I had used the negative loadings, Factor 1 would have been "not local leadership and wealth." Conversion of the scores does not alter the meaning of the statistical analysis.

36. Factor scores are composite scores (based on the factors) that are created for each case (see Chapter 4). The method used for constructing the factor scores was least squares regression (see Nie et al. 1975:486).

37. One problem with path analysis and other procedures is that, as in this study, they are usually used on synchronic data. That is, variables measured during the course of my research all refer to the period around 1973. However, most researchers are interested in making diachronic statements on the basis of data. Without data measured at different points in time it is impossible to be certain that the relationships posited (especially with regard to the direction of causality) are true. We should also keep in mind, especially with regard to simple recursive path analysis, that the procedure does not allow for any feedback in the system. For example, if local leadership and wealth is seen as a cause of extralocal orientation, it must be assumed that extralocal orientation is not a cause of local leadership and wealth. Although in the real world it is to be expected that there are many such reciprocal causal effects, such simplifying assumptions must often be made. Despite these reservations, path analysis has been shown to have considerable utility in the social sciences (Boudon 1965; Duncan 1966; Werts and Linn 1970; and Hadden and DeWalt 1974).

38. One advantage of path analysis is that assumptions such as this are made explicit. Other researchers, using a different theoretical model, may revise the causal ordering and test their idea, as can be done with the data from Tables 12.3 and 12.4.

39. Figures 12.3 through 12.7 contain the path models for the five different adaptive strategies. The portion of the model that includes paths to sociopolitical manipulation, local leadership and wealth, and extralocal orientation is exactly

equivalent to Figure 12.2. However, in order to avoid some of the clutter that arises from including all possible paths, I have eliminated all paths below plus or minus .10. This figure was an arbitrary cutoff point and does not correspond to any level of statistical significance. The reader who is interested in these small path coefficients can obtain them from either Figure 12.2 or Table 12. 5.

40. The regression coefficient for local leadership and wealth is not statistically significant (see also Table 12.5). However, I will discuss all of the variables and their effects on the adaptive strategies. The reader should be cautioned that only those direct effects so indicated in Table 12.5 are statistically significant.

41. As I indicated in Chapter 4, this scale is a summation of the scores on the four other adaptive strategies. I inverted the scores so that those individuals who had not adopted any adaptive strategies would come out highest on this scale. These individuals have not adopted any other adaptive strategy and thus can be said to be maintaining a traditional corn cultivation strategy. Those scholars who are interested in a summary measure of innovation adoption can also use this scale. Simply transposing the signs in Figure 12.7 will result in the predictors of this summary measure of innovation adoption.

42. I should note that Bennett did not focus on adoption of innovations in order to identify adaptive strategies in his study of *Northern Plainsmen.* Instead, he identified adaptive strategies in broad, general terms based upon the way the social and natural environment was exploited (e.g., ranchers, farmers, and communal society). Bennett would probably identify *ejidatario* as a broad, general adaptive strategy in contrast with merchants, private farmers, and workers without land. However, I believe that within these large groups, more specific adaptive strategies can be identified, and I made an effort to do this for the *ejidatarios.* By focusing on the innovations adopted (or not adopted), it is possible to delineate adjustments that people are making to better obtain and use resources.

43. Wheat was rotated with corn in the *ejido* until the 1950s. A combination of falling market prices and a fungus disease resulted in the elimination of wheat as a cultigen in the area.

Bibliography

Acheson, James. 1972. Limited Good or Limited Goods? Response to Economic Opportunity in a Tarascan Pueblo. *American Anthropologist* 74:1152–69.

Adams, R. N., ed. 1957. *Political Changes in Guatemalan Communities*. Publication 24. New Orleans: Tulane University Middle American Research Institute.

Adams, Richard. 1970. *Crucifixion by Power*. Austin: University of Texas Press.

Aguirre Beltrán, Gonzalo. 1967. *Regiones de Refugio*. México: Instituto Indigenista Interamericano.

Alland, Alexander. 1970. *Adaptation in Cultural Evolution: An Approach to Medical Anthropology*. New York: Columbia University Press.

Anderson, R. 1965. Studies in Peasant Life. In *Biennial Review of Anthropology 1965*, ed. B. J. Siegel. Stanford: Stanford University Press.

Armer, M., and Schnaiberg, A. 1972. Measuring Individual Modernity: A Near Myth. *American Sociological Review* 37:301–16.

Bailey, Frederick G., ed. 1973. *Debate and Compromise: The Politics of Innovation*. Totowa, N.J.: Rowan and Littlefield.

Banfield, Edward C. 1958. *The Moral Basis of a Backward Society*. New York: Free Press.

Barkin, David, and King, Timothy. 1970. *Regional Economic Development*. Cambridge: Cambridge University Press.

Barnett, Homer. 1953. *Innovation: The Basis of Cultural Change*. New York: McGraw-Hill.

Barth, Fredrik. 1967. On the Study of Social Change. *American Anthropologist* 69:661–9.

Beal, George H., and Sibley, Donald N. 1966. Adoption of Agricultural Technology Among the Indians of Guatemala. Paper presented at the Rural Sociological Society, Miami Beach, Florida.

Beals, Ralph. 1975. *The Peasant Marketing System of Oaxaca, Mexico*. Berkeley: University of California Press.

Bee, Robert. 1971. Unpublished field notes. July 21.

Belshaw, Cyril. 1976. *The Sorcerer's Apprentice: An Anthropology of Public Policy*. New York: Pergamon Press.

Belshaw, Michael. 1967. *A Village Economy: Land and People of Huecorio*. New York: Columbia University Press.

Bendix, R. 1967. Tradition and Modernity Reconsidered. *Comparative Studies in Society and History* 9:292–346.

Benedict, Ruth. 1934. *Patterns of Culture*. New York: Houghton Mifflin.

285

Bennett, John W. 1969. *Northern Plainsmen: Adaptive Strategy and Agrarian Life.* Chicago: Aldine-Atherton.

———. 1976a. Anticipation, Adaptation and the Concept of Culture in Anthropology. *Science* 192:847-53.

———. 1976b. *The Ecological Transition: Cultural Anthropology and Human Adaptation.* New York: Pergamon Press.

Blalock, Hubert. 1960. *Social Statistics.* New York: McGraw-Hill.

Boudon, R. 1965. A Method of Linear Causal Analysis: Dependence Analysis. *American Sociological Review* 30:365-74.

Bricker, Victoria Reifler. 1973. *Ritual Humor in Highland Chiapas.* Austin: University of Texas Press.

Bunzel, Ruth. 1940. The Role of Alcoholism in Two Central American Cultures. *Psychiatry* 3:361-87.

———. 1967. *Chichicastenango: A Guatemalan Village.* Seattle: University of Washington Press.

Campbell, Donald. 1966. *Human Evolution: An Introduction to Man's Adaptations.* Chicago: Aldine.

Cancian, Frank. 1965. *Economics and Prestige in a Maya Community: The Religious Cargo System in Zinacantán.* Stanford: Stanford University Press.

———. 1972. *Change and Uncertainty in a Peasant Economy.* Stanford: Stanford University Press.

———. 1974. Economic Man and Economic Development. In *Rethinking Modernization,* ed. John Poggie and Robert Lynch. Westport, Conn.: Greenwood.

Carrasco, Pedro. 1950. *Les Otomíes: Cultura e Historia Prehispánicas de los Pueblos Mesoamericanos de Habla Otomiana.* México: Editorial Jus.

———. 1961. The Civil-Religious Hierarchy in Mesoamerican Communities: Pre-Spanish Background and Colonial Development. *American Anthropologist* 63:483-97.

Chattopadhyay, S. N., and Pareek, Udai. 1967. Prediction of Multi-Practice Adoption Behavior from Some Psychological Variables. *Rural Sociology* 32: 324-33.

Chayanov, A. V. 1966. *The Theory of Peasant Economy.* Homewood, Ill.: Richard D. Irwin for the American Economic Association (original ed. 1925).

Chodak, Szymon. 1973. *Societal Development: Five Approaches with Conclusions from Comparative Analysis.* New York: Oxford University Press.

CIMMYT. 1969. *The Puebla Project, 1967-1969: Progress Report of a Program to Rapidly Increase Corn Yields on Small Holdings.* México: Centro Internacional de Mejoramiento de Maíz y Trigo.

Colby, Benjamin N. 1966. *Ethnic Relations in the Chiapas Highlands.* Santa Fe: Museum of New Mexico Press.

Cortés Ruiz, Efraín C. 1972. *San Simón de la Laguna.* México: Instituto Nacional Indigenista.

Darling, Malcolm. 1930. *Rusticus Loquitur: The Old Light and the New in the Punjab Village.* London: Oxford University Press.

De La Fuente, Julio. 1968. Ethnic and Communal Relations. In *Heritage of Conquest,* ed. Sol Tax. New York: Cooper Square.

DeWalt Billie. 1975a. Changes in the *Cargo* Systems of Mesoamerica. *Anthropological Quarterly* 48:87–105.

1975b. Inequalities in Wealth, Adoption of Technology, and Production in a Mexican *Ejido: American Ethnologist* 2:149–68.

1975c. Modernization in a Mexican *Ejido:* Choosing Alternative Adaptive Strategies. Ph.D. dissertation. Storrs: University of Connecticut.

1978. Appropriate Technology in Rural Mexico: Antecedents and Consequences of an Indigenous Peasant Innovation. *Technology and Culture* 19:32–52.

DeWalt, Billie; Bee, Robert; and Pelto, Pertti. 1973. The People of Temascalcingo: A Regional Study of Modernization. Mimeographed. Storrs: University of Connecticut.

DeWalt, Kathleen Musante. 1977. The Illnesses No Longer Understand: Changing Conceptions of Health and Curing in a Rural Mexican Community. *Medical Anthropology Newsletter* 8:5–11.

n.d. Personal communication.

n.d. Nutritional Correlates of Economic Microdifferentiation in a Highland Mexican Community. In *Nutritional Anthropology,* vol. 1, ed. N. Jerome, R. Kandel, and G. Pelto. Pleasantville, N.Y.: Docent, in press.

Dirrección General de Estadistica. 1963. *VIII Censo General de Población: Estado de México.* México: Secretaría de Industria y Comercio.

1971. *IX Censo General de Población: Estado de México.* México: Secretaría de Industria y Comercio.

Dobyns, Henry F. 1951. Blunders with *Bolsas:* A Case Study of Diffusion of Closed-Basin Agriculture. *Human Organization* 10:25–32;

DuBois, C. 1944. *The People of Alor: A Social-Psychological Study of an East-Indian Island.* Minneapolis: University of Minnesota Press.

Duncan, O. D. 1966. Path Analysis: Sociological Examples. *American Journal of Sociology* 72:1–16.

Ennis, W. B. Jr.; Dowler, W. M.; and Klassen, W. 1975. Crop Protection to Increase Food Supplies. *Science* 188:593–8.

Epstein, T. S. 1962. *Economic Development and Social Change in South India.* Manchester: Manchester University Press.

1973. *South India: Yesterday, Today and Tomorrow.* London: Macmillan.

1975. The Ideal Marriage Between the Economist's Macroapproach and the Social Anthropologist's Microapproach to Development Studies. *Economic Development and Cultural Change* 24:29–45.

Erasmus, Charles. 1961. *Man Takes Control: Cultural Development and American Aid.* Minneapolis: University of Minnesota Press.

Excelsior. 1973. 'Sociedad Mortal' al Alcoholismo y la Desnutrición. June 8:19A.

Firth, Raymond. 1956. *Elements of Social Organization.* London: Watts.

Fliegel, Frederick, and Kivlin, Joseph. 1966. Attributes of Innovations as Factors in Diffusion. *American Journal of Sociology* 72:235–48.

Foster, George. 1967. *Tzintzuntzan: Mexican Peasants in a Changing World.* Boston: Little Brown.

Francis, E. K. L. 1945. The Personality Type of the Peasant According to Hesiod's Works and Days: A Culture Case Study. *Rural Sociology* 10:275–95.

288 *Bibliography*

Frank, Andre Gunder. 1969. *Latin America: Underdevelopment or Revolution.* New York: Monthly Review Press.

Franke, Richard W. 1973. The Green Revolution in a Javanese Village. Ph.D. dissertation. Harvard University.

Friedl, Ernestine. 1962. *Vasilika: A Village in Modern Greece.* New York: Holt, Rinehart and Winston.

1963. Studies in Peasant Life. In *Biennial Review of Anthropology 1963,* ed. B. J. Siegel. Stanford: Stanford University Press.

Friedrich, Paul. 1970. *Agrarian Revolt in a Mexican Village.* Englewood Cliffs: Prentice-Hall.

Fromm, Erich, and Maccoby, Michael. 1970. *Social Character in a Mexican Village.* Englewood Cliffs, N.J.: Prentice-Hall.

Geertz, Clifford. 1962. Studies in Peasant Life. In *Biennial Review of Anthropology, 1961,* ed. B. J. Siegel. Stanford: Stanford University Press.

Gibson, C. 1964. *The Aztecs Under Spanish Rule.* Stanford: Stanford University Press.

Gillin, John. 1951. *The Culture of Security in San Carlos: A Study of a Guatemalan Community of Indians and Ladinos.* Publication 16. New Orleans: Tulane University Middle American Research Institute.

Goldberg, David. 1974. *Modernism: The Extensiveness of Women's Roles and Attitudes.* Occasional Papers of the World Fertility Survey. Voorburg, Netherlands: International Statistical Institute.

Goldkind, Victor. 1965. Social Stratification in the Peasant Community: Redfield's Chan Kom Reinterpreted. *American Anthropologist* 67:863–84.

González Casanova, Pablo. 1970. *Democracy in Mexico.* New York: Oxford University Press.

Gorer, Geoffrey, and Rickman, John. 1949. *The People of Great Russia: A Psychological Study.* London: Cresset.

Graves, Theodore. 1970. The Personal Adjustment of Navaho Indian Migrants to Denver, Colorado. *American Anthropologist* 72:35–54.

Greenwood, Davydd. 1974. Political Economy and Adaptive Processes: A Framework for the Study of Peasant-States. *Peasant Studies Newsletter* 3 (3): 1–10.

1976. *Unrewarding Wealth: The Commercialization and Collapse of Agriculture in a Spanish Basque Town.* New York: Cambridge University Press.

Griffin, Keith. 1974. *The Political Economy of Agrarian Change: An Essay on the Green Revolution.* Cambridge, Mass.: Harvard University Press.

Gusfield, Joseph R. 1967. Tradition and Modernity: Misplaced Polarities in the Study of Social Change. *American Journal of Sociology* 72:351–62.

Guttman, Louis. 1944. A Basis for Scaling Qualitative Data. *American Sociological Review* 9:139–50.

Hadden, Kenneth, and DeWalt, Billie R. 1974. Path Analysis: Some Anthropological Examples. *Ethnology* 13:105–28.

Halpern, Joel, and Brode, John. 1967. Peasant Society: Economic Changes and Revolutionary Transformation. In *Biennial Review of Anthropology 1967,* ed. B. J. Siegel and A. R. Beals. Stanford: Stanford University Press.

Handlin, Oscar. 1951. *The Uprooted.* Boston: Little, Brown and Company.

Harris, Marvin. 1968. *The Rise of Anthropological Theory.* New York: Thomas Y. Crowell.

———. 1975. *Culture, People, Nature.* New York: Thomas Y. Crowell.

Helms, Mary W. 1975. *Middle America: A Culture History of Heartland and Frontiers.* Englewood Cliffs, N.J.: Prentice-Hall.

Hernandez, Mercedes; Chávez, Adolfo; and Bourges, Hector. 1974. *Valor Nutrivo de los Alimentos Mexicanos.* México: Instituto Nacional de la Nutrición.

Hill, Polly. 1963. *The Migrant Cocoa-Farmers of Southern Ghana: A Study in Rural Capitalism.* Cambridge: Cambridge University Press.

———. 1970. *Studies in Rural Capitalism in West Africa.* Cambridge: Cambridge University Press.

———. 1972. *Rural Hausa: A Village and a Setting.* Cambridge: Cambridge University Press.

Huizer, Gerrit. 1970. "Resistance to Change" and Radical Peasant Mobilization: Foster and Erasmus Reconsidered. *Human Organization* 29:303–12.

Inkeles, Alex, and Smith, David H. 1974. *Becoming Modern: Individual Change in Six Developing Countries.* Cambridge, Mass.: Harvard University Press.

Iwańska, Alicja. 1971. *Purgatory and Utopia: A Mazahua Indian Village of Mexico.* Cambridge, Mass.: Schenkman.

Johnson, Allen. 1974. Ethnoecology and Planting Practices in a Swidden Agricultural System. *American Ethnologist* 1:87–101.

Junghare, Y. N. 1962. Factors Influencing the Adoption of Farm Practices. *Indian Journal of Social Work* 23:291–96.

Kahl, Joseph. 1968. *The Measurement of Modernism: A Study of Values in Brazil and Mexico.* Austin: University of Texas Press.

Kaplan, Bernice. 1965. Mechanization in Paracho: A Craft Community. In *Contemporary Cultures and Societies of Latin America,* ed. Dwight Heath and Richard Adams. New York: Random House.

Kardiner, Abram. 1945. *The Psychological Frontiers of Society.* New York: Columbia University Press.

Katz, Elihu. 1961. The Social Itinerary of Technical Changes: Two Studies on the Diffusion of Innovation. *Human Organization* 20:70–82.

Kay, Paul. 1964. A Guttman Scale Model of Tahitian Consumer Behavior. *Southwestern Journal of Anthropology* 20:160–67.

Kearney, Michael. 1972. *The Winds of Ixtepeji: World View and Society in a Zapotec Town.* New York: Holt Rinehart and Winston.

Kennedy, John G. 1966. "Peasant Society and the Image of Limited Good": A Critique. *American Anthropologist* 68:1212–25.

Kerblay, Basile. 1971. Chayanov and the Theory of Peasantry as a Specific Type of Economy. In *Peasants and Peasant Societies,* ed. Teodor Shanin. Baltimore: Penguin.

Kroeber, Alfred L. 1948. *Anthropology.* New York: Harcourt.

Lerner, Daniel. 1958. *The Passing of Traditional Society: Modernizing the Middle East*. New York: Free Press.

Levine, Robert. 1973. *Culture, Behavior and Personality*. Chicago: Aldine.

Lewis, Oscar. 1951. *Life in a Mexican Village: Tepoztlán Restudied*. Urbana: University of Illinois Press.

Lopreato, Joseph. 1965. How Would You Like to be a Peasant? *Human Organization* 24:298-307.

McClelland, David C. 1961. *The Achieving Society*. New York: Van Nostrand.

Madsen, William, and Madsen, Claudia. 1974. The Cultural Structure of Mexican Drinking Behavior. In *Contemporary Cultures and Societies of Latin America*, ed. Dwight B. Heath. New York: Random House.

Mead, Margaret. 1953. National Character. In *Anthropology Today*, ed. A. L. Kroeber. Chicago: University of Chicago Press.

  1955. *Cultural Patterns and Technical Change*. New York: Mentor.

Miller, Roy. 1974. Are Familists Amoral? A Test of Banfield's Amoral Familism Hypothesis in a South Italian Village. *American Ethnologist* 1:515-35.

Myrdal, Gunnar. 1968. *Asian Drama: An Inquiry into the Poverty of Nations*. New York: Twentieth Century Fund and Pantheon Books.

Naroll Raoul. 1970. What Have We Learned from Cross-Cultural Surveys? *American Anthropologist* 72:1227-88.

Nash, June. 1970. *In the Eyes of the Ancestors: Belief and Behavior in a Mayan Community*. New Haven: Yale University Press.

Nash, Manning. 1958. *Machine Age Maya: The Industrialization of a Guatemalan Community*. Memoir 87. Menasha, Wis. American Anthropological Association.

  1961. The Social Context of Economic Choice in a Small Community. *Man* 61:186-91.

  1964. Capital, Saving and Credit in a Guatemalan and a Mexican Indian Peasant Society. In *Capital, Saving and Credit in Peasant Societies*, eds. R. Firth and B. S. Yamey. Chicago: Aldine.

  1971. Market and Indian Peasant Economics. In *Peasants and Peasant Societies*, ed. Teodor Shanin. Baltimore: Penguin.

Nie, Norman. 1975. *Statistical Package for the Social Sciences*. New York: McGraw-Hill.

Niehoff, Arthur. 1966. *A Casebook of Social Change*. Chicago: Aldine.

Nutini, Hugo. 1968. San Bernardino Contla: Marriage and Family Structure in a Tlaxcalan Municipio. Pittsburgh: University of Pittsburgh Press.

Ortiz, Sutti Reissig. 1973. *Uncertainties in Peasant Farming*. New York: Athlone Press.

Papousek, Dick. 1974. Manufactura de Alfarería en Temascalcingo, México, 1967. *América Indígena* 34:1009-46.

Parsons, E. C. 1936. *Mitla: Town of the Souls*. Chicago: University of Chicago Press.

Pelto, Pertti, J. 1970. *Anthropological Research: The Structure of Inquiry*. New York: Harper and Row.

  1973. *The Snowmobile Revolution: Technology and Social Change in the Arctic*. Menlo Park: Cummings.

Pelto, Pertti, J., and Pelto, Gretel. 1975. Intra-Cultural Diversity: Some Theoretical Issues. *American Ethnologist* 2:1–18.

1976. *The Human Adventure: An Introduction to Anthropology.* New York: Macmillan.

Poggie, John. 1972. Toward Quality Control in Key Informant Data. *Human Organization* 31:23–30.

Poggie, John, and Lynch, Robert, eds. 1974. *Rethinking Modernization: Anthropological Perspectives.* Westport, Conn.: Greenwood.

Pollnac, Richard, and Robbins, Michael. 1972. Gratification Patterns and Modernization in Rural Buganda. *Human Organization* 31:63–72.

Porak, René. 1943. *Un Village de France: Psycho-physiologie du Paysan.* Paris: G. Doin and Cie.

Pozas, Ricardo. 1971. *Juan the Chamula: An Ethnological Re-Creation of the Life of a Mexican Indian.* Berkeley: University of California Press.

Quezada Ramírez, María Noemi. 1972. *Los Matlatzincas: Epoca Prehispánica y Epoca Colonial Hasta 1650.* México: Instituto Nacional de Antropología E Historia.

Redfield, Robert. 1930. *Tepoztlán: A Mexican Village.* Chicago: University of Chicago Press.

1941. *The Folk Culture of Yucatán.* Chicago: University of Chicago Press.

1950. *A Village that Chose Progress: Chan Kom Revisited.* Chicago: University of Chicago Press.

1960. *Peasant Society and Culture.* Chicago: University of Chicago Press.

Robbins, Michael, and Thompson, Richard. 1974. Gratification Orientations and Individual Modernization in Buganda. In *Rethinking Modernization,* ed. John Poggie and Robert Lynch. Westport, Conn.: Greenwood.

Roberts, John M., and Sutton-Smith, Brian. 1962. Child Training and Game Involvement. *Ethnology* 1:166–85.

Robinson, W. S. 1950. Ecological Correlations and the Behavior of Individuals. *American Sociological Review* 15:351–7.

Rodale, Robert, ed. 1971. *The Basic Book of Organic Gardening.* New York: Ballantine.

Rogers, Everett. 1962. *Diffusion of Innovations.* New York: Free Press.

1975. The Anthropology of Modernization and the Modernization of Anthropology. *Reviews in Anthropology* 2:345–58.

Rogers, Everett, with Shoemaker, F. Floyd. 1971. *Communication of Innovations: A Cross-Cultural Approach.* Toronto: Collier-Macmillan.

Rogers, Everett, with Svenning, Lynne. 1969. *Modernization among Peasants: The Impact of Communication.* New York: Holt, Rinehart and Winston.

Romanucci-Ross, Lola. 1973. *Conflict, Violence, and Morality in a Mexican Village.* Palo Alto, Calif.: National Press.

Romney, A. Kimball, and Romney, Romaine. 1966. *The Mixtecans of Juxtlahuaca, Mexico.* New York: Wiley.

Rummel, R. J. 1970. *Applied Factor Analysis.* Evanston: Northwestern University Press.

Ryan, Bryce, and Gross, Neal. 1943. The Diffusion of Hybrid Seed Corn in Two

Iowa Communities. *Rural Sociology* 8:15-24.

Sahlins, Marshall, and Service, Elman, eds. 1960. *Evolution and Culture.* Ann Arbor: University of Michigan Press.

Salisbury, Richard. 1970. *Vunamami.* Berkeley: University of California Press.

Schneider, Harold. 1975. Economic Development in Anthropology. In *Annual Review of Anthropology 1975,* ed. B. J. Siegel, A. R. Beals, and S. A. Tyler. Stanford: Stanford University Press.

Schryer, Frans J. 1976. A Reinterpretation of Treasure Tales and the Image of Limited Good. *Current Anthropology* 17:708-10.

Schumacher, E. F. 1973. *Small is Beautiful: Economics as if People Mattered.* New York: Harper & Row.

Sexton, James. 1972. *Education and Innovation in a Guatemalan Community: San Juan La Laguna.* Los Angeles: U.C.L.A. Latin American Center.

Shapiro, Kenneth H. 1975. Measuring Modernization Among Tanzanian Farmers: A New Methodology and an Illustration. In *Formal Methods in Economic Anthropology,* ed. Stuart Plattner. Washington, D.C.: American Anthropological Association.

Silverman, Sydel. 1966. An Ethnographic Approach to Social Stratification: Prestige in a Central Italian Community. *American Anthropologist* 68: 899-921.

Simon, Barbara D. 1972. Power, Privilege, and Prestige in a Mexican Town: The Impact of Industry on Social Stratification. Ph.D. Dissertation. University of Minnesota.

Simpson, Eyler. 1937. *The Ejido: Mexico's Way Out.* Chapel Hill: University of North Carolina Press.

Soustelle, Jacques. 1935. Le Culte des Oratories Chez les Otomis et les Mazahuas de la Région d'Ixtlahuaca. *El México Antiguo* 3:97-117.

  1937. *La Famille Otomi-Pame du Mexique Central.* Paris: Institut D'Ethnologie.

Southworth, John R. 1910. *El Directorio Oficial de las Minas y Haciendas de México.* México: J. R. Southworth.

Spicer, Edward H., ed. 1952. *Human Problems in Technological Change: A Casebook.* New York: Russell Sage Foundation.

Stavenhagen, Rodolfo. 1970. Social Aspects of Agrarian Structure in Mexico. In *Agrarian Problems and Peasant Movements in Latin America,* ed. Rodolfo Stavenhagen. Garden City, N.Y.: Anchor Books.

Steinhart, John, and Steinhart, Carol. 1974. Energy Use in the U.S. Food System. *Science* 184:307-17.

Steward, Julian. 1955. *Theory of Culture Change: The Methodology of Multilinear Evolution.* Urbana: University of Illinois Press.

Stone, Martha. 1975. *At the Sign of Midnight: The Concheros Dance Cult of Mexico.* Tucson: University of Arizona Press.

Swadesh, Morris. 1960. The Oto-Manguean Hypothesis and Macro-Mixtecan. *International Journal of Linguistics* 26:79-111.

Tax, Sol. 1953. *Penny Capitalism: A Guatemalan Indian Economy.* No. 16. Washington, D.C.: Smithsonian Institution Institute of Social Anthropology.

Tipps, Dean C. 1973. Modernization Theory and the Comparative Study of Societies: A Critical Perspective. *Comparative Studies in Society and History* 15: 199–225.

Villas, Enrique C. Antonio. 1851. Unpublished letter to the municipal officers in Temascalcingo.

Vogt, Evon Z. 1969. *Zinacantán: A Maya Community in the Highlands of Chiapas.* Cambridge, Mass.: Harvard University Press.

Wade, Nicholas. 1975. E. F. Schumacher: Cutting Technology Down to Size. *Science* 189:199–201.

Wagley, Charles. 1949. *The Social and Religious Life of a Guatemalan Village.* Memoir 17. Menasha, Wis.: American Anthropological Association.

Wallace, Anthony F. C. 1970. *Culture and Personality.* New York: Random House.

Weber, Max. 1930. *The Protestant Ethic and the Spirit of Capitalism.* London: George Allen and Unwin.

Werts, C. E., and Linn, R. L. 1970. Path Analysis: Psychological Examples. *Psychological Bulletin* 74:193–212.

Whetten, Nathan. 1948. *Rural Mexico.* Chicago: University of Chicago Press.

Whittenbarger, Robert, and Maffei, Eugenio. 1966. Innovativeness and Related Factors in a Rural Colombian Community. Paper presented at the Rural Sociological Society meeting, Miami Beach.

Wilkie, Raymond. 1971. *San Miguel: A Mexican Collective Ejido.* Stanford: Stanford University Press.

Wittwer, S. H. 1975. Food Production: Technology and the Resource Base. *Science* 188:579–84.

Wolf, Eric R. 1955. Types of Latin American Peasantry: A Preliminary Discussion. *American Anthropologist* 57:452–70.

    1956. Aspects of Group Relations in a Complex Society: Mexico. *American Anthropologist* 58:1065–78.

    1957. Closed Corporate Peasant Communities in Mesoamerica and Central Java. *Southwestern Journal of Anthropology* 13:1–18.

    1966. *Peasants.* Englewood Cliffs, N.J.: Prentice-Hall.

    1974. Aspects of Group Relations in a Complex Society: Mexico. In *Contemporary Cultures and Societies of Latin America,* ed. Dwight Heath. New York: Random House.

Woods, Clyde M., and Graves, Theodore. 1973. *The Process of Medical Change in a Highland Guatemalan Town.* Los Angeles: U.C.L.A. Latin American Center.

Zabala Cubillos, Manuel. 1961. Sistema Económico de Zinacantán: Estructura Económica de Nivelación. Dissertation. Escuela Nacional de Antropología e Historia, México.

Index

adaptation
  decision making, 20
  definition of, 19
  see also adaptive strategies; decision
    making
adaptive dynamics, 268–71
  see also modernization, methodolo-
    gy for studying
adaptive strategies
  community differences in, 86–8
  definition of, 59–60, 251
  diversification of, 257, 259, 261
  factionalism and, 138–9
  intracultural variation in, 269
  predictions about, 60–1, 63,
    258–60
age
  operationalization of, 209–10
  relationships with adaptive strate-
    gies, 210–11
  relationships with independent vari-
    ables, 210–11
alcohol use
  animal improvement and, 239–40
  drunkenness, 175, 177
  economic costs of, 117, 119–20,
    179–80, 183, 188–9
  ethnographic comparisons of,
    170–2
  fertilizer use and, 244
  forage production and, 239
  health effects of, 172
  historical perspective on, 169–70
  Indian-ness and, 234–5
  operationalization of, 180–3, 228
  relationships with adaptive strate-
    gies, 183–5, 231
  relationships with independent vari-
    ables, 185–9
  religious activities and, 160, 176
  subsistence agriculture and, 245

  tractor use and, 241–2
  violence and, 175–6, 178
  see also pulque
animal improvement adaptive strategy
  age, 209–10
  alcohol use, 184, 231
  cargo system participation, 163
  cash value of animals, 121–3
  change agent contact, 204–5
  community differences in, 86–8
  community leadership, 142
  cosmopolitanism, 204–5
  definition of, 61–2, 70–3
  distance from land, 99–100, 231
  education, 204–5
  ejido leadership, 142
  extralocal orientation, 231
  income from other pursuits, 121–3
  Indian language ability, 218
  Indian-ness, 231
  land quantity–quality, 99–100
  local leadership and wealth, 229–31
  mass media exposure, 204–5
  material style of life, 121–3
  number of people in the house, 213
  political knowledge, 204–5
  predictors of, 252
  religiosity, 163
  sociopolitical manipulation, 231
  value of agricultural equipment,
    121–3
  wealth ratings, 121–3
  see also path analysis
anthropology
  public policy and, 260–1
appropriate technology, 263–4

Banfield, Edward, 6, 249
Barth, Fredrik, 18, 19
Bee, Robert, 30, 105, 130, 194
Belshaw, Cyril, 260–1

295

Cambridge Latin American Studies

302